£15

KW-326-432

P3

DEFINING THE DIVINITY

MEDIEVAL PERCEPTIONS
IN WELSH COURT POETRY

Defining the Divinity

MEDIEVAL PERCEPTIONS
IN WELSH COURT POETRY

N. G. COSTIGAN RSM

ABERYSTWYTH
UNIVERSITY OF WALES
CENTRE FOR ADVANCED WELSH AND CELTIC STUDIES
2002

© Copyright N.G. Costigan, 2002.

All rights reserved. No part of this book may be reproduced, stored in a retrieval system, or transmitted, in any form or by any means, electronic, mechanical, photocopying, recording or otherwise, without prior permission from the University of Wales Centre for Advanced Welsh and Celtic Studies, National Library of Wales, Aberystwyth, Ceredigion, SY23 3HH.

ISBN 0 947531 85 8

A catalogue record for this book is available from the British Library.

Typeset in Monotype Bembo 11/12pt by Ann and Andrew Hawke, Llanilar.
Cover design by Elgan Davies, Welsh Books Council, Aberystwyth.
Printed by Creative Print & Design Group, Ebbw Vale.

UNIVERSITY OF GLASGOW LIBRARY
WITHDRAWN

In gratitude to my Parents and all
Family members
living and deceased

Contents

Acknowledgements

In the preparation of this work I have incurred many debts, both in Wales and Ireland. I must mention the Congregation of the Sisters of Mercy, without whose support this project would have been impossible. Especially helpful was the hospitality and encouragement received from the communities in Haverfordwest, Cahir, Portlaw and finally in St Maries of the Isle, Cork.

This *Duw* project was the brainchild of the late Professor Emeritus J.E. Caerwyn Williams and it has benefited, especially in its final stages, from his vast experience and erudition. Professor Emeritus R. Geraint Gruffydd, too, kept a caring eye on progress, giving unstintingly of his time in reading through the entire text and suggesting emendations. Hence it is true to say that the encouragement and challenge of both these renowned scholars ensured the completion of this work, enabling it to assume its present shape and see the light of day. *Diolch o galon i chwi eich dau a hefyd i Gwen a Luned.*

In formatting the text I have been helped and guided by Dr Ann Parry Owen and she, as well as Dr Rhiannon Ifans, read through translations of the poems, thus saving me from error and myriad pitfalls. I owe a great debt to Glenys Howells for her care and attention to detail in copy-editing the text. Other friends at the University of Wales Centre of Advanced Welsh and Celtic Studies helped too and I am especially thankful to Morfydd E. Owen for sharing ideas with me and for giving useful pointers at the start of this project. Staying with Wales I must record my thanks to a number of other friends, especially Daniel Huws and Sr Margaret O'Connor. Tad John Fitzgerald kindly read the script, and kept his eye on theological aspects. To Ann and Andrew Hawke goes the credit for preparing the camera-ready text for printing. My thanks are also due to Mr Elgan Davies of the Welsh Books Council for his striking cover design and to the printers, Creative Print & Design of Ebbw Vale, for their care and skill in printing the volume. Last, but by no means least, I thank Professor Geraint H. Jenkins, Director of the Centre for Advanced Welsh and Celtic Studies, for accepting this book for publication. In Cork I received support from Professor Terry O'Reilly and Aidan MacDonald and I was blessed in having Professor Máire Herbert, who gave freely of her time to read through the script and offered invaluable advice. It is true to say that it was her friendship which enabled me to complete the project. The National Library of Wales,

Aberystwyth; the Bodleian, Oxford; The Religious Libraries—Benedict-ine, Glenstal Abbey, Co. Limerick; Jesuit, Milltown Park, Dublin; Aug-ustinian, Cork—and The Boole, UCC, have all helped me greatly. But ultimately I am responsible for any shortcomings in this work.

Final thanks go to *Duw*, Himself, for the inspiring words of the Psalmist:

I will instruct you and teach you the way to go
I will be with you and guide you.

Abbreviations

ANT	*The Apocryphal New Testament*, M.R. James (Oxford, 1986).
Arch Camb	*Archaeologia Cambrensis*, 1846– .
B	*Bulletin of the Board of Celtic Studies*, 1921– .
BaTh	*Beirdd a Thywysogion*, ed. B.F. Roberts and M.E. Owen (Cardiff and Aberystwyth, 1996).
BibT	*Bible Themes*, T. Maertens (Brughes, 1964).
Bl BGCC	*Blodeugerdd Barddas o Ganu Crefyddol Cynnar*, ed. M. Haycock (Llandybïe, 1994).
CBT	*Cyfres Beirdd y Tywysogion* I–VII.
Célí	*Célí Dé*, P. Ó'Dwyer (Dublin, 1977).
CMCS	*Cambridge Medieval Celtic Studies*, 1981– .
Cy	*Y Cymmrodor, the Magazine of the Honourable Society of Cymmrodorion*, 1857–1951.
R.R. Davies: CCC	R.R. Davies, *Conquest, Coexistence, and Change: Wales 1063–1415* (Oxford and Cardiff, 1987).
DIL	*Dictionary of the Irish Language* (compact edition; Dublin, 1983).
DrOC	*Drych yr Oesoedd Canol*, ed. N. Lloyd and M.E. Owen (Cardiff, 1986).
DWB	*Dictionary of Welsh Biography down to 1940* (London, 1959).
Eger	*Egeria's Travels*, J. Wilkinson (London, 1971).
ERLMA	*The English Religious Lyric in the Middle Ages*, R. Woolf (Oxford, 1968).
EWGT	*Early Welsh Genealogical Tracts*, ed. P.C. Bartrum (Cardiff, 1966).

GPC	*Geiriadur Prifysgol Cymru* (Cardiff, 1950–).
H	*Llawysgrif Hendregadredd,* ed. J. Morris-Jones and T.H. Parry-Williams (Cardiff, 1933).
HG Cref	*Hen Gerddi Crefyddol,* ed. Henry Lewis (Cardiff, 1931).
HW	*A History of Wales,* J.E. Lloyd (London, 1911, 1912, 1939).
JB	*Jerusalem Bible,* general ed. A. Jones (London, 1966).
LBS	*Lives of the British Saints,* S. Baring-Gould and J. Fisher (London, 1907–13).
LlB	*Cyfreithiau Hywel Dda yn ôl Llyfr Blegywryd,* ed. S.J. Williams and J.E. Powell (Cardiff, 1942).
LlCy	*Llên Cymru,* 1950– .
LlDC	*Llyfr Du Caerfyrddin,* ed. A.O.H. Jarman (Cardiff, 1982).
LlyB	*Llywelyn y Beirdd,* ed. J.E. Caerwyn Williams, Eurys Rolant and Alan Llwyd (Caernarfon, 1984).
MCE	*Modern Catholic Encyclopaedia,* Glazier and Hellwig.
Missal	*St Andrew's Daily Missal,* G. Lefebvre (Brughes, 1962).
MWRL	*The Medieval Welsh Religious Lyric,* C.A. McKenna (Massachusetts, 1991).
NCE	*New Catholic Encyclopaedia* (New York, 1967).
NLW	National Library of Wales.
NLWJ	*National Library of Wales Journal,* 1939– .
NOJ	*The Name of Jesus,* I. Hausherr, trans. C. Cummings (New Riegel, 1983).
ODCC	*Oxford Dictionary of the Christian Church,* ed. F.L. Cross (London, 1958, reprinted with corrections 1963)

Ott	Ludwig Ott, *Fundamentals of Catholic Dogma*, trans. P. Lynch (Cork, 1955).
PapM	*The Papal Monarchy*, C. Morris (Oxford, 1989).
PBA	*Proceedings of the British Academy*, 1903– .
Peritia	*Journal of the Medieval Academy of Ireland*, 1982– .
PL	*Patrologia Latina;* J.P. Migne (Paris, 1844–5).
P Tal	*The Poems of Taliesin*, ed. I. Williams, English version by J.E.C. Williams (Dublin, 1968).
PWP	*The Poets of the Welsh Princes*, J.E.C. Williams (Cardiff, 1978, 1994).
R	*The Poetry in the Red Book of Hergest*, ed. J. Gwenogvryn Evans (Llanbedrog, 1911).
Raby	F.J.E. Raby, *A History of Christian-Latin Poetry from the beginnings to the close of the Middle Ages* (Oxford, 1953).
RC	*Revue celtique*, 1870–1934.
SC	*Studia Celtica*, 1966– .
D. Stephenson: GG	David Stephenson, *The Governance of Gwynedd* (Cardiff, 1984).
Studies	*Studies* (Dublin), 1912– .
TCHSG	*Trafodion Cymdeithas Hanes Sir Gaernarfon*, 1939– .
THSC	*Transactions of the Honourable Society of Cymmrodorion*, 1892/3– .
ThU	'A Study of the Themes and Usages', R.T. Davies (1958).
Trin	*The Trinity*, K. Rahner (London, 1975).
TYP	*Trioedd Ynys Prydein*, ed. R. Bromwich (Cardiff, 1961).
TYP²	*Trioedd Ynys Prydein*, ed. R. Bromwich (second edition; Cardiff, 1978).

Vul   *Biblia Vulgata,* A. Colunga and L. Turrado
                             (Madrid, 1982).

J.E.C. Williams: ByT   J.E.C. Williams, *Beirdd y Tywysogion: Arolwg*
                             (Cardiff, 1970).

J.E.C. Williams: CCG   J.E.C. Williams, *Canu Crefyddol y Gogynfeirdd*
                             (Llandysul, 1977).

WLW   *The Welsh Law of Women,* ed. D. Jenkins and
                             M.E. Owen (Cardiff, 1980).

YB   *Ysgrifau Beirniadol,* ed. J.E. Caerwyn Williams
                             (Denbigh, 1965–).

Jerusalem Bible abbreviations

Ac	Acts	Jn	John
Am	Amos	Jr	Jeremiah
Ba	Baruch	1 K	I Kings
1 Ch	1 Chronicles	2 K	2 Kings
2 Ch	2 Chronicles	L	Leviticus
1 Co	1 Corinthians	Lk	Luke
2 Co	2 Corinthians	Mi	Micah
Col	Colossians	Mk	Mark
Dn	Daniel	Mt	Matthew
Dt	Deuteronomy	Nb	Numbers
Ep	Ephesians	NT	New Testament
Est	Esther	P1	1 Peter
Ex	Exodus	P2	2 Peter
Ezk	Ezekiel	Ph	Philippians
Ezr	Ezra	Pr	Proverbs
Ga	Galatians	Ps	Psalms
Gn	Genesis	Qo	Ecclesiastes
Heb	Hebrews	Rm	Romans
Ho	Hosea	Rv	Revelation
Is	Isaiah	1 S	1 Samuel
Jb	Job	2 S	2 Samuel
Jg	Judges	Si	Ecclesiasticus
Jl	Joel	Ws	Wisdom
Jm	James	Zc	Zechariah

Foreword

It gives me immense pleasure to write this foreword to a volume which is based on published research carried out at the University of Wales Centre for Advanced Welsh and Celtic Studies. Sister Nora Costigan was a highly valued member of the research team at the Centre which produced *Cyfres Beirdd y Tywysogion* (The Poets of the Princes Series) in seven volumes between 1991 and 1996. Subsequently Sister Costigan decided, with the encouragement of her former colleagues, to undertake a survey of the seven volumes from the viewpoint of her own special field of interest, namely theology. This book is the result, and the Centre is pleased to publish it as an example of the many studies which could, and doubtless will, be undertaken on the basis of the series. For instance, plans are afoot to prepare a complete, albeit curtailed, English version of the series. This enterprise is likely to take several years and in the meantime Sister Costigan's study will provide a valuable preliminary insight into the riches of thought and expression manifested in the work of Welsh court poets in the twelfth and thirteenth centuries.

Geraint H. Jenkins

Preface

The Welsh Court Poet and God begins with a short general introduction, giving a brief overview of Wales in the twelfth and thirteenth centuries, and an account of the *Gogynfeirdd* or court poets. The poets' place in the society of the period and their relationship with their prince-patrons leads to a discussion of their religious outlook. Possible similarities with other lyric poetry of the period in England, on the Continent and in Ireland are considered, and sources for the religious themes are traced.

The main work is presented as a tripartite study:

Part I offers translations of 27 poems of dedication to God, three of which are classed as deathbed poems. *Incipits* of three secular poems are also included: these address God and Christ, and are given here as examples of a strict adherence to the legal requirement that the poet sings first to God and then to the patron.[1] A short biographical note on the author precedes each translation, or group of translations. Translations in both Part I and Part III seek to combine literal accuracy with normal English usage, and follow the interpretations given in *Cyfres Beirdd y Tywysogion* I–VII.

Part II is a commentary on the poems, noting points of special interest and difficulty. Necessary cross-references involving the Introduction, Part I and Part III, appear in footnotes. Where more than one poem is attributed to a poet, each is examined separately, and features of similarity or difference between these poems are considered.

Part III opens with a brief general review of Gogynfeirdd religious belief and understanding of the faith in accordance with the general religious norms of the twelfth and thirteenth centuries. This is followed by a classified survey of all references to the Godhead in both the religious and secular poems of *Cyfres Beirdd y Tywysogion* Volumes I–VII. This part is mainly lexical and is presented in eight sections—1. God, 2. Father, 3. Son, 4. Holy Spirit, 5. Trinity, 6. Christ, 7. Jesus, 8. Alternative words for God, e.g. 'Lord', for which a large number of Welsh equivalents occur. Section 1 is further divided, with each subsection giving examples of a particular concept or description of the Godhead, e.g. True God, Eternal God, Creator God, Angry God, Wise God, God as King, &c. All other sections of Part III follow a similar pattern. Prefatory notes consider the particular aspect of the Godhead in each section.

---

[1] For an account of this legal requirement, see the prefatory note to Poem 28, Part I.

Modernised Welsh spelling, as found in CBT, is the norm for all examples in the Appendix and an English translation and source detail for each citation is given. The Appendix accords with the section sequence employed in Part III.

Throughout the study reference is made to volume numbers of CBT in Roman capitals, while poem and line are indicated in Arabic numerals, e.g. II 11.1 denotes Volume two, poem eleven, line 1. Arabic numerals in bold are used in numbering the individual citations in Part III, e.g. **1. 1. 1** = 1. God, 1. True God: example one.

Scriptural references follow the abbreviation system of *The Jerusalem Bible* and this system is also used when citing Old Testament or New Testament examples from the *Biblia Vulgata*.

Introduction

The scope of *The Welsh Court Poet and God* spans the twelfth and thirteenth centuries, when professional poets plied their trade in the courts of native Welsh princes. These princes gave them support and patronage as they composed within a privileged and defined system. While recognizing the social structures within which the poets worked, the main emphasis of this study remains firmly focused on religious aspects of their compositions, and particularly on the dedication poems to God, and the references to the Godhead. The entire corpus of compositions is now edited and available in seven volumes as *Cyfres Beirdd y Tywysogion* I–VII, and this is used as the basis for the present study.

The historical context is of importance in understanding the poets' reaction and response to their contemporary experiences.[1] Throughout this period Britain remained in the throes of political upheavals, following the Norman conquest of England (1066 AD) and the subsequent invasions and annexations of land in different parts of Wales. Norman and Welsh attack and counter-attack, as well as intervening compromise, peace-treaty and alliance, are recorded in contemporary, or near-contemporary Welsh chronicles. To corroborate chronicle evidence, Welsh historians quarry the works of the court poets and often find references of considerable worth.

It is interesting to remember that both chroniclers and poets give us glimpses of their theological orientation. Neither manifests an involvement with 'school theology', which was gaining ground from the eleventh and twelfth centuries onwards: both chroniclers and poets seem rather to operate within the norm of a long-established 'community theology', which derives its faith and practice from the liturgy and especially the weekly Mass and the homilies.[2] It is of vital importance to keep these points in mind as attitudes to God emerge from a careful reading of the religious content of the court poetry. Before dealing in detail with this material, however, it is necessary to glance back and take brief cognisance of the church tradition which nurtured the faith of these poets.

---

[1] For an excellent account of early invasions and settlements in Wales, see W. Davies, *Wales in the Early Middle Ages* (Leicester, 1982), 5–90, and especially helpful are the maps on pp. 15, 17, 20, 86 and 87.
[2] M. de Verteuil, *Your Word is a Light for my Steps: Lectio Divina* (Dublin, 1996).

At the opening of the period of our interest we find the Welsh with a natural pride and confidence in their military record, as well as in their rich and varied cultural heritage. In the context of this study the most significant feature of this heritage was the introduction of Christianity. After the Edict of Constantine, Christianity became the official religion of the Roman Empire, and gradually it changed or affected all earlier cultures. Owing to the dearth of evidence we have very little knowledge of the establishment and the development of the Christian religion in Britain. Bishops from there, and possibly from that part now known as Wales, were however summoned to attend important Councils at Arles in 314 and at Rimini in 359 to determine Church policy. According to Raby,[3] Britain rapidly became a Christian country, although he believes that neither Christianity nor Roman culture took such a firm hold there as in Gaul or Spain. Through trading with the East the British came into contact with, and were influenced by, certain practices of the Eastern style of Christianity, which they brought back and introduced into the British Church. Monasticism was the most significant and far-reaching of these aspects, and this they adopted and planted on their home-soil. From an early date it took root and flourished.

With the passage of time there emerged in Britain an expression of church organisation which in Wales developed about the *llan* or *clas,* a church under abbatial rule. This organisation continued until Norman times, when it was replaced by a distinctive Roman style. However, very little archaeological evidence survives, and only some four hundred Christian stone monuments bear witness to Church presence in the country during this period, from the fifth to the twelfth century; literary sources are fewer still. Gildas in *De Excidio,* a sixth-century document, clearly favours the Roman way of Christian living[4] and does not throw very much light on the contemporary situation in Wales. From perhaps the seventh century there is the *Life of St Samson,* but this is the only early hagiographical *vita* that has survived. However, in the twelfth-century *Book of Llandaff* there are some early church charters, and in the *Book of Lichfield* there are interesting survivals of Church legislation.[5]

In the wake of the Norman conquest the Church in Wales underwent a considerable degree of change. During this period the Cistercians and other Religious Orders, notably the Franciscans and the Dominicans, arrived from the Continent, each bringing a fresh approach to the ex-

---

[3] See Raby 131.

[4] See *ib.* 132, where he speaks of Gildas's *Lorica* poem, whose authorship is uncertain. He points out that it was certainly composed by a Celt; see also V.E. Nash-Williams, *The Early Christian Monuments of Wales* (Cardiff, 1950).

[5] See W. Davies *op.cit.*, also 'The Latin charter tradition in western Brittany and Ireland in the early medieval period' in *Ireland in Early Mediaeval Europe,* ed. D. Whitelock, R. McKitterick and D. Dumville (Cambridge, 1982), 258–80.

pression of the faith. The teaching of the Fourth Lateran Council also affected Welsh religious practice and attitude in this post-Norman era.[6] Details of these changes will be dealt with later in this study and concentration on the court poets and *Duw* (God), will reveal certain facets of this Church, showing something of religious belief and practice during the twelfth and thirteenth centuries. Before proceeding to look at their compositions in greater detail it seems necessary to make some general remarks about these poets.

Older Poetic Traditions

Beirdd y Tywysogion, the Poets of the Princes, are also known as *Gogynfeirdd* (the 'not so early poets') to distinguish them from the *Cynfeirdd,* the first or earliest Welsh poets. In Parts I and II we shall be dealing with eleven of the thirty-five named *Gogynfeirdd,* whose poems are edited in the series *Cyfres Beirdd y Tywysogion.* For the kingdoms associated with poets see Rees, Plates 38–41.[7] In her essay 'Noddwyr a Beirdd', Morfydd Owen makes the point that the more powerful the patron the greater the number of poems in his honour which survive, and her chronological tabulation of patrons and poets in the kingdoms of Gwynedd, Powys and Deheubarth corroborates this statement.[8] Gwynedd certainly enjoyed political dominance in the *Gogynfeirdd* period and it was there, too, that the earliest reference we have to bards in Wales occurs. Writing before 547, Gildas, in castigating Maelgwn, King of Gwynedd, accuses him of paying excessive attention to his bards:

> When the attention of the ears has been caught, it is not the praises of God, in the tuneful voice of Christ's followers, with its sweet rhythm, and the song of church melody, that are heard, but thine own praises (which are nothing); the voice of the rascally crew yelling forth, like Bacchanalian revellers, full of lies and foaming phlegm, so as to besmear everyone near them.[9]

---

[6] S. Victory, *The Celtic Church in Wales* (London, 1977), and K. Hughes, 'The Celtic Church: Is this a valid concept?', CMCS i (1981), 1–20. See also D. Walker, 'Church in Wales' in his *Medieval Wales* (Cambridge, 1990), 67–89; note too O. Davies, *Celtic Christian Spirituality* (London, 1995), 12–13, who states that perhaps the most important single feature of the Welsh Church in the early Middle Ages was its remoteness from the urban centres of ecclesiastical power and hence its tendency to retain customs that elsewhere were rapidly overtaken by a harmonization process that was characteristic of the Christian Church throughout Europe at this time.

[7] See W. Rees, *An Historical Atlas of Wales* (London, 1952, 1971).

[8] See BaTh 78, 79, 81, 83.

[9] See *De Excidio,* 80–1; for Gildas this decadence was particularly odious in Maelgwn who, as a young man, had become a monk and had studied for a time under St Illtud. For an account of St Illtud, see LBS iii, 303–17, also G.H. Doble, *Lives of the Welsh Saints,* ed. D. Simon Evans (Cardiff, 1971), 88–145.

As well as being hostile to Maelgwn, Gildas shows his contempt for the bards, whom he regarded as illiterate. *Annales Cambriae*[10] gives Maelgwn's *obit* as 547, the very year, if *Historia Brittonum*'s entry is correct, when King Ida began his reign in Northumbria. During the period of his reign (547–59), several poets seem to have been famous:

> Talhaern (Talhaearn) Tad Aguen (Tad Awen) gained renown in poetry; and Neirin (Aneirin) and Taliessin (Taliesin) and Bluchbard (?Blwchfardd) and Cian who is called Gueinth Guaut (?Gwenith Gwawd, 'Wheat of Song') gained renown together at the same time in British poetry.[11]

Not a line of work from these poets survives, apart from that of Taliesin and Aneirin.[12] These two are regarded as the founding fathers of Welsh poetry and both bear witness to a developed poetic style cast in a heroic mode consonant with the general ethos of Heroic Age Britain.[13] In the main their poetic works emanate from that region of Britain, embracing Southern Scotland and Northern England, i.e. the kingdoms east and west of the Pennines, which has long been referred to as the Old North. To this region, as well as to the rest of Britain, including Wales, the Romans had brought Christianity, so we must assume that both Taliesin and Aneirin, composing in the late sixth century, were Christians. Yet evidence of this is slight indeed. Except for a formulaic greeting to God in a couple of introductory lines, and the recommending of a patron's soul to the mercy of God, Taliesin's poems are devoid of religious references, while, throughout the whole of Aneirin's *Gododdin,* there is not a single direct reference to God. On the contrary there are lines that suggest a pre-Christian outlook, retaining as they do traces of ancient pagan values. In his tirade against Maelgwn[14] Gildas expresses outrage at finding Christian poets in Gwynedd flattering a patron in a pagan manner. A similar survival of pagan influence marks the *Beowulf* poem, whose author seems quite definitely to have been a Christian.[15] If,

---

[10] See Cy ix, 143–83; also *Gildas: New Approaches,* ed. M. Lapidge and D. Dumville (Woodbridge, 1984), where the dating of Maelgwn's death and also that of *De Excidio* has been reconsidered.

[11] *Historia Brittonum,* c. 62. For an English translation, see A.W. Wade-Evans, *Nennius's 'History of the Britons'* (London, 1938); *Nennius British History and the Welsh Annals,* ed. and trans. by J. Morris (1980); note a discussion on this passage in P Tal i–xi; also *The Beginnings of Welsh Poetry,* ed. R. Bromwich (Cardiff, 1972).

[12] On Taliesin, see the introductory discussion in P Tal, and for the poetry attributed to Aneirin, see Ifor Williams, *Canu Aneirin* (Cardiff, 1938), K.H. Jackson, *The Gododdin: The Earliest Scottish Poem* (Edinburgh, 1969), and J.T. Koch, *The Gododdin of Aneirin* (Cardiff, 1997).

[13] See de Vries, *Heroic Song and Heroic Legend* (London, 1963); C.M. Bowra, *Heroic Poetry* (London, 1964); A.O.H Jarman, 'The Heroic Ideal in Early Welsh Poetry'. (This article appeared as 'Y Delfryd Arwrol yn yr Hen Ganu', *Llên Cymru,* viii (1965), 125–49.)

[14] See footnote 10 *supra.*

[15] See *Beowulf,* 29–33, and 51 ff.

as has been suggested, the *Beowulf* poem originated in the Northumbrian area, it was an Old North composition but dating from about two hundred years later than the compositions of the *Cynfeirdd*. Another suggestion is that it emanated from some part of Mercia during the reign of King Offa II, who built a dyke—Offa's Dyke—along the eastern border of Wales against the marauding Welsh at the close of the ninth century.[16] There may be a possibility then of an affinity with the Llywarch Hen[17] cycle of anonymous poems, which deal with Welsh resistance to Mercian incursions along this same border. Certain similarities mark both compositions, e.g. the beginnings of a breakdown in the old heroic ideal and an admixture of Christian and pagan values. These same characteristics are noticeable in the Myrddin poems[18] which seem to derive from the close of the *Cynfeirdd* period. Heroic elements are still evident in both secular and religious poems of the *Gogynfeirdd*, while *Cynfeirdd* standards of composition and outlook continue to inspire and sustain Welsh poets during and beyond the period of the court poets.

Poet and Patron

Perhaps at this point we can consider some of Stacey's remarks that neither Ireland nor Wales shared extensively in the general medieval trend towards feudalization, urbanisation or monarchical consolidation although those developments were common to the emerging European states around them. Furthermore, she comments:

> In Ireland and Wales literary sources together represent the largest body of pre-twelfth-century vernacular material extant from anywhere in Western Europe, and yet they remain essentially unknown to the vast majority of early medieval historians.[19]

The *Gogynfeirdd* or court poets were the beneficiaries of a rich poetic inheritance, and, thanks to their professional skills and enthusiasm, this ancient tradition was not only kept alive but developed and honed to a perfection hitherto unknown. These poets operated in a privileged sector of medieval Welsh court society under the patronage of the princes, with whom they shared the uncertain political fortunes of the period. Michael Richter, citing *Unde et poetas, quos bardos vocant ... in hac natione multos*

---

[16] See Cyril Fox, *Offa's Dyke: a field survey of the western frontier works of Mercia in the seventh and eighth centuries A.D.* (Cardiff, 1953); also W. Davies, *Patterns of Power in Early Wales* (Oxford, 1990), 64–7, and for a map on English attacks on Wales see *ib.* 68; also D. Walker, 'Church in Wales' in *Medieval Wales* (Cambridge, 1990).

[17] See I. Williams, *Canu Llywarch Hen* (Caerdydd, 1935), *passim*, and J. Rowland, *Early Welsh Saga Poetry* (Cambridge, 1990).

[18] See A.O.H. Jarman, 'The Welsh Myrddin Poems', 20 ff.; also TYP² 469–74.

[19] See R.C. Stacey, *The Road to Judgment: from Custom to Court in Medieval Ireland and Wales* (Philadelphia, 1994), Intro., p. 3 and footnote 17, following D. Walker *op.cit.*

invenies,[20] points out that Giraldus Cambrensis was sufficiently familiar with Welsh society for his statement to be accepted as well informed and valid and, since he was also familiar with other societies, particularly in England and France, this statement must be understood as saying that it was characteristic of Welsh society to have numbers of persons competent and well versed in their native learning.[21]

As the momentum of Norman aggression and power extended ever further into Wales during the twelfth century, an inevitable patriotic reaction was kindled, with the native princes as the vanguard of this struggle. Under their patronage, a Welsh literary revival was spearheaded by the *Gogynfeirdd*. Meilyr Brydydd is regarded as the first of these poets whose work survives. In 'Cerdd Ddarogan Meilyr' ('Meilyr's Prophetic Poem') (CBT I 5) the defeat and dispatch of Trahaearn ap Caradog and Meilyr ap Rhiwallon by Gruffudd ap Cynan's army at Mynydd Carn 1081 is predicted. (However, it must be remembered that 'Meilyr's Prophetic Poem' is almost certainly confused from the point of view of defeated allies.) The two anonymous poems in *Llyfr Du Caerfyrddin* (Black Book of Carmarthen) (see CBT I, pp. 1–44) mark the beginning of the *Gogynfeirdd* period as we know it, which ends with the elegies lamenting the failure and treacherous death of the last prince of Wales, Llywelyn ap Gruffudd and his brothers, Dafydd and Owain, in 1282–3. It can truly be said that these poets stood for the independence of Wales and fell with it.

The varying fortunes of this politico-military struggle are reflected in the poems of the *Gogynfeirdd*, where patrons are challenged and goaded on by the poets to a continuing and ever greater effort to counter the Norman menace and restore freedom to Wales. (However, we cannot forget that the *Gogynfeirdd* could also be ambivalent in their allegiance and at times praised patrons who sided with the English.) If the prince-patron accepted the challenge and emerged victorious, with territories restored and wealth increased, the poet's part in this achievement had to be recognized. Woe betide a patron who, on such an occasion, failed to meet the poet's expectations for gifts of land, horses or other valuables! Thus poet and patron realized and accepted their interdependent relationship and, to a certain degree, lived in salutary respect of one another. Listen to Cynddelw:

---

[20] Giraldus Cambrensis, *Descriptio Kambriae* i, xii.

[21] M. Richter, *The Formation of the Medieval West* (Dublin, 1994), 112, and in 'The Celtic Countries', Chap. 9, he says that while we speak of 'people of native learning' we must remember that this does not necessarily mean that these people had to be literate in the sense of having the skills of reading and writing; see B. Stock, *The Implications of Literacy and Models of Interpretation in the Eleventh and Twelfth Centuries* (Princeton, 1983), 15, who maintains that 'the single great storehouse of meaning is memory'.

Hanpwyf well honawd, gwasgawd gwosgor,
Hanpych well honaf [   ]heiror.

Let my life be the better because of you, protector of hosts,
Let your life be the better because of me ...[22]

Certainly loyal devotion and even real love for the patron may be a part of the poet's professional ethos, but no patron can presume too much on this! The poet, confident in his power to generate political benefit and prestige, was not shy in declaring this quite openly to his patron. A good example is:

Na ddilysa fi yfelly,—fy naf,
Nid ef it lesaf o'm dilysy.

Do not thus cast me aside,—my lord,
I shall not be of benefit to you if you cast me aside.[23]

Dadolwch ('appeasement / reconciliation') poems, too, can veil a mordant threat:

Neud tau o'r barau a berydd—i'm plaid,
I'm plygu heb ddefnydd,
Ai cardd ai cerdd o newydd,
Ai cabl ai cwbl gerennydd.

Yours it is, in the wake of the sorrows which you cause me,
By belittling me without cause,
Either [to choose] disgrace or an eulogy once more,
Either censure or full reconciliation.[24]

Bygwth ('threatening') poems alert the patron to his continuing indebtedness to and dependence on effective eulogy:

Gwynygawd dy glod hynod honni
O angerdd a'm cerdd a'm cymelri.

Your fame shines forth because of its [being] publicly proclaimed
By the force of my song as well as my [inspired] passion.[25]

---

[22] Cynddelw, 'Arwyrain Owain Gwynedd' ('Exaltation to Owain Gwynedd'), IV 2.57–8.

[23] Dafydd Benfras, 'Mawl Llywelyn ab Iorwerth' ('Praise of Llywelyn ab Iorwerth'), VI 26.37–8.

[24] Llywelyn Fardd (I), 'Dadolwch Owain Fychan' ('Appeasement of Owain Fychan'), II 3.37–40.

[25] Llywarch ap Llywelyn, 'Bygwth Dafydd ab Owain Gwynedd' ('Threatening Dafydd ab Owain Gwynedd'), V 2.59–60.

then Dafydd's open threat:

> Na orsang dy len, dy les wyf i,
> Na orsaf arnaf er neb ynni.
>
> *Do not trample on your own mantle, [for] I am of benefit to you,*
> *Do not oppose because of any compulsion.*[26]

If a poet of high standing felt slighted or belittled he could transfer his service and allegiance to another prince, possibly a rival of his former patron. While the poets held power and exercised it to sway the fortunes of patrons and of their country, we also know that some of them fought side by side with their patrons in battle.[27] Like the Irish *Rosc Catha,* 'battle-cry' poems can sound a rallying cry like that of the *Chanson de Roland.*[28]

Since the point of this study is the poet's references and attitudes to God, one might question the emphasis on the poet-patron relationship. However, in the translations of the poems in Part I, and in the references cited in Part III, it will be abundantly clear that the poet-patron attitudes are expressed alike for the secular and the heavenly patron, God. To quote R.R. Davies:

> Churches throughout Europe took on the colour of the society in which they oper-
> ated, and assumed, often unconsciously, many of its values; but rarely had a church so
> submerged itself into the local social landscape as in Wales. It had adopted many of
> the values and assumptions of a heroic and violent society. God was a 'ruler' or 'sov-
> ereign' (W. *gwledig mechteym*), incomparable as were worldly heroes. Christ likewise
> was saluted as a 'hero'(W. *arwr*), and his 'prowess' was construed in terms borrowed
> from the secular world. 'He seized the plunder of hell into his possession', vaunted
> one poet; thereby, according to another, 'he had bought reconciliation' (*ni'th oes
> gystedlydd*) between God and man, much as a feud might be terminated by buying off
> hostility' (see HG Cref 66).[29]

Poetic Expression

Before turning our full attention to the religious aspects of this poetry, we must pause to consider briefly some stylistic features of the *Gogyn-feirdd* compositions, both secular and religious. In the main, secular poems, both elegies and eulogies, show a highly developed and sophistic-ated style of composition, and this is also true of the religious poems. A

[26] *Ib.* 59–60. See also BaTh 108–21, esp. 114–19.
[27] In ByT 33–4, J.E.C. Williams deals with evidence for poets fighting in battle along-side their patrons.
[28] See *La Chanson de Roland,* ed. and trans. G.J. Brault (Pennsylvania, 1978); also J.E.C. Williams, *op.cit.* 34.
[29] See R.R. Davies: CCC 172–210, esp. 175.

preoccupation with perfecting stylistic expression, coupled with abstruse allusions to events and personages, can at times obscure meaning or make the interpretation of particular passages very difficult for modern editors.[30] Study by experts reveals that the poetry never falters in grammatical and syntactical correctness which the strict system of the period required.[31] On the basis of the frequent citations in *Gramadegau'r Penceirddiaid*,[32] it would appear that court poetry was regarded as a model of technique for poets in the schools of the fourteenth, fifteenth and subsequent centuries. Adroit choice of word and phrase combined with complicated or simple rhythms, can not only produce harmony of sound and meaning but can also evoke emotional responses. Achieving these effects required exceptional skill in poetic art and poets vied with one another in aspiring to attain this much-desired excellence.

A long and careful training in the intricacies of *cynghanedd*, 'a system of consonance or alliteration in a line of Welsh poetry in strict metre and internal rhyming' (GPC 737), ancient lore, and every other aspect of poetic composition, including genealogical expertise, was necessary before a poet could master the skills required to qualify as *pencerdd*, 'chief poet', the highest official rank to which he could aspire. Line, couplet and section-construction of these poems demonstrate a deep and studied understanding of the essentials of poetry.

Where compositions are divided and presented as cantos we find them cleverly interlinked by word and theme, as in Poem 1 (Part I), which is a good example of this particular skill. Linking in this way may have been a memory device in poems composed for public delivery. Excellent recall, by the poet himself or by a specially-trained reciter, was essential in order to render, with verbal exactitude and interpretative fidelity, these long and stylized productions. Agreeing with the general opinion that trained reciters spoke or chanted the poems, perhaps to the accompaniment of a harp, we can visualize the performance before an assembly in the royal court, on festive occasions, e.g. at a prince's inauguration or perhaps to celebrate his victory on the field. In order to meet and satisfy the expectations of an audience, whose ears were attuned to well-known runs and cadences in familiar phrasing and melodic variation, certain standards of excellence were required on the part of the poet himself and of the reciter. The audience was also alert for the novel in ideas or expression and, if both the familiar and the innovative blended into a subtle and

---

[30] See 'The Court Poet and his work' in *Irish Classical Poetry* (Dublin, 1957), 41 ff. for Eleanor Knott's view of the Irish Court Poets.
[31] See J. Vendryes, *La poésie galloise des XIIᵉ–XIIIᵉ siècles dans ses rapports avec la langue*, Zaharoff Lecture (Oxford, 1930); J. Lloyd-Jones, 'The Court Poets of the Welsh Princes'; J.E.C. Williams: CCG; *id., The Poets of the Welsh Princes* (Cardiff, 1994); *id.*, ByT *passim*.
[32] G.J. Williams and E.J. Jones, *Gramadegau'r Penceirddiaid* (Cardiff, 1933).

happy interweave of idiomatic vigour, the poet was assured of success
and reward. The aspiration of all such poets was to be unimpeachable in
vocabulary, grammar and syntax, but they also strove, by means of familiar themes and sequences interspersed with elements of the unexpected,
to produce a rounded semi-masterpiece on every occasion. A *caveat* is
necessary here. There is a danger of ascribing unqualified and impeccable
perfection to *Gogynfeirdd* poems. The truth is that authors vary in standard and, even within the confines of a single composition, certain irregu-
larities can occur. Perhaps an over striving for the *non pareil* explains some
rather forced and turgid lines or couplets.

Dedications to God

It is not certain when or where the poems of dedication to God were
presented but, judging by the length and number of them which survive,
in a context of limited scribal transcription, it is clear that they must have
been quite popular. *Marwnadau* (elegies)[33] were probably sung for
mourners and courtiers of the deceased prince near the grave or within
the church itself following the celebration of Requiem Mass.[34]

Certain questions arise regarding religious aspects. From a study of
these religious poems, what do we learn about the faith and religion of
the poets? What do the references, attitudes and content of their laudatory and exhortative responses tell us of the Church during the two
century span of Welsh court poetry? What are the themes which occur
and recur in their poetry? Undoubtedly the *Gogynfeirdd*, their patrons and
their audiences were familiar with contemporary Church teaching and, as
far as can be gathered, loyal in their faith, though we have very little
direct evidence of the extent to which they practised that faith. We do
not know, for instance, if they attended Mass on Sunday, a practice
which has always given a certain indication of commitment to faith and
Church. There is one reference to the 'sin of [desecrating] Sundays'

---

[33] The death of a patron was the occasion for an elegy but in general the focus was less
on the subject of death than on the glory of the subject's life. Kennings such as 'bed',
'covering of earth' or 'green sod' are usually substitutes for direct mention of death and
much metaphorical language is employed to give grave imagery. However, this changes
and by the time of Gruffudd ab yr Ynad Coch's *marwnad* for Llywelyn ap Gruffudd there
is a more realistic approach, with death being regarded as a subject worthy of prayerful
contemplation, and as a salutary help towards the reform of one's life.

[34] See *Missal* 1585; elegies were probably sung after the Requiem Mass for the celebration of the Month's Mind, on the thirtieth day after the death; see E.D. Jones, 'Presiden-
tial Address', Arch Camb cxii (1963), 4–5, where he cites from George Owen Harry,
Well-spring of True Nobility; also R.G. Gruffydd in YB i (1965), 134. For further details,
see CBT VI, p. 425 on 27.55 and the note, p. 440.

I. 22. 26 *infra),*[35] which might, perhaps, indicate the poets' acceptance of the precept 'to keep holy the Sabbath Day' under pain of sin. From the preoccupation, if not obsession, with sin and its punishment and the emphasis on death, judgement, hell and heaven, we can deduce that the Church to which these poets owed allegiance retained certain elements of Old Testament rather than Gospel values and teaching.[36] Large sections of these religious poems spread a pall of gloom as details of sin and its consequences, horrific descriptions of hell, and graphic and lurid accounts of satanic machinations succeed one another. Yet in the midst of the darkness an unexpected line or couplet may reveal the poet in a change of mood, hoping for, or actually engaging in, a friendly and even intimate relationship with God. Again the scene may light up as he breathes a sigh for the bliss of heaven, there to enjoy companionship with the saints and angels. In general, the poets looked upon God with awesome respect, which at times borders on an unholy fear; to them, He is a remote Being—One wielding supreme power and a force to be reckoned with and placated. R.R. Davies points out:

> In 1070 the church in Wales was archaic and backward-looking, isolated (probably more so than in earlier centuries) from England and Europe, and idiosyncratic in many of its customs. Two centuries later it was an integral part of a papally dominated Western Christendom.[37]

There we see the *Gogynfeirdd,* while geographically distant from the Continent, apparently influenced by Christian thinking both in England and on mainland Europe, and we note W.P. Ker's explanation:

> In the Middle Ages, early and late, there was very free communication all over Christendom between people of different languages. Languages seem to have given much less trouble than they do nowadays. The general use of Latin, of course, made things easy for those who could speak it; but without Latin, people of different nations appear to have travelled over the world picking up foreign languages as they went along, and showing more interest in the poetry and stories of foreign countries than is generally found among modern tourists.[38]

Interest in languages and their importance appears in some of the compositions of the *Gogynfeirdd.* Gwalchmai ap Meilyr, in his 'Arwyrain Owain' ('Exaltation of Owain Gwynedd') towards the end of the twelfth century, speaks hyperbolically of 'seven score languages of eulogy' (I 8.52), but in his 'Mawl Rhodri ab Owain' ('In Praise of Rhodri ab Owain') (I 11.30–3) he is more specific:

---

[35] See Bl BGCC 308–9, where, in 'Ymddiddan Arthur a'r Eryr', we have examples of the stress placed on Mass attendance and Sunday observance.

[36] See prefatory note to Part III.

[37] R.R. Davies: CCC 179.

[38] See W.P. Ker, *Medieval English Literature* (Oxford, 1969), 35.

Caraf Rodri draws drais gyffredin,
Ei enw yn Efrai ac yn Lladin,
Ac ym mhob cyfaith yn gyfiewin
Hyd yd breswyl hwyl haul Fehefin!

I love Rhodri strong and upright his force,
His fame in Hebrew and in Latin,
And in every language worthily
As far as the course of the June sun lasts!

and Cynddelw in his 'Arwyrain Owain fab Madawg' ('Exaltation of Owain ap Madog') (III 13.51–2) boasts:

Nid wyf fardd dylaw, wyf dylaith—ar gerdd,
    Wyf diludd ym mhob iaith,

I am not an unskilled poet, I put finish on a poem,
I am most free in every language.

Gwalchmai also notes the value of language in his dedication to God, Poem 3.11–14. Apart from the two just mentioned, what were the other languages the poets had in mind? Possibly French, English, and Irish. Subsequent to the coming of the Normans and intermarriage with the native Welsh, one would expect that French, for some in Wales, would be a lingua franca, and that as the English language evolved, from its parent Anglo-Saxon, it, too, may have made an impact within Wales. There is a possibility that some Irish was heard and spoken in the North West and the South of the country. Assuming that language need not have posed an insurmountable barrier to extra-Cambrian contacts, we can perhaps view the *Gogynfeirdd* of Wales as at one in matters of faith with their European neighbours. In this context it may interest us to reflect on what P.S. Diehl says in his discussion on 'Genres, Forms and Structures':

> ... the very familiarity of Marian, or Christological, penitential, mystical, meditative, hymnic, or supplicatory motifs guarantees a medieval religious lyric a degree of coherence. In this case, however, the difficulty lies not in the internal relationships of the text, but in its external, intertextual attachments. Not only does a lyric cohere within itself, it coheres so completely with poetic and religious tradition that it lacks a distinct identity. General unity makes particular unity almost impossible; it is as if one were trying to make out a white disc against a white wall—where are the edges? ... it and the wall are of a piece.[39]

Even a cursory reading of *Gogynfeirdd* work shows these poets in tune with the beliefs, practices and general attitudes of the Western Church of

[39] 'Genres, Forms and Structures' in P.S. Diehl, *The Medieval European Religious Lyric: an ars poetica* (Berkeley, 1985), 129.

their day. Yet it is hard to accept unreservedly Diehl's general thesis. A reading of individual compositions attests their internal cohesion and unity. However, until these religious poems are studied in minute detail it is impossible to make dogmatic pronouncements on their cohesion or the lack of it.

Influences and Sources

These poets knew the Principal Mysteries of the Christian Religion—the Unity and Trinity of God, the Incarnation, Death and Resurrection of our Saviour and the theological virtues of Faith, Hope and Charity, whether reference is made to these latter by name or by implication. All this leads us to a consideration of the influences which shaped religious court poetry in twelfth- and thirteenth-century Wales. To deal with this we must bear in mind four ecclesiastical developments in that period[40] which must have affected the *Gogynfeirdd* compositions. The first of these was Cistercian spirituality and the teaching of St Bernard of Clairvaux with its emotional approach to God through love of Christ and fear of hell. The second was the preaching of the Franciscans which stressed in detail the awful suffering of Christ and the horrors of hell. The third, which came as a direct result of the decrees of the Fourth Lateran Council 1215, was that priests should instruct their flocks in the essentials of the Faith and make available copies and translations of Latin Church documents in vernacular languages. The fourth was the influence of new hymns such as *Stabat Mater*[41] and the *Dies Irae,*[42] which were included as part of the liturgy during the thirteenth century. In different countries these hymns or sequences were the impetus for poets to compose in a similar vein in their own languages. Part III will contain several references to different Psalms which are echoed in lines of *Gogynfeirdd* poems both religious and secular.

Since, with a few possible exceptions, the poets were laymen, what was the source of their knowledge and how did they acquire the proficiency to draw upon scriptural sources and use them to such effect? The immediate answer is the Mass. Throughout the Ordinary of the Mass (that part of the service which remained unchanged whatever the season or occasion), copious extracts from Psalms occurred.[43] Those who attended Mass heard these every Sunday of the year, while whole Psalms

---

[40] For a full discussion on religious changes and developments, see MWRL 42–6.

[41] ODCC 1285.

[42] *Ib.* 398, '*Dies Irae* (Lat., "Day of Wrath"), the opening words, and hence the name, of the sequence in the Mass for the Dead in the W. Church. Its author is almost certainly a 13th cent. Franciscan. It was not originally intended for liturgical use, as it is in the 1st person sing.' For a translation, see Raby 443–50, which also includes the original text.

[43] Ps 42 *Judice me*, Ps 50 *Miserere mei*, etc.

were essential to special liturgical celebrations, e.g. those of Holy Week, when the great mysteries of Redemption were re-enacted with particular emphasis on the sufferings, death and resurrection of Our Saviour. The importance of the Easter Vigil liturgy, with the singing of the *Exultet*[44] followed by the Preface on the Saturday night, cannot be over-emphasized. In the latter the enslaving Egyptians are dramatically depicted as the powers of night, while the deliverance of the Hebrews to attain the Promised Land represented the deliverance of all humankind and their right to enter heaven.[45] With symbolic ingenuity expressed through the initial darkness in the Church followed by the lighting of the paschal candle (representing Christ) from which all other lights are lit, events of the Old and New Dispensations are brought together in an interrelated significance.[46] It seems beyond question that poets, like other officials of the royal court, would have attended Requiem Masses, whose texts were compiled, to a large extent, from scriptural passages including a number of Psalms or excerpts from them. Through attendance at these services the poets would have become familiar with at least some verses of the better-known Psalms. But we must also take into account that, depending on the location of the court in which they functioned and the proximity of a monastery, they could have attended the singing or recitation of the Canonical Hours. The royal chaplain or priest-officials in the court[47] may have celebrated some at least of these seven hours, especially Vespers on Sunday. The bond of friendship and favour between the Cistercians and the prince-patrons would have given the poets easy access to members of the order and also to the perusal of monastic service books. For those poets who were literate in Latin, this would have provided a rewarding opportunity.[48] We may accept that poets who combined the practice of poetry with that of a civil service could have acquired some Latin.

---

[44] This is an ancient hymn, going back to the seventh century, in which the Church expounds the beautiful symbolical meaning of the Paschal Candle. It is sung by a deacon, as part of the proclamation of the Easter message; see ODCC 486, also J.W. Tyrer, *Historical Survey of Holy Week* (Oxford, 1932).

[45] See *Peregrinatio Etheriae (Silvae)* Latin 490–523 and English trans. 541–71, where we find a first hand account of the services of the Holy Sepulchre at Jerusalem in the time of St Jerome.

[46] See *Missal* 471 ff.

[47] See LIB 16.31–17.3, where *caplan y brenhin* 'king's chaplain' is mentioned and some of his duties are described. Two other priests are listed among the court officials, once as *offeiriat teulu* 'household priest' (31.1–20), and again as *offeirat brenhines* 'queen's priest'; and in 9.25–6 the chaplain's residence *llety* is said to house both of the priest-officials, *Llety yr offeirat a'r yscolheigyonn* ('and the scholars', *ysgolhaig* could also mean 'cleric') *yw ty caplan y tref, a llety offeirat brenhines y gyt ac wynt.*

[48] At that period Latin was the language used in all Church Service Books.

Lateran IV; The Franciscans

As the thirteenth century progressed, the Church throughout Christendom experienced the tremendous impact of the Fourth Lateran Council of 1215, the 'Great Council' as it has been called. Part of this impact was the greater stress on the confessing of sin in the Sacrament of Penance.[49] The Council also emphasized the importance of instructing the laity and in this the Franciscans played a prominent role. From the middle of the thirteenth century, with the coming of the Friars Minor (Grey Friars, as they were familiarly known) founded by St Francis,[50] Wales would have experienced a type of preaching that was simple, but also eloquent and precise in its exposition of the Gospel message in its mysterious power, which in time was described as Franciscan.[51] In St Francis's mind the basic conception of the Order of Friars Minor which he founded was quite simple: it was the literal, deliberate imitation of the way of the life of Christ and His Apostles as described in the Gospels. In practical application this meant an itinerant life divided almost equally between prayer and preaching and supported by work (if possible manual) or by begging, with the greatest stress laid on voluntary self-denial and renunciation of property—all for the single purpose of enabling oneself and inducing others to live a life of ever-closer union with Christ in His Church.[52] The Friars regarded themselves as missionaries and evangelists and as they went through the country they sought every opportunity of preaching, whether in their own church, the parish churches, or in the open air. Another facet of their lives, as members of religious communities, was the daily recitation of the Divine Office. Even as they walked from place to place the Friars recited the Psalms, reading from breviaries[53] which they carried, and perhaps the poets had the opportunity to join them in this prayer, and may even have borrowed or secured a copy of the breviary for their own personal use.

---

[49] For a discussion on the history and theology of the Sacrament of Penance and the practice of confession, see Ott 416 ff.

[50] See *Francis and Clare: the complete works,* English trans. by R.J. Armstrong and I.C. Brady (New York, 1982), *passim.*

[51] See E. Hutton, *The Franciscans in England* (London, 1926), 88, where Llan-faes is listed as one of the nine Franciscan houses under the custody of Worcester, and the only one subject to Worcester in Wales. Llan-faes near Beaumaris, Anglesey, was founded before 1245 (Pat., *(sic)* 29 Hen. III, m.2) *op.cit.* 90. The surrender of the convent was signed by Friar John and three others on August 19, 1538. (*L. and P. Hen. VIII,* XIII (2), 196), and its inventory noted in *Letters and Papers,* XIII (2), 138. For references to the Friars in Carmarthen, Shrewsbury and Hereford, see *op.cit.* 82, 83, 89–90.

[52] See R. Brown, *Little Flowers of St Francis* (New York, 1958), *passim.*

[53] Breviaries, as the name suggests, were shortened texts of the Canonical Hours; see ODCC 196.

The Franciscans are important because Madog ap Gwallter, one of whose compositions appears as Poem 18 in Part I, was, in all probability, a Grey Friar in the second half of the thirteenth century.[54] Furthermore, the preaching of the Grey Friars seems to have had considerable influence on other thirteenth-century Welsh poets, as the biographical notes in Part I and comments on poems in Part II reveal. At this point it is of interest to recall the words of R.R. Davies:

> In many ways Wales was and remained unpromising ground for the friars; it has neither the large urban centres nor the university schools which were their natural habitat. It is not surprising, therefore, that only three Franciscan houses (Llan-faes (pre-1245), Cardiff (pre-1284), Carmarthen (pre-1284), five Dominican houses (Cardiff (pre-1242), Haverfordwest (pre-1246), Bangor (pre-1251), Rhuddlan (pre-1258), and Brecon (pre-1269), and one Carmelite house (Denbigh pre-1289) were founded in Wales ... By teaching and, above all, by preaching, the friars introduced new standards into the life of the parish clergy and laity alike; ... they used the vernacular to communicate the intensity of their religious sentiments and vision—as in Brother Madog ap Gwallter's touching meditation on the nativity of Christ, the earliest such nativity poem in Welsh, or in *Y Cysegrlan Fuchedd* ('The Consecrated Life'), the most important work of piety and devotion produced in medieval Wales and one whose author may have been a Dominican friar. ... It was the friars, not the Cistercians, who were moulding the shape of popular devotion and religious practice in later medieval Wales.[55]

Themes

A list of certain themes which occur in the dedications to God in Part I highlights the religious interest and emphasis of the *Gogynfeirdd:*

Sacraments
  Baptism: Poems 3, 5, 15.
  Penance / Confession: Poems 21, 28.[56]
  Holy Eucharist / Communion: Poem 21.
  Extreme Unction: Poems 22, 25.

Sin Poems 3 (2), 6 (2), 9 (2), 10, 11, 14, 15 (2), 16, 17, 19, 20, 21 (2), 22, 23 26.

---

[54] See CBT VII, p. 347, which deals with the question of Madog the Franciscan; see also *id.* note 2, on the suggestion that he was, perhaps, a member of the Dominican Order.

[55] See R.R. Davies: CCC 201–2; and also D. Knowles and R.N. Hadcock, *Medieval Religious Houses: England and Wales,* 226, which mentions that the monastery at Llan-faes was built by Llywelyn the Great as a memorial for his wife Joan of England who had died in 1237. D. Walker, *op.cit.* 83, also confirms this, saying that Llywelyn buried his wife Joan at Llan-faes, and during the next few years established the Franciscans there.

[56] See Part II footnote 33 and B. Poschmann, *Penance and the Anointing of the Sick* (Freiburg, 1964); P. Anciaux, *La théologie du sacrement de pénitence au XIIᵉ siècle* (Louvain, 1949).

Repentance

Poems 3 (2), 6 (2), 9, 10 (2), 11, 13, 16, 17 (2), 19, 27.

Sufferings of Christ

Passion: Poems 9, 15 (2), 19, 20, 21, 23, 24 (3).

Cross: Poems 3 (2) 6, 7 (2), 9, 11, 15, 19, 20, 21, 23, 25, 28.

Ages of the World

Five ages: Poems 1 (2), 9, 10, 17, 21, 28.[57]

Six ages: Poem 9.[58]

Transience of life Poems 1, 15, 17, 20, 23.[59]

Hell

Harrowing of hell: Poems 1, 2, 5, 7, 9, 10, 21, 22, 28.[60]

Descriptions of hell: Poems 2, 7, 9, 10, 15, 17, 20, 21, 22, 24, 25, 27.

Judgement

Three hosts coming to Judgement: Poems 1 (2), 2, 6, 10, 17, 19, 24.[61]

Judgement Day: Poems 3, 5, 6, 10, 12, 13, 14, 19, 24.[62]

Heaven Poems 4, 5, 6, 7, 11, 12, 13, 14, 15, 17, 19, 20, 22, 23, 24, 25, 26.[63]

This list does not include references to personages, e.g. Mary or saints, because these will receive adequate treatment in Parts I, II and III. In view of the wealth of contemporary poetry in other countries and the many dedications to Mary, it is striking that not a single poem is dedicated to her in all the extant *Gogynfeirdd* compositions.

Procedamus in nomine Domine ut poëtarum voces audiamus!

---

[57] See Part II footnote 18.

[58] The idea of six ages of the world was fundamental to cosmic chronology in the Middle Ages. The usual division was 'from Adam to Noah, from Noah to Abraham, from Abraham to Moses, from Moses to David, from David to Christ and from Christ to judgement day'. References to five ages of the world also occur in *Gogynfeirdd* poetry; see Poem 9 and CBT I, p. 469; H. Tristram, *Sex Aetates Mundi* (Heidelberg, 1985); the Introduction to D. Ó Cróinín, *The Irish Sex Aetates Mundi* (Dublin, 1983).

[59] This links with the *Ubi sunt?* and *memento mori* themes, which occur elsewhere in *Gogynfeirdd* poems, and also in the literature of other countries; see Bl BGCC 210, also CBT VI, p. 376.

[60] See P 1: 3:19, 4:6; The Apostles' Creed; M. MacNamara, *The Apocrypha in the Irish Church* (Dublin, 1975), 68–75; ANT 'Acts of Pilate', 117 ff.; C. Perrot, 'La Descente aux Enfers et la Prédication aux morts', *Lectio Divina*, cii (1980), 231–46.

[61] See Part II, footnote 4.

[62] As a parallel, or possibly an exemplar for many of these themes, see *Early English Christian Poetry*, trans. C.W. Kennedy (New York, 1963), 'The Last Judgement', 268–89, and the commentary, 254–8.

[63] See Part III 1. 4.

Part I

Biographical Notes and Translations

Poems 1–24
Dedications to God

Cynddelw Brydydd Mawr

Cynddelw's floruit has been established as *c.*1155–95.[1] Virtually irrefutable evidence shows him as a poet with his roots in Powys. Among his patrons were some of the most important princes of the period—Madog ap Maredudd, prince of Powys (*ob.* 1160), Owain Gwynedd (*ob.* 1170), the Lord Rhys ap Gruffudd from Deheubarth (*ob.* 1197) and possibly Llywelyn ab Iorwerth, along with lesser princes, as Hywel ab Owain Gwynedd, Owain Cyfeiliog and his son Gwenwynwyn, Cadwallon ap Madog ab Idnerth from Maelienydd, Iorwerth Goch (brother of Madog ap Maredudd), and noblemen of note—Rhirid Flaidd and Arthen his brother, Einion ap Madog ab Iddon, Ednyfed, Lord of Crogen, Heilyn ap Dwywg and Ithel ap Cedifor. Thus we find that his poetry celebrates patrons in Powys, Gwynedd and Deheubarth, as well as including two odes to God and one deathbed poem. He also sang a long celebratory ode to St Tysilio (CBT III 3), who had definite connections with Powys. In Powys, too, he addressed a love song to Efa, daughter of Madog ap Maredudd (CBT III 5).

On the basis of the number of poems and lines in his canon, Cynddelw was the most prolific of all the *Gogynfeirdd*: his 48 poems total 3,847 lines. These compositions are now edited and available in volumes III and IV of *Cyfres Beirdd y Tywysogion*. Obviously the preservation of so much of Cynddelw's work bears witness to his reputation and popularity as a poet. D. Myrddin Lloyd suggests that he may have been given the pseudonym *Mawr* ('large') because of his large physique.[2] Our concern here is with his two religious poems and his *marwysgafn* or deathbed poem, below Poems 1, 2 and 27.

Poem 1 (IV 16)
May my destiny be at the right hand of my Lord!

One mighty Lord, law-loving Ruler
Who rules serenely
Only Son of God, immense His plan,
Only Son of Mary, powerful, invincible,

---

[1] For a full summary of the life, works, etc., of Cynddelw, see CBT III, pp. xxv–l.
[2] See DWB *s.n.* Cynddelw Brydydd Mawr.

5   One eternal [and] merciful God,
        One King, Sovereign of heaven and earth,
        One Hero heroic His design,
        I desire [to present to Him] a sacred song in tender prayer.
        May I be a friend of my Lord before the presence of peril,
10   Let me embrace repentance for my sin.
        Where a blind and deaf person gives up his [sinful] ways
        God redeems him as a best friend,
        While fiercely the ungodly one is hurled into hell
        [By the] Lord of hell, Prince of the swamp.
15   This Sovereign they approach in threefold belligerence,
        A meeting-place of unfortunate tribes,
        A mottled crew, associates avid for fight,
        Second, a hateful mob, very dark [and] raucous,
        Third, a host to whom He does not deny comfort,
20   Bright, blessed company whom He loves.
        In a splendid refuge, in a heaven abounding in riches
        May I have a delectable dwelling;
        Before I become the prize of the enemy on a weak pretext,
        Let me be a servant of God, the blessed and joyful sustainer;
25   Before I be a humble wretched one in need,
        Already [full of] anxiety [and] looking like a dismal corpse,
        Before the merciless inevitability of death,
        The pain [and] anguish of the greensward earth,
        Before the very great moment of separation,
30   Ere I be borne to my final bondage
        Before wretched tribulation of a miserable grave in captivity
        In the covering of oak and blood,
        Noble King extensive his sway, gentle Lord,
        King and Judge, beloved dispenser of gifts,
35   Bountiful Redeemer, distributing favour
        To the intercessor, fine Bestower of gifts,
        Meet it is for me through my learned and eloquent gift
        [To give You] unceasing praise, with delight unstinted;
        I am an intercessor full of fervour and in sadness,
40   I pray to God in order to placate His anger.
        Because of the anger of our lord, Chief of wise liberality,
        Substantial his sadness will be,
        In our age morality is ever in decline,
        Great evils from treacherous minds.
45   Because of unchristian disbelief
        There is, alas, ungodliness;
        It is better to attain to rewards once again

Without old age, illness and yearning
Before the grave of noble cavalry,
50   Before the shame of the strife of devilry.
Faulty and treacherous plotting was not part of the Son of God
In His plan for mankind;
When the Great One suffered death
On the wood of the cross, our Creator went [from us].
55   He, our friend, led us then
Out of hell, a foul swamp of cruelty.
To Him belongs the blessings of graciousness
Above nine choirs, nine principalities;
Below the heavens, above the heavens, above the nine shores is He
60   Whose rule cannot be swayed.
He is our Guide in joyous supremacy,
Blessing-sharing One, a fine Gift-giver;
He it is who governs, [and] rules according to His plan,
The strongest King, feast [giver] of the ages past,
65   He is strong, all-embracing is His heart,
He will come to reveal what He has achieved.
Let us present to Him before the horror of mortality
A service of willing gift;
By Judgement Day, terror will God's judgement be,
70   He will judge the free and the slave;
When every arrogant one will be restrained,
Cowardice in warfare will not avail;
The One who watches over us with foresight,
Clearly will be seen there.
75   The Ruler of men loves greatness more
Than a lover of poetry loves avarice,
Less does He love the garrulous one than the meek one,
More does He love the open-handed person than the niggardly
        person!
The joy of the heavenly host, make joyous my mind
80   In Your blissful land, in Your blessed dwelling-place,
Son of the living God, my Ruler who will settle me
From my wretched place, and who will bring me to my well-
        being.
The graciousness of my King will free me:
May I be free along with my Ruler who has accomplished it.
85   A King brilliant His law, Lord of perfect grace,
Gracious and wise, Prince of the memorable realm,
From our stay [full] of adversity here,
From our sinfulness [He] will take us back again.

Merciful Lord, have mercy on me,
90   Do not drive me away from You;
I am far off straying in passion,
He who is not mindful will not be mindful [of Him].
But will not tarry for a moment, he will not make arrangement,
The happiness of mortal man is of transient duration,
95   Merciless, piercing sadness stabs him.
Extinguisher of battle-tumult, who loves me, do not hate me,
Do not impede me in my petitioning.
Because of the tumult of this world comes punishment
[For] the taste of an apple, the greed of Eve,
100   From disobedient and obstinate intent,
From many a sinful indulgence [in eating].
If there was desire to covet pride,
[And if] it was sweet it turned sour later.
The world laughs, constant is our undoing,
105   [But] in mocking us it moves into oblivion:
According to [the] report of destruction all shall perish
Of the peoples of whom none will remain.
He, the Prince of heaven, provided a refuge,
A fair dwelling, a place of honour [in] Paradise,
110   A place of fair renown there
For Adam, a habitation not of benefit [to him]:
A covering laden with fruit, a constant blessed provision
Laden with fruits of the earth.
Bright Saviour, save [us],
115   A poet worships You, praises and glorifies You.
Noble cause of Christendom, blessed King,
Chief of spoils whom it is easy to praise,
Praise of God, I extol those who proclaim it,
I will not acclaim anyone who praises [Him] if he desists;
120   For a reward, in order to deserve that which I must have,
[I] delight in praising Jesus.
I love the tribute which chanters present,
Blessed declamation to purify the soul.
From the leap into the cold-hot confusion of hell-swamp,
125   From the loud moan because of cold,
From an unmoving army of constant complaint,
From the roar of fire of persistent leap,
From destructive, fated, craving,
From the seriousness of sad contemplation,
130   From a lifetime with sinners,
From squandering happiness in vast and perdurable pain

In great regret through animosity of underlings,
From the shame of demons' provocation,
A devilish band horrific to beholders,
135   From grievous oppression at the time of sinning,
From familiarity with sin,
Make me familiar, O strong King, Chief of warfare,
With generous privilege, in the company of blessed saints,
Perfectly at ease cogitating wisdom,
140   In a free right not diminishing and slow to vanish,
In the precious order of the assembly of supporters,
In the precious and learned song of an excellent realm,
In the urgency of [the] labour of book producers,
In this world, in the dwelling-place of the soul.
145   In the faithful support of very splendid fearless ones
And the elevation of holy ones, a shining host,
God grant that I consider the will of the Prince,
The joyful portion of the sublime choir of higher chanters,
A splendid group and most eminent as need requires.
150   Salutary for your singer are welcomers in face of the judgement,
In face of the wrath of the judgement of the judges;
When the three hosts [will] be judged according to their lot,
May God decree that we be brought to the blessed host
Of heaven as befits wise ones.
155   Not a wise one is the presumptuous person who does not
          arrange protection
Before taking on the mantle of sadness,
When heavy grief weighs upon the breast of a lonely one,
How fortunate will be the contented and commendable one;
What an affliction when everything sweet turns bitter,
160   How consoling it is to make amends for what one may do.
May Christ the Lord be ready to reach me,
If benefit does reach me, let [Him] not reject my petition!
God will lead me from my evil ways to follow
His way, to the beauty of [His] pathway.
165   How fortunate that person who proceeds and dies on the way
While journeying towards the generous-hearted One,
Since God fetched the defenceless ones
(Praiseworthy encounter sequel to bitter punishment),
Five ages of people from the violence of burning,
170   The five ages of the world and even longer.
Woe to one indulging in his sin
In evil rather than working for a reward,
Sin and increasing greed it is

To desire iniquity for too long and excessively.
175   He guards perfectly anyone who seeks [His] will,
      Who does penance for whatever his sin,
      [But] a sinner indulging in sins
      That deserves anxiety in its main portion.
      May we aim, before familiarity with agony,
180   To seek heaven, gentle home of affability.
      Since our God has purchased us
      With nails and blood and suffering,
      Since the Creator grants salvation to the one who believes in Him,
      Since he saved Noah's ark and people.
185   Since the Trinity rescued the three youths from the fire,
      Three fine youths going to the saints,
      Because He rules over whatsoever He wishes,
      Since that is His will, I desire whatever He desires;
      The friend of a loving host is beloved,
190   Protector of Christendom, let Him grant me devotion!
      Since the Lord of the splendid sphere reigns
      Over the brilliant circuit of the sun that cannot brighten Him
            [further],
      Let the Patron bestow ever greater support
      Upon Cynddelw, the help of [His] encouragement.
195   Since God has fashioned our transient short life
      Brilliantly in faith,
      May the One who created us ordain on our behalf
      Mercy before possession by the grave.
      He who brings us into being, our praiseworthy Lord,
200   One excellently wise, complete His fine realm,
      The One who knows us and redeemed us from the fate of those
      The five ages of the world through the baptism of John.
      The One who is not lacking in devotion or worship,
      The One on a gibbet, on a four-pointed cross,
205   The One who is recognized, who hastens to the judgement seat,
      He will come to us (not to him [a sinner]).
      When God may show forth His anger,
      It will erupt and come down upon our heads,
      An uproar will amazingly strike fear into crowds,
210   A roaring wind will sweep along its strident way,
      A foam-crested wave will ravage the seashore,
      The deep will surge forward, the sea will overflow,
      Sparks will assume noisy fury,
      Rage from heat of flaming fire will burst forth.
215   After New Year gift-giving, after pleasant New Year

When brave ones are feasted around a drinking cup,
After love and armour and graceful white steeds,
War horses of a royal court reared on equine fare,
After payment [as reliable] as the proclamation of John,
220 Before a grave under the green turf, before my visage pales,
God will give me, because of my gift of craftsmanship,
Great confidence from labour in the vineyard,
And then will come judgement [with its] total panic,
May my lot be at the right hand of my Lord.

Poem 2 (IV 17)
Sic transit gloria mundi

Lord Possessor of the ten orders, true Claimant of honour,
Ten grades of Your blessed land [which is] so fortunate, so vast,
God strong and true, comprehensively is our discord
    considered,
Destruction of the world when it is rushed upon us.
5   There are two habitations which are considered,
Two [so] dissimilar in the face of death:
The home of heaven [which is] a land full of wisdom, a fine large
    erection [for] Adam,
Hell is the other, a cruel [and] bitter construction,
[A place] vain [and] useless, as is read in writing,
10   It is believed through faith and religion.
Through great praising of [the] Three in a perfect treatise,
By means of the restrictions of language, by means of the
    alphabet,
The riches of the Lord will be spread abroad,
Not well has a mother raised a son who does not consider them.
15   The Protector who is the support of mankind maintains blessings
    for the world,
Ruler on behalf of people, Head of all liberality;
The gracious Prince apportioned [to me] a gift which will be
    purified,
Support for my poetic art, [for me] Your bondsman.
A fine wisdom-laden kingdom will shine out forever
20   Around Christendom which is laden with riches, around the face
    of the earth,
After the concealment of the day by darkness,
After the treacherous aspect of the light of dawn.
By praising God before [marriage] union with the earth—burial,
Gentle merciful One, let Your friend be a bard to You;

25   Though I be accustomed today to a happy life on earth,
      Yet I know not if I shall be long-lived.
      God knows our need, numerous prayers without ceasing
      Lest we be put in danger without a priest;
      We have known that One awaits us who holds the entire world
          intact,
30   One of certain dominion over death in sanctuaries.
      It is so sad for anyone to lose utterly [the] great God,
      A wise person does not neglect Him from his early life;
      There is a Guide, He makes us tremble,
      [Our] Defender in the final dissolution of [our] death.
35   A curse comes [to us] from denying Christ,
      Intricate, most sad and most painful punishment;
      It is a crime for anyone to scorn His will,
      The devil will take hold of evil in the mind.
      Persecution which is oppressive will bring great sorrow [in its
          wake],
40   An inevitable decree before a sad death:
      The truly wise one avoids the stratagem of the betrayal of the will,
      [And the] grievous hardship [that comes after] the greatest anger
          resulting from the greatest sin.
      The full intent [of God] to punishment because of the [full]
          intent of [my] deceit
      ([By] praising battles) makes me reflect in my danger:
45   In spite of that [sc. praising battles] very usual to my mind is the
          practice of
      Aligning myself with [the] sweet [which turns] bitter after a long
          while.
      An essential for me and [for] my cause was
      Contemplating my coming close to my grave;
      In the way of the inhabitants of the earth the Lord will place us
50   In the earth [that causes] worry to many, [in] a comfortless grave;
      He consigns us wholly to the soil of the earth
      [And] in the space of one moment he will raise us
      (From the sadness of death, terror of battalions,
      From a grief-laden cold grave) all of us to life.
55   From enjoyment of the world we all come on Judgement Day,
      Because of bearing sin, sadness will abound;
      The merciful God does not like excessive arrogance,
      Bounty does not accrue from the love of that [excessive
          arrogance].
      Let me not offend a Leader who has saved me from misery,
60   It is not easy for His adversaries to hide themselves [from Him];

Let me not lose [sight of] God because of the splendour of the
    world,
Those who are not foolish did not lose heaven!
Folly is the desire for the emotional activity of lust,
Inordinately we love the leader's load [of wealth-gift]
65   Without regard for our need, [the] assured refuge,
And without realizing that the world is so corrupt.
There was [a] lesson for us: Arthur has been of yore,
He was [like] the wind's onslaught, attacking [with] blows
    beyond count;
There was Julius Caesar, he had tried to win Fflur
70   From the lord of Britain, it was costly to claim her.
There was Brân son of Llŷr, a good binder of an army
Of valour in enemy territory, in battle, in conflict;
There was great Hercules, with terrible attack of steel,
With the passionate and strong courage of Greiddur.
75   Criminal was Madog, [the] renowned leader,
He had a warning, gnawing anxiety:
There was Alexander, prince of the world,
Even as far as the signs of the zodiac, he was not idle.
Do not peoples recognize that all [are] in the misery of plague,
80   [That] every thing [is] laid waste, and in ruins,
[That] every lord in his retinue, every prince, every leader,
Every defender in the present world is perishable?
To reject the absolute Lord of all the extensive scripture,
Doing so is an unrewarding task;
85   According to desire beyond sight [and] beyond the perception of
    a watchman,
On the day of victory over the world will come the perfect One.
May the supreme King, strong Ruler of the cosmos,
Banish from my mindset the danger of [the] sinner;
Prince of heaven, bright temple,
90   May Christ the Creator be not sorrowful in my regard!
Creator of heaven, blessed protection of [the] saints,
A rulership [that is] so great a pardon,
Sin [that is] an innate force within me, I nourished it
Praising and consenting to [practices of] my youth.
95   I shall worship, I shall extol the Three by the excellence of my
    gift,
A refuge that will save me by virtue of my excellence,
Since the Lord God bestows bounty in abundance,
Since He shares bright blessing, fine and generous rewards.
Since the bounty of the Leader liberates all,

100   Since the Prince, the strong Lord, binds both the strong and swift
            man,
        Since He hears, since He understands my composition,
        The splendid Ruler, the Creator, let us believe that it was He
            who made everything.
        The conflict of the present world is vexation, unsure habitation,
        For brittle as glass is [its] strong enchantment;
105   Upon the Three cosmic Persons let your purpose be,
        To the Three rightly and truly [let you render] just homage.
        To the one God, one Man, let treachery not be vocal,
        To the blessed Son, to the Father of fine longevity,
        Since the five wounds of Christ brought the five ages from
            captivity,
110   From anguish, from a distressed region.
        Because of the unyielding strength [of the world] (to consider the
            sorrow of humanity),
        Because of treachery, because of a deceitful reign
        He [Christ] entered humanity, and [human] form and the womb,
        In sorrow, in pain, in bodily form.
115   The great One conquered death [and] extensive His suffering
        In endeavouring to win the supreme proprietorship;
        Let us, without grievous experiences, [endeavour to] win
        Kingship on high with our God.
        Head of monarchs, when You were born, Excellent One,
120   The world was a captive, [its] desire was [for freedom].
        King of every frontier, of every illustrious fate,
        Consumed by fear we fell into the horror of unbelief:
        Amidst the hosts of hell, piercing slavish abode,
        In the affliction of heat, of wretched welcome,
125   With a device of savage hatred including fire,
        In the chaos of a place where motion avails not.
        Where Cain went because of his sinful act,
        Let me not go [to] the society of wickedness;
        We know that every evil one comes to the earth
130   To endure the ready and unrelenting furrow [of the grave].
        Let us endure, and be vigilant, in our sadness,
        [We who are] an angry assembly in church, a full congregation;
        And me with my [religious] fervour so uncertain
        To hold God in infinite contempt.
135   I pray through the intercession of Mary for peace before death,
        So that my playfulness may not cause me painful hurt,
        Before setting out in misery for a home in the earth,
        Paying back to God what is His due.

With a host of angels, fair hope of the race,
140   Before death [and] in front a very great assembly,
       Let me receive a boon through worshipping Christ the Lord,
       Finding refuge in the dwelling of the nine heavens!

Gwalchmai ap Meilyr

Gwalchmai ap Meilyr was a close contemporary of Cynddelw, being perhaps slightly earlier, with his floruit spanning the years 1132–80. He was one of a family of poets; his father, Meilyr Brydydd (c.1081–c.1137), is regarded traditionally as the first of the *Gogynfeirdd*. Gwalchmai's two sons, Einion and Meilyr, and Elidir who was also probably his son, were also professional poets and their seventeen dedications to God appear below as Poems 4–15. A tradition survived in Anglesey at the beginning of the fourteenth century that Gwalchmai ap Meilyr was an 'advocate' in the court of Owain Gwynedd.[3] More is known of him than of most of the other court poets, see CBT I, pp. 129 ff. Nine of his poems survive, four of which are dedications to secular patrons, Madog ap Maredudd of Powys, Owain Gwynedd and his two sons, Dafydd ab Owain and Rhodri ab Owain. Gwalchmai followed his father, Meilyr, as *pencerdd*, 'chief poet', to Owain Gwynedd, who had succeeded Gruffudd ap Cynan (*ob.* 1137) as prince of Gwynedd, and who was the most note-worthy of all Gwalchmai's patrons. This is evidenced in the poem entitled 'Gorhoffedd Gwalchmai' (CBT I 9).

A study of his poetry reveals that his poetic duties were performed at a period slightly earlier than Cynddelw (c.1155–95). It seems reasonable, therefore, to assume that the full-length dedication to God, Poem 3, is the earliest example of its kind in *Gogynfeirdd* poetry. The general mood and attitude in the poem suggest that its author, at the time of com-position, was advanced in years and painfully conscious that death is fast approaching.

Poem 3 (I 14)
Mea Culpa!

       I beseech God, [as] divine service,
       [For] conversion that will come to goodness,
       [For] free-flowing energy in keeping with my desire,
       Guidance for my success in all my aspirations.
5   I will sing, I intend by means of such energy

---

[3] For further details on legal posts held by poets in the Court of Gwynedd, see D. Stephenson: GG 14, which refers to J. Fisher (ed.), *Tours in Wales* (1804–13) by Richard Fenton (London, 1917), 306.

(Unnecessary [is that] in my need to arouse me)
An association with toil, and in praise worshipping the Creator,
And attaining complete devotion.
And effort and pain and subjugation of the body,
10 And preparing properly for sailing the sea,
And obtaining from God the eradicating of lust,
And the sincere prayer of a Welshman in exile,
[And] uprooting and change where there used to be desire and
  anger,
Scorning this world's state of constant hardship,
15 And toil which would be better than evil riches,
The will of the Trinity, a force that would not fail.
From the Creator, from community [with Him], will come my
  understanding,
From the Son, from the Spirit, from the power of fine intent,
From the unity of the Trinity, of the same stock as I am:
20 Mercy from the same substance, dignity of the same kind.
Three persons equally fine over the archangels,
Heavenly ones equally endowed, of undying power,
Let them be united in granting me peace as I extol them;
They are One God and truly Three.
25 A wretched nature we have through the folly
Of loving the world too much with its dark oppression:
While I might have God to praise with my talent
My mind wanders in duplicity and deceit.
Merciful God, lessen my sinfulness,
30 So that according to the faith my song be not treacherous.
I believe in Christ [from] heaven (a candle in time of need)
[And] the excelling baptism of my God on the Epiphany.
On the Epiphany the one of the true essence of God considered
(Unfailing comprehension) accepting baptism;
35 The young and blessed John held
The true Son of the God of heaven in running water.
Since the One of sublime power came to the womb
Of Mary in order to raise up the multitude of joy,
Happy will God be in His glory;
40 She will long be loved for that.
She the mother to her Father, she an undeniable virgin.
She wholly gracious, a bestower of blessing,
She a daughter to her Son the way things are,
She a sister to God of holy faith,
45 She carried lovingly the well-being of the race of her fellow-man

Against the burden of the eight sins, the proper possession of the
   chief Three.
The Son of God purchased a happy reconciliation;
The one who would not belittle it, deserves a reward.
Let us be mindful of the time of the Lord's coming
50   With drops of His blood upon His cross.
The twelve chosen apostles, wise [and] gentle,
Trusted joyfully in His power:
We believe in their being together, and it ends not,
In the unity of the Trinity eternally.
55   Eternal God, while I may speak
I shall take pains to make a song about You;
Through the gift you have bestowed [on me] may I speak
[Though it is] in the grip of falsehood that I sing.
And in the spate of ready excitement [of inspiration] I am
60   Accorded dignity which is no dignity because of what I compose,
With my mind set on possessing, according to my desire,
A gift of wealth wherever I may obtain it,
And I have a God to whom I shall pay recompense for my evil
Because of His mercy before I should die;
65   And when I may be in peril may the Lord grant me [that I make]
A composition perfect in structure which I shall handsomely
   dedicate [to Him].
The abode of merit, a holy home,
It is recited [that it is] beyond [the] sea, beyond [the] vast
   boundary,
The land which Christ has taken through the painful cross of
   nails
70   Because of the complete loss of man's goodness:
May God bring me there on a profitable journey,
Pleasant travelling [to] the noble fortress.
I prefer, since proper it is,
To grow familiar with exile rather than [drink] golden mead.
75   Sweet is sin when a weak person pursues it,
So sad is the soul when it languishes.
Inheritance of the profligacy of my conduct pursues me,
Wretched sadness of hostile terror.
The good repentant man, God will honour him,
80   He will receive forgiveness in virtue of his ardent faith.
I beseech You, O King, generous Lord, right now,
That I might merit easily a speedy journey on a voyage with a
   quick and sharp wind.
[The man] eager in his journey to a dwelling across the seas

To diminish sin, he desires to go
85   Where Christ walked on the fair face of the earth:
Before I become a corpse, may I have the exhaustion [of
        penance].
May my purpose be successful in true belief,
In devotion, in faith, in illustrious company,
To be borne by my God to my deserts
90   From the tumult of this life with its very great oppression.
Helpless is the beginning of life [even] for one with abundance of
        splendour
And its certain end as painful as death,
And there is no avoiding the bitter lodging
Of a cold bed in the covering of earth.
95   Alas for us the fate that has been given to us
In excessive habit of sin leading to failure,
Lest something pleasant in appearance deceives us eternally
To forfeit the attributes of the fullness of peace.
And we have a physician who can rid us of our falsehood,
100   And let us put our trust [in Him];
He, Lord of heaven, let Him strengthen us
To abandon sin after [our] arrogance.
And of my blessed Lord a weak supporter am I,
And mine it is to request a noble request,
105   Pardon for all the great wrong-doing
Which I have committed through any evil deed.
And my merciful Lord, let Him have mercy for me.
And let Him not drive me away from Him:
And God will faithfully rescue me
110   Ready for the judgement of the Trinity of the Three in One.

Elidir Sais

We assume that Elidir was the son of Gwalchmai ap Meilyr and grandson of Meilyr Brydydd. He is generally known as Elidir Sais, Elidir the Englishman, and he lived c.1195–1246. How he acquired the cognomen Sais is a moot point, and different suggestions have been advanced. The most likely one is that he may have spent time in England either as exile or on some official mission.[4] Ten poems, comprising 333 lines, make up his poetic canon. Of the ten, five are secular and the remainder are dedications to God, Poems 4–8. There is some doubt about the authorship of Poem 8, and whether or not it should be included in this study. It has been edited as an ode to God, but in fact the word 'God' does not occur

[4] See CBT I, pp. 317–18.

throughout its 22 lines. Poem 29 is an example of a long *incipit*, in Elidir's eulogy 'To God and Dafydd ab Owain'.

Poem 4 (I 21)
Deliver me, O Lord!

Mighty warrior, His gift came in the form of
Jesus, child of Mary.
Blessed was the gift of her breast born from her womb
Through growing under privileged favour.
5   He knows us thoroughly, He triumphed,
He is [the subject] of the greatest praise that was;
He created the world before entering the womb,
On high from heaven he beheld us.
He made the sun with its shining in a great sweep,
10   He made the moon and light in darkness;
He made ebb and flow [of tides], and complete ruling of the world,
And the governing of worlds.
How just was His giving of gift,
How impeccable was His adhering to His intention!
15   Traitors had insisted on betraying Christ,
Ineffectual cruelty that!
Had they succeeded, we could have not believed [in Christ],
Standing amazed for too long amidst the terror of the world.
We have done wrong, and a great wrong it has been;
20   That was over-indulgence, amazing that it was permitted:
The children of Adam seeking to hide from the Lord,
From admitting the sinning;
Both Eve and he [Adam] knew that:
God knows, knowing what happened.
25   Best for me is to excel through [the help of] the Lord
Composing a fine song in the best language;
Proclaiming a song about the Trinity,
A eulogy in language [to] One deserving worship.
Wisest it is for us to put things in order with God,
30   A faithful Warrior to help me.
Acts [imbued with] hateful forces I practised,
The work of a fortunate man is to make peace!
Before the wound of confining burial subjugates,
Before the grave (odious deed)
35   Before my flesh is placed in an unseemly and distressing manner
        under the earth,

With a sod on each side [of it],
Let me be a servant of God, before being muted
(Necessary suffering in the death of a host).
Let me be placed in the same place where there is submitting
40   By servants to serve Him.
May God call me to summon me to heaven
Under His protection and that of His household.

Poem 5 (I 22)
Preserve me God, I take refuge in You

It will be necessary for us to prove, though the world be
    shattered,
Our physical baptism.
God the Magician, privileged King,
You are privileged, generous [One] who defends the land.
5   Place me with the baptized host,
Do not place me in the fearful place [hell],
Do not take me from my dwelling-place in the world
Amidst the clamour of mortal men.
Christ will come gently, doughtily on the Day of Judgement
10   In order to free the people of the world;
[He] who is good, he will be called godly,
[He] who is evil will continue to be without recompence
In the persistent painful infernal fire
Of deep hell, with its deepest declivity.
15   Many a one will come with his soul in fetters
In bodily garments.
Mine it is to enlist a Virgin to pray for me,
Mary and Peter, Maria and Paul.
Mine to utter [the] mighty word
20   Of the Lord Ruler who grants control.
He who made the birds of the firmament
And earthly refuge,
Listen to me, rightful Lord,
May the Master of the heavenly temple listen:
25   Let me be in whatsoever part where You are praised,
[In the] land of the Spirit of our spiritual Father.

Poem 6 (I 23)
O God be our protector and strength

It is a necessity that we reject the concordance of this world,
For we are diligent in its vanity.
I have fled from sin of no little import
Through a desire of keeping [my share of] mercy.
5   Let the Trinity take me from my sadness
To the mercy of redemption [which is] the whole of my desire.
In three ways will they, the race, come to God
When all shall come to the place of judgement on Judgement
        Day:
[The] highest [way] (chaste is the cause of truth)
10   Is the way of virginity [as regards] sexual intercourse (let it be a
        virtue on Judgement Day!);
The second is the proper esteem of wisdom
In order to enjoy the dwelling-place of mercy;
(Three good [Ones] made us) [and] the third way is bequeathing:
The good repentant one, God does not refuse him.
15   He refused Eve and her fall on account of the apple;
Her rebellion was a sadness to her kin.
Concerning the Lord is the discourse in poetry,
Concerning Jesus did Joseph declaim.
May God, defender of Israel, give to me
20   [My] share of life through which I may come to His peace
[The] day when some will be placed in honour
[And] others be placed on the left side.
Christ will make an assembly after the cross,
Assemblies of peoples, all in His dwelling-place.
25   It is wisest for man before his end
To make peace with God before removing to a grave.
Ours it was to accept complete reconciliation
Before God found fault with our life.
We have sinned through bad transgression:
30   I desire Your mercy, [O] Trinity!
A limit is placed on every wantonness:
It is Moses who said that, and God will arrange it.

Poem 7 (I 24)
Memento homo quia pulvis es!

The best thing for man on Shrove Tuesday is to persuade
A priest to accept him,

For the faithful God caused
The redemption of [His] children from plague and sadness.
5   The One who was destined to redeem them, multitude of the
            world,
Undertook the burden of penance in Lent.
Very great was the fast by intention:
[For] forty days was God's self-denial.
On Spy Wednesday came Judas's purpose,
10   To betray our Spirit,
And Thursday there came discouragement to us,
The taking of Jesus of gentle and consoling speech.
Friday, it was harsh, bloody was
The cross / crucifixion of our Father: our total oppression.
15   For His sake let us make appropriate profession,
He caused every species to be alive from its beginning.
Saturday he departed, He went to the grave,
An unhappy parting.
The next day he performed a second feat,
20   [He], true Son of God, demonstrating that He was alive.
Sunday (most profound memory) when the sun arises,
He rose up from His grave.
Great news excites us, it will excite,
[The event] of Christ the Lord's awakening, our [poetic?] art.
25   [O] Lord who made us and will redeem us
[   ]
Sustainer, [O] Son of grace, One who was imprisoned for too
            long,
He was the one who fulfilled His intention.
The Son of God led [souls] out from fire and terror,
30   From the cold marsh of hell, redemption from its morass,
[And] from the earth's disturbance, from trepidation,
[And] from a cold comfortless prison.
In large numbers did the children / men fall on account of Him
Around a Lord with His cross bloody.
35   Eight chief sins there are (dangerous are they):
From amongst the eight vicious [sins], pride [is the] worst.
I call, my Lord, for I will be accepted by you:
Every one of evil mind is called an outlawed one.
There will be no undoing of human happiness
40   With the Son of God in His blessedness.
Manifestly may my love be
For heaven, for God's refuge and His protection!

Poem 8 (I 20)
Have mercy on me, O God

I extol the glorious Lord,
King of Glory, the divine Seer,
Defend me, my King, spiritual Ruler,
Mighty prosperous Lord, victorious Noble [One],
5   Blameless Father, against the treachery of the mortal community
Of extreme sharp hellish pain of penance.
Generous and blessed Christ, gainful [His] cross,
Splendidly He saved us on [Good] Friday.
[O One of] faithful holy standard, I supplicate
10   That I may not be a cruel fetter on You, my Ruler,
Supreme Ruler, privileged Redeemer,
You received, you led forth a baptized host.
Receive me, my Leader, to the rightful place of virtues
For the sake of your painful nails and your nailed [body as]
    testimony.
15   Lord of heaven and earth, holy Lord,
I claim your protection against the molten fiery material
Of the torment of the fierce oppressive instruments of hell,
Host of the dreadful cold swamp, an enslaved mortal host.
Because of the pain of your suffering, strong Lord,
20   Supporter of glory, heroic guarantor,
Hear wretched poor flesh often in supplication
To You for mercy, my King of laudable blessing.

Einion ap Gwalchmai

Einion was a son of Gwalchmai ap Meilyr and was trained as a professional poet in the tradition of his father and grandfather. Five of his
compositions survive—two sung to secular patrons, one of whom was
definitely Llywelyn ab Iorwerth. Regarding the second of these poems,
'Marwnad Nest ferch Hywel' ('Elegy for Nest daughter of Hywel'), this
Hywel cannot be identified, so it is impossible to say who Einion's
patron was at the time of its composition. For a full analysis of the
difficulties and possibilities, see CBT I, pp. 443–4. Einion, like his father
Gwalchmai, is remembered for having held some legal post in the court
of Llywelyn ab Iorwerth.[5] This could not have been as seneschal,[6] a post

[5] See D. Stephenson: GG 14, where he cites from the *Calendar of Various Chancery Rolls
... 1277–1326)*, 195, *Eynon ap Walchmayn associatus fuit Justiciariis Domini Regis ap West-
monasterium et ipsi judicaverunt.*

which Ednyfed Fychan held from 1216 until his death *c*.1246. Weighing the evidence, Stephenson asserts that in the persons of Gwalchmai and his son Einion, we see men who may have retained the functions and the eminence of the *ynad llys* of the legal texts.[7] Einion's other three odes are dedications to God, translated as Poems 9, 10, 11.

In view of the uncertainty regarding whether Elidir Sais was a son of Gwalchmai, it would seem preferable that Einion and Meilyr ap Gwalchmai should precede Elidir in this study, but the order of presentation of their works, given in *Cyfres Beirdd y Tywysogion I,* has been followed.

Poem 9 (I 27)
Praise and thank you O God

       [O] God, supreme wonder-worker of miracles,
       Dispense to us a share of your blessings.
       You made use of men for your purpose,
       I also am a talented mortal man.
5   I have appropriately a gift as a man of genius
       And ready thoughts.
       I am a man of the holy profound Masses,
       [O] Lord God, [the] Giver of enlightened law;
       I am a wicked son of Yours, Master who created me.
10   If I were good, I would be without uncertainty
       Before a cemetery of loathsome activities;
       Though I be evil, be You merciful.
       Because of worthy devotion, may tears of atonement
       Flow unceasingly on my cheeks
15   Gaining appeasement for my sins
       Before I be on the way to the grave amongst graves.
       Before the bitter time of [rendering] an account comes,
       Before the disappearance of the desire for sins,
       God who will grant me love within the battlements of heaven;
20   God will hear my cry in my anxieties.
       May God ordain that I avoid the fierceness of the current's chill
       Of the flood of wicked hell, ferocious torrents.
       May God arrange that I because of my own effort avoid wounds,
       May God see that I eschew the foul sin of [desecrating] Sundays.
25   May God defend me from my intentions,
       [O] God, bring me unto You, my Great Father!
       [O] God, do not punish me because of my transgressions

[6] Official adviser of the prince; OED definition: 'the steward or major-domo of a medieval great house'.
[7] For a note on *ynad llys,* see WLW, 220–1.

The day that sins are punished.
For You there will be no end, nor was there a beginning:
30   May I be not sad in your assembly.
May I repay Him, generous Lord of kings,
On the bank of Jordan in order to receive His gifts,
Through pain and sorrow upon knees,
Through assuming the penance of elbows
35   In an altogether useless life because of words of wantonness
Which came beyond measure across my lips.
You suffered for the sake of the five ages the hurt of blue spears,
Five wounds, Lord of arts;
May I endure the place of pain on the Alps
40   In the interest of going to the place where I heard that You were.
The climax of faith was to see Your wounds
When you were wounded in Your wounds.
With the help of bright gentle angels
It does not belong to You, blessed Father, to put me one side.
45   Since You, [O] God, caused life to be mine
Do not for the sake of your nails abandon me to the devil.
Your Rood formed from a wooden cross of royal privileges
Saved six ages of the world from the danger of punishments.
Emperor Creator, because of Your blood (bloody it was)
50   Scornful of Your laws I shall not be.
Blessed [the] monks in churches,
They who love the Church, who are loving, observing well the
        afflictions [of penance],
A gentle assembly of holy songs,
Men, unflinching persons.
55   Alas for him who caused [them], dangerous treacheries,
When Jesus was pierced in His ribs.
After he had reached his [godly] goal
He brought the spoils of hell in His grasp,
And after that he did this
60   (It is truthfully that the sermons are preached!):
[The One of] fine attributes was seen going away
[On] the Feast of the Ascension (do not entertain doubt!).
On Thursday the Son of God ascended to heaven above
(A small amount of sins is too much)
65   As a noble King on the right hand side of [the Father],
As a generous brave [One] with [the] saints.
Let our end be on the shores
Of [the] sea of Bardsey until our [going to] heaven.
After telling a lie through ill nature,

70   And also after the wickedness of adulterers,
        After agreeing to join in battles,
        After bearing envy towards the best [ones],
        After zealous loving a multitude with oaths [of love]
        And many a reason for sighs,
75   After causing too much scandal, after worldly poems,
        After sin because of [?distractions at] the office of matins,
        After quarrelling over decisions on verdicts,
        After long pursuing merit [for] rewards,
        After fierce rejection of the assembly of ceremonies [of the Mass],
80   After serving the chieftains,
        After difficult bouts of [the illness of] humanity,
        After the wrath of pursuing in battles,
        Let me receive from God on high, after transgressions,
        [The] winning of a resting-place in the land of Paradise
85   Where man will not be older nor younger,
        Where the anguish of far-reaching need does not stab.
        I present a petition to God of the dwellings of heaven
        That Peter may not place obstacles
        To prevent me from my desert, from what is mine,
90   From my inheritance, from my dear love.
        May Michael come to me to bring me [in his] keeping
        As Cwyfan brought learning and books,
        As the coming of Elfodd to the land of Gelau,
        Like the obvious devotion of the prosperity of Cenau.
95   Mary and Saint Silin, Martin, Matthew,
        Mark and Luke, [with] the utterance of John,
        To [the] God of my soul, [in] need of speech,
        Make a request, do your share!
        Paul can intercede for me whenever death may come to me,
100   The generous strong [one] who will not separate me from my
                righteous One.
        Before I become silent, let me not be burdened;
        Gentle is piety and faith and [the] graces of blessing.
        The intercession of the steadfast achieves the hierarchies [of
                heaven]
        Where it befits Your powers, [O] wise God;
105   Let gentle thoughts demand, for the sake of my redemption,
        Praise of the Trinity in the form of prayers;
        Recourse to the treasures of God
        And the rejection of arms will achieve my forgiveness.
        May there be for me a perfect period of the best work
110   Before lying down in a grave.

Poem 10 (I 28)
Let us pray, keep watch and be ready

Lord of heaven, cleanse my heart,
Grant me, O God, to speak of You
True speech when melodious song is proclaimed
Like pure sweet paean.
5   Perilous for man is his age
Whenever he is in the evil of a life of sin.
When the three hosts of tribulation come before Jesus,
All will come to Him as terrified people to the judgement;
People of the miserable world, their destruction will be achieved,
10   Those who would not give alms on His behalf.
The good repentant ones, God will receive them,
And sinless men in their holiness.
The evil host will not endure;
Alas for those, Lord of heaven, who are not prepared.
15   There is no warning beforehand, wretched weak one,
Of the One who caused us to eschew drunkenness:
Believe that there will come later on the path of trouble
One day (and it is the Lord that has told us this)
When the transgressor will be punished, when
20   The war alliance will bring punishment on the human race.
And yet, before the pang of a fresh green grave of sand,
Let us do penance, let us humble ourselves in our dereliction;
Let us give food [as alms] and provide drink for God's sake,
Christ Lord and Master, with [submissive] humility.
25   Let us not be content to lack the welcome
Of the habitation of the blessed land of heaven in gentleness.
Fair habitation of the Lord, of the mode of its blessings
No tongue can declare.
Let us give precedence to religion, faith and blessing
30   Before stealthy death, deceitful treachery.
Let us pray, keep watch and be ready
For the valiant Hero who has saved us.
When Jesus came from His kingdom on high
The five ages of the world were in common bondage
35   In distraint, in a wretched condition, in the depths of hell,
Imprisoned in the grip of the cold swamp.
O revered God, avow You
I shall, Lord [and] Sovereign, strength of all peoples.
Let us uphold the midnight [service] prerogative, for it is the
       custom;

40   The Lord God will not accept a false excuse.
      Let us not sleep, let us chant the religious song of the rule,
      Since it is not through sleeping that protection [from hell]
            comes.
      To the home of God in heaven will go my cry
      Echoing on high before the Trinity,
45   Asking my Lord, Ruler of the rich ninefold host,
      To receive my soul when it leaves my flesh.
      Grant that, after my burial, I may be
      In the company of the One great God in His Unity.

Poem 11 (I 29)
Exaudi me Domine!

      Sustainer of the home of heaven, of Your grace (may it be great)
      Hear my prayer, [O] Lord God;
      Support me, Lord [who are] ready [with Your] protection,
      Supporter, Ruler, control my cupidity.
5   Upon the deceit of sins I would have desired [to put] the sign of
            the cross
      [And] to carry the cross for Christ's sake on my shoulder.
      Death for the soul (an unfortunate, unnecessary thing)
      Comes from desiring sinfulness.
      Little honour there is in [extending a] welcome [to] transgression
10   In a life of an immeasurable extent of folly.
      A burden of sins, not a small matter,
      Mote of the blind, foolish, unknowing [one]!
      Before my face pales, before the green grave of the cemetery,
      Sods [covering the] fall [of the] hosts buried in the earth,
15   Before the coming of the appointed time of our prison
      [And] the messengers of death as witness [to us],
      Before I have a cold grave, may I have a Lord!
      Let me atone graciously [and] extensively
      With ready repentance to my Jesus,
20   After [His] giving to me worthiness.
      Before there comes the falling of tears on cheeks,
      Before the enclosure of earth, [let] not shame [be mine]!
      Grievous will be the expense of a man of sixty years,
      After this there will be [the] letting go of life, it will not succeed!
25   Pleasant is every stratagem when it succeeds,
      Another pleasant thing is a mantle [for] arranging an appointment
            [under it]!
      Pleasant is the mead and feast of a successful leader,

Pleasant is a long and bright summer, lovely is a grove with growth,
Pleasant is the speedy stallion of April's stable,
30   Pleasant is plying spear and standard,
Pleasant will be a shield on a courageous shoulder,
Pleasant [and] strong is a hero and steed,
Pleasant are fiery warriors zealous [in the] unremitting fury of
     battle
When stalwart ones are in battle-fury:
35   More pleasant, more noble (let it be plentiful with me)
Is the magnificent praising of the Lord of magnanimity!

Meilyr ap Gwalchmai

Meilyr ap Gwalchmai was a professionally-trained poet, but no evidence exists of his being in the service of the princes of Gwynedd. The only poems of his which survive are religious in character and content and, although they embody a great deal that is definitely personal, they throw little light on Meilyr's own history. These four poems have all been edited as dedications to God and, varying in length, they amount to 213 lines. His poetry, revealing a deeper knowledge and experience of the Catholic faith than we would expect from a layman of the period, may suggest that Meilyr had studied theology and had entered a monastery. However, he makes no direct reference to becoming a monk and no historic record exists to corroborate that possibility.

Poem 12 (I 30)
Miserere mei, Deus!

May I receive from God, may I receive mercy,
Let it not be fearful need that overcomes me.
May being in the right through my gift free me from plague;
The world which I know through and through shall see tumult.
5   Let me please God, may the Lord deem me worthy,
May it be in the dwelling of heaven that he shall suffer me to be.
Certain heaven will there be for him who seeks it, freely,
Royal triumph of the religion of the creed.
May the God of seas and stars take account of me,
10   Rightful His claim over whomsoever He may claim!
May the privilege of the land of paradise welcome me,
That is a just and sure kingdom.
On great and perfect meaning may my mind contemplate
(Wise combination); may art make me skilled.

15   [The] One of discernment does not come close to one who may
          utter
      A ready lying word, no matter who may proclaim it.
      I believe in Christ, joyful teacher,
      Undiscerning is the poet who does not believe in Him.
      May I believe and may I consider that which a wise man may
          consider,
20   I shall put my trust in God and the saints and the privilege of
          their region.
      I am a Christian (unwavering blessing) under the rightful claim of
      Christ, may I be blessed whenever He may bless!
      May my nurturing in Christianity liberate me,
      May Christ the Lord, my King, free me,
25   And may He, King of heaven, protect me from stain [of sin],
      May his grace and understanding fulfil me fully.
      Let not the unfailing God scorn me,
      Without deceit is his thought, he who praises Him!
      Undeceiving is His love whenever He loves,
30   Unsullied glory it is for the one who believes in Him.
      May God the Creator and Ruler guide me until Judgement Day,
      A sinless life for me He desires.
      According to [my] desire may He give me great fulfilment of
          desire,
      May [His] shining gifts purify me;
35   May acceptable ceremonies prepare my body for burial,
      May the blessings of counsels instruct me.
      Heroic Counsellor, gentle towards the one who seeks Him,
      He does not like envy towards him who loves Him.
      That I love at all, may that free me from censure,
40   Let not love and its purpose fail in me.
      May the Lover of our safe cause choose me,
      May the friendship of God be mine each day.

Poem 13 (I 31)
God of heaven my certain refuge

      O Lord God, listen to Your praise,
      God Gift-giver who gives me remorse of conscience;
      Steadfast God of the hosts of glory,
      God of heaven, my refuge for sure;
 5   Privileged God who ransomed His friends
      From the pains and the sin they had committed.
      The descendants of Adam, [like] plants were they,

In this world they tarried.
With God in light, they [will] shine, host of Christendom,
10   Happiness they [will] have.
In the presence of Mary of greatest authority,
Spotless saints will our surety be,
And fine Michael, they will bring him as a helper
To the hosts from perdition.
15   Men of religion, they professed the faith,
In the Creator who created them they believe.
In the fair blessedness of the Trinity they will abide
In splendour as reward for the sublime song they sing.
I too must have a place according to privilege,
20   Paradise for ever is my aspiration.
Through the intercession of thousands and a hundred thousand
    of the [heavenly] host,
They will set me side by side with them.
Gabriel and Raphael will honour me wisely,
My reconciliation they have effected.
25   On the [Last] Day they will affirm me to my Owner,
To the One God in the unity they will admit me.
According to the merits of virtue they will place me.
Unceasingly they will maintain my dwelling-place.
To the blessedness, from depression, to happiness,
30   The rulers of the royal land will bring me;
From the throne of the Lord God they shall rule,
They demand that they be respected with universal respect.

Poem 14 (I 32)
May all believe in God!

It would be most proper for me, most needful for my life
To love the company of the fiercest conflict.
[About] sincere love I mention
[   ]
5   Sin in the form of transgression, the worst wickedness,
From my mind I shall expel it before [the] grave.
To love God would be the finest [thing] for all
As the saints most favoured in privilege love,
For loving God is the most perfect activity,
10   Henceforth I shall consider it before [the] law.
He [is] blameless and generous [and] of the utmost right,
He [is] sinlessly excellent, I shall be His bard,
He [is] a steadfast protector, supreme His peace,

He fashioned heaven, home of Adam.
15   He [is] one true God, the most faithful One,
Unity of generous grace, least cruel,
He [is] Three, and I, I wish not His anger,
He [is] the merciful and gentle, most loving [One].
He is the Father, He is the greatest good,
20   He is the Son, He is the highest Father,
He [is] the Holy Spirit most brilliant of nature,
He [is] generous majesty (I am not amazed),
He will ratify His vow, finest vow,
[The] hidden secret vow which I profoundly proclaim.
25   Let all believe in God, strong Lord of glory;
Belief as a thing desired I desire.
I consider a belief of meditative significance,
Faith without concealment it is, the surest.
He is credible, I believe in His intention,
30   Christ Lord and Master, and I shall not hide it.
To trust in unjust law, it is most repugnant:
To learn faith with magistrates and lord,
Devotion of belief daily, greatest glory,
Trusting in God and His grace, it is most righteous.
35   May You have faith in me, for the sake of the most skilful Lord,
May I have faith in You, my King, when I have most need [of it!]

Poem 15 (I 33)
Holy is the Most High King of saints, resplendent His Kingdom

Majestic King of the tempestuous might,
[O] King, I attain through your gift [the ability] to praise You
      with ready will,
A fine share of praise which has the characteristics of song
To my merciful Lord, Chief of heaven,
5   For He is our goodness, [the subject] of our wise service.
Rich and gracious God, we beseech You
That we go not to our place, a place of anguish
For the destruction of a wicked accursed host.
Well does a godly person multiply prayers,
10   A task the Prince of reconciliation urges upon me.
I have great fear in going to it;
Lord of battlements, do not blame me
Since I know not my way nor my manner [of acting] on it.
A pain for man is that he was created
15   [As one] giving inadequate service to God

Which could lead him astray to the tumult of hell,
[The] grasp of unhappy sleepless trouble.
The appropriate longing of a man of transient honour
Is [to make] peace when [Saint] David may be a patron.
20 Sadness arises after death
For him who is an exile in his shame.
The shame of exile! Certain affliction!
Without hope is [the] man who is without faith [and] of hapless
      words,
Evanescent is his wealth [and] his practices,
25 A bad offensive neighbour of the frail rejected multitude,
[The] first man whom the tribulation of death overcomes
([In the] deprivation of poverty) in battles.
Let me pray to the King, Ruler of forces,
Since God made from His materials
30 (God did it) the virtue of plants.
Ruler of speech and crops,
One of ready gifts who made evident our evil and our deceit;
Let not the Lord leave us deprived of our share.
At our beginning God gave to us
35 The fine gift of paradise (light abides!).
God had made us without any need
Until our acts did us harm.
Woe to the one who may anger God of the fullness of riches,
The God who makes the two forms of streams and fruits.
40 Earth was made sterile through the transgressions of man;
Without blemish it would have been [otherwise, it was] God
      who made it.
Finest deliverance is [the] praiseworthy Passion,
[In order to] win merit, contemplate it!
Since you have given audience to me, a human person,
45 I shall give you advice without enmity in it:
When God may wish to uproot you
From the order of the present world with its constant fear,
Though you have wealth (an evident endowment)
Let not regret entice you though leaving it
50 Nor greater bitter anxiety of pain that is, because of it;
Do not reproach God for taking away that which is His.
A man's desire is to be brought in his life
To accept the calling of the Christian cross,
Strong confidence against disbelief,
55 Since our mind knows not how long our life.
Necessary is it to consider for a while, in spite of that,

In the midst of a hard struggle, the achievement of life in this
    present world:
He who was long-lived yesterday, today is no more,
God did not intend human life to be abiding.
60 Honour for a life in the presence of the host of the faithful
Instead of grief is what the Lord ordains.
He who receives it will be found without the reproach
Of sin and conflict and angry mockery.
Since death faces us,
65 All the people of the world, wretched death,
But for what he might say about God the Son of Mary,
It would not be right for man to say a word.
Harsh-tongued word of evil, act of a bitter mind,
Miserable will they be at home with him together [in hell].
70 Alas for those who may offend God through pride,
Arrogance that plunges them into pain, in lengthy gnashing of
    teeth.
Alas for him who does not labour for benefit in his soul
[And] undertake a short period of penance in the world.
Alas for him who may go astray in the company of Cain
75 Before the perilous corruption of burial as a result of war.
Alas for whoever may be there, a sad exile,
Pain will reach him [and] suffering of severe anguish.
God will accept our longing
For it is He who made us and who will save us.
80 Most High Lord, defending the rule [of religion],
Wealthy Lord, light of the world,
Let me receive, [O] Creator of heaven, strength from You
[And the] reward of seeing a feast in peace for ever.
For ever in peace may I be at ease in His family,
85 Holy is the Most High King of saints of resplendent kingdom;
Lord of heaven and earth and complete refuge,
Generous Lord of many, Patron of the happy ones.
Alas for him who makes no effort before his death
[Nor] makes peace with the Creator who has made him.
90 Let us believe in the Lord who has blessed us,
[The] world that came to His part, obvious was its hatred.
I shall call on the blessed dwelling to pray for me
And the entire grades of heaven in their merit.
May Peter of fair practice pray for me
95 And the holy peoples so gentle as to their lineage.
May Saint Ezechias pray for me
To Mary mother of her Father, her fine honour.

May Mary pray for me to her Boy
That I go not defiled to the abode of Judas.

100   Let not the Lord, who has fairly ransomed us, permit me [to be]
In the ruin of Cain along with Satan.
From peoples with agony as their company
Let Him, my God of heaven, be my defence.

Llywelyn Fardd (II)

An examination of the two secular poems ascribed to Llywelyn Fardd (II) suggests that he belongs to the thirteenth century, and for the general argument in favour of placing his floruit *c*.1216, see CBT VI, pp. 101–2. The other two poems, which are dedications to God, represent more than half of the poet's work. In themes and style they accord with *Gogynfeirdd* religious poetry of the same period, and bear a marked resemblance to that of Einion ap Gwalchmai (Poems 8, 9, 10) in the early thirteenth century. They also have a certain affinity with two compositions by Gruffudd ab yr Ynad Coch (Poems 41, 42) in the later part of that century. (His namesake Llywelyn Fardd (I) belongs to the twelfth century, see CBT II, pp. 3–5).

Poem 16 (VI 9)
Contrite, contrite am I

Regretful, regretful am I
For loving the comfortless, sad world.
The second worry is remorse
For destroying a man and falsely accusing an abject person.

5   The third [grief] will be, when the lamentable day comes,
Pride due to arrogance, due to vexation.
The fourth will be the greed of the wealthy
For a store of riches too vast, too showy.
The fifth pain is when there is rebellion:

10   [Eating] meat at a forbidden time, a companion to [i.e. evidence of] disrespect.
The sixth, bitterly did it happen early on,
Eve's luscious eating became [an occasion of] sadness.
I ask the Lord of so great purity of joy
Who created a variety of seeds, and birds,

15   That I may always be with the just Son of Grace,
May I be a servant of God before [entering] a habitation in [the] earth.

Poem 17 (VI 10)
The Lord in seeing understands

O may it be God who may turn me from my great wickedness
    towards Him,
To rightful hoping in that which is known,
To do penance before the sin [that leads to] enervation,
To contemplate, holy joyful profundity,
5   To faith, to devotion, to strength in order to go
On a vowed journey, while that is permitted to us.
It is to grasp protection that may not be denied that I go
To two elders of the Lord, not in vain will it be.
Asking the help of [Saint] Dewi wherever one goes
10   That is not a forbidden or untimely petition.
When Mary and Michael are encountered,
May I be skilful in the meeting-place before evening,
Where it is not righteous to turn [back] because of foolishness
Nor to seek a retreat in the oppression.
15   It will not defend or save us there
To express arrogance through evil activity.
The sin of vanity will not save us
Nor give us his reconciliation with wantonness.
Heaven is not reached by dint of fury
20   Nor at the same time through force of aggression.
It is better in seemly fashion at morning and evening prayer
To pray to the saints with the seven petitions of the Lord's
    Prayer.
It is Holy Peter that receives us in the time of need:
You it is who rejects whoever may be rejected!
25   Into the presence of the Trinity will come the three hosts
And one of the three led by Lucifer
And the [other] two on the right hand in light,
In the dwelling of light that will be blessedly praised.
Our leader was glorious, in the commendable scripture
30   His soul shall have a very sweet rest.
No one has been born fortunate or will be born fortunate
Who is deprived of the sight of God.
No one took up a weapon auspiciously who does not do
    penance
Since he does not at any time know how long [he] will be left.
35   Not auspiciously does a man pursue any boldness
In the turmoil of this world without [due] circumspection.
There will always be regret whilst one is in it,

It is for our renewal that there is our great cunningness,
It is to move us [forward] that there is our great courage,
40   Our wrong-doing alters our thought.
Very greatly does it concern me what may be given to me of
        wealth,
Ephemeral it goes, it is scattered.
Miserably does man pine [away] when he is deceived,
Sad, O God, is his destruction when he is destroyed.
45   The saddest [thing] I hear regarding the brilliance of the world
Is the excessive love of pride, [which leads to] a burden of penance.
Very idle and foolish are diverse [kinds of] frivolity,
The day of its retribution will come upon him.
Christ came to the womb in wisdom for our sakes,
50   We shall come before Him on the Mount of Olives.
Michael will come, in such a manner that he may be [clearly]
        seen,
Before a host of angels gentle and kind.
There will come to him those who may have been placed in the
        grave;
Let me come from my evil-doing, God will receive me,
55   Let Him come to protect me before the time of grief,
He who saved Paul will save all.
Saviour of great blessing, exalting a great law,
God of Israel, chosen race:
May God be with me, may I be a companion to you,
60   And you, Lord, a hundred times over with me.
And as for me, may I be yours, may I be on a journey without
        fear,
In a godly nature best utterance has been tested.
Alas for the proclaimer [i.e. the poet], before the agony of death,
Who does not proclaim a declamation of praise in Your honour.
65   Alas for the one without shame, impudent, heedless concerning
        his word,
Who does not speak at length of the great Son of Mary.
Alas for him who does not believe in the Trinity before the
        onrush of judgement:
It is usual for the hearth of the unbeliever to be[come] desolate!
When God willed a special punishment for him,
70   Towards the desire of his helper he was not kind:
Cain in league with lawbreaking,
Closed is hell on the captive host.
He who redeemed the five ages of the world from hell's captivity,
From among the innumerable captive multitude,

75   Before I become a man [buried] in the earth, let the Saviour
        Save me from pain, from all suffering.
        He who may perform an act of devotion, let him constantly ask
        The Lord who in seeing [him] discerns
        And who hears us, as we listen to him,
80   And who knows us fully according to fate
        And who loves us tenderly and again saves us
        And who loves not arrogance, an act of great insolence,
        And who seeks not oppression or violent practice
        And who praises not treachery through [exploitation of] trust
85   And who does not award of necessity his due debt to a man
        Unless he seeks it with righteousness.
        I present my petition to Mary,
        For the sake of her two loves let her not reject me:
        When I am standing [before the judge], let her stand to help me,
90   To bring me to the entrance leading to the Trinity.
        Let strong Michael welcome me,
        Let him take me from confinement to the expansive abode
        When one asks that his sin be removed,
        It is most just for his Lord to hear him.
95   I ask God for two petitions:
        One faith with devotion, and belief.

Madog ap Gwallter

Nothing is known of the life of Madog ap Gwallter except what can be
gleaned from his three surviving poems, two of which are dedications to
God (Father and Son) and one to St Michael, giving a total of 168 lines.
Since all three are religious poems we are obliged to rely on them and
their manuscripts to establish broadly the period of their composition.
The two main manuscripts in which Madog's poems were preserved are
Llyfr Coch Hergest, The Red Book of Hergest, and NLW 4973B. In both
of these Dr John Davies, Mallwyd (*ob.* 1644) has recorded evidence of
what was by then probably an accepted tradition. In the Red Book he
records the name *y brawd Fadog ap Gwallter,* 'Brother Madog ap Gwallter', and in NLW 4973B he gives 'fl. A.D. 1250'. There is also a
tradition, based on certain historical evidence, that Madog ap Gwallter
was a Franciscan[8] and therefore his surviving poems are accepted as
belonging to the second half of the thirteenth century. The first Franciscan friary was established in Wales before 1245.[9] It is believed that

---

[8] See CBT VII, pp. 347–8.
[9] Glanmor Williams, *The Welsh Church from Conquest to Reformation* (Cardiff, 1962), 21
and Intro. footnotes 50 and 54.

Madog was a native of a place called Llanfihangel since, in a series of *englynion* which he composed to Mihangel, St Michael the Archangel, he states that Michangel was patron saint of his parish. In a discussion on the Cardiff 2.611 Manuscript, Sir Ifor Williams has attempted to locate this particular parish, namely Llanfihangel Glyn Myfyr in Denbighshire.[10]

Although poem 33 in *Cyfres Beirdd y Tywysogion* VII has been edited as a dedication to God, a translation has not been given here because of interpretive difficulties caused by defective manuscript readings.

Poem 18 (VII 32)
Gloria in Excelsis Deo!

A Son was given to us, a Son [who was] born favoured, having
    privileges,
Son of glory, Son to redeem us, the best Son,
Son of a virgin mother, gentle [her] faith, mature [her] words,
Without a father of flesh, He is the grace-filled Son, giver of
    blessings.
5   Let us wisely meditate and wonder at [the] marvels!
There never will be henceforth, no lips will speak of, anything
    more marvellous:
God came to us, [a] man creating creatures,
As God, as man, and the God [a] man, of the same endowments,
Great giant [yet] small, [a Son] strong and steadfast [yet] weak,
    white [his] cheeks,
10   [A Son] rich [yet] poor, our Father and our Brother, author of
    judgements:
Jesus is He whom we receive as supreme king,
[A Son] humble [yet] exalted, Emmanuel, honey sweet his
    thoughts.
Ox and ass, Lord of the world, a manger they have,
And a bundle of hay instead of a throne for our Lord of hosts;
15   He will not have embroidered silk, he has no white linen
    napkins,
Instead of fine linen around his bed rags were seen.
Yet heaven, that performed miracles, revealed that He
Was Son of the Lord God, He of whom literature and books
    declare
And learned and sensible wise men, of special excellence,
20   And [the] foretelling of holy prophets, of clear utterances.
A voice to shepherds, watchers of folds,
Will be an angel, and night became bright as day;

[10] See footnote 8 *supra*.

Then was spoken and believed [the] news of joy:
The Lord being born indeed in the city of David.
25   Men hear the sound of angels with thanks,˙
Great joy and many outbursts of songs:
'Glory to God, on the earth peace to our boundaries,
Peace to the world, complete salvation after death'.
Of yore men watched, with memory of long duration, according
    to ancestors,
30   Wise watchers, men of the east on hilltops,
All one after the other, in turn, performed a share of watchings
From night to night, as though in covetousness expecting
    rewards.
They saw a star of a different hue with haloes
And of a different portent from the stars on high above their
    heads:
35   Then the birth of the good King, a certain sign
That was first [seen] by [the] three kings, great their privileges.
Then they believe, then they travel on a successful journey,
And their sign was a star before them giving light;
[To] Jerusalem and the city of Bethlehem (not for stratagems)
40   They came freely on swift steeds [fed on] fine fodders.
Dismounting speedily (a star guides them, reliable its directions),
They go to the house without a door, without a wall, windy its
    entrances;
The Son it was that had been born under its signs,
And His mother on the floor, and her precious breast to His lips.
45   A man they saw, God they believed Him to be, good were their
    beliefs,
They worship Him (they delay not) on noble knees,
They open treasure, they offer gold and more besides:
Myrrh and incense, adornment of a sanctuary, [and] virtues of
    song.
Wisely they return by another way, without losses,
50   Towards their country, for fear of the deceit and treachery of the
    false king;
Herod was frustrated, cruel [his] attack, with his weapons,
Innocent blessed sons were killed: alas for their mothers!
But not alas for them: blessed are they to be saints
And martyrs for the sake of their King, in their swaddling
    clothes,
55   Before there was yet good will, absence of revenge,
Nor doing good, nor expressing goodness with tongues.
Those things brought about the birth of fine miracles

Of the only Son of the true God, if the beginnings be looked at;
Christmas night: a night unlike evil nights,
60   A night of joy for the host of Christendom: let us also be [joyful]!
Blessed is Christmas, worthy [its] feasts,
When [the] Son was born, Lord of all priests, who owns
    everything,
Of a Lady who ensures our good, [and] who prevents suffering
    from reaching us,
And who makes a place for us on the most splendid hill, amidst
    rewards.

Gruffudd ab yr Ynad Coch

This poet belongs to a family of famous lawyers, Llwyth Cilmin Droetu, in Arfon,[11] though Gruffudd's father, Madog Goch Ynad, seems to have moved from there to Anglesey where he held land in Llandyfnan. Since it was customary for a son to follow his father's profession we may presume that Gruffudd was himself a lawyer as well as a poet.[12] Some documentary evidence shows that, during the conflict between Llywelyn ap Gruffudd and Edward I in 1277, the poet supported King Edward, who handsomely rewarded him with a sum of £20.[13] Gruffudd is best known for his lament on the death of Llywelyn ap Gruffudd in 1282. The last native Welsh prince is also believed to be the one addressed in the only *englyn* composition of the poet which has survived. Six religious poems form the remainder of his canon and it is with these we are now concerned; each has been edited under the title 'Awdl i Dduw' ('Ode to God').

Poem 19 (VII 38)
We humans are mortal

Is not the sinner's burden unfortunate and wretched
With his innumerable transgressions,
That man does not see that the time of his death approaches,
That he does not see [the] dishonour of cunning,
5   That his hand does not tremble in plotting corruption,
That he believes not in God, prophet of faithfulness,
That he would not be always trembling for fear of falling
Into the same destruction as Lucifer,

---

[11] See EWGT 117, 157.
[12] The only suggestion of this in his poetry is his condemnation of the evil practices of lawyers in Poem 22 *infra*.
[13] See CBT VII, p. 415.

And into the world's lack of sorrow, [namely] being frivolous?
10   Neither arrogance nor pomposity is good;
[He] will not be unashamed on Judgement Day when is seen
[The] reading out of every sin as it was committed,
And Christ on the wood of the cross because of cruelty
In the agony He was in on Good Friday,
15   With the five streams [of blood], [the] five blessings that [are not]
        without benefit,
And their drops [descending] upon the crowd,
And an unworthy host along with Lucifer,
And on the forehead of each saint his sign ,
And the angels of heaven, [the] loving host,
20   Quaking in distress.
Let us understand, let us contemplate through the wisdom of the
        Lord
How worthless is man [on the] day he is born:
Now a little boy, wasteful as to [his] childhood,
Now a youth, fickle in craftiness,
25   Now an adult nurturing bitterness,
Now a man [of years] fostering sadness;
He humpbacked like a villein's hook,
He voraciously rushing [through] Friday['s fast],
He with farting between his two legs,
30   He without sense because of pugnacity,
He, weak [and] useless [his] spearing hand and without strength,
Without help, without support;
His head, from which derives his pride, is grey,
[His] eye [is] damaged without colour, without light,
35   [The empty] space [where were] the teeth [is] bruised when felt,
The cheek is [as] leather, dry when touched,
[His] skin [is] bare, dry and spotted, horrible,
[It is a] remarkable place [for] arrogance and pomposity!
Let no [man] under the stars be too proud,
40   Let him not have the same pseudonym as Lucifer.
The covering of [the] hand that is punished will not be mottled
        white,[14]
Man will not be white-spotted on [the] day he is buried;
Of his wealth there will not follow him, from his career of
        deceit,
Only his shroud, a very poor garment.

[14] This is an extremely obscure line; see Part II footnote 101.

Poem 20 (VII 39)
Subvention from heaven

[The] protection of the Father and the Son of Grace between me
    and my enemies,
[The] protection of the Holy Spirit [is the] objective [of my]
    thoughts,
[The] protection of the loving Jesus, crown of peace,
Discipline of sin and its followers!
5   [The] protection of the auspicious cross sending forth blessings,
Which You have undertook [O] God, for the sake of Your
    people,
Against the unbelieving fettered host of hell,
And its wholly bloody enemies!
[The] protection of the gracious love between me and my enemies,
10   [The] protection of the seas and Mary along with her virgins!
I pray to [the] majestic archangels [for] protection,
[O] Lord of heaven and earth, that they may cause success for me,
[The] protection of the incomparable Peter, supporter of lections,
[The] best helper of prayers of [all] the helpers!
15   [The] protection of the four gentle, pure [as] virgins,
Evangelists, [of the] company [of] proclaimers of Scripture!
[The] protection of John [of] fine complexion, foremost [of the]
    faithful ones,
Whom Christ blessed [with] signs of [the] cross!
[The] protection of the kindly [and] accredited [ones], unceasing
    [are] their prayers,
20   Excellent prophets of the Lord!
[The] protection of the Unity of the Trinity of the Three Persons,
[The] protection of all the saints, a sinless assembly,
[The] protection of [the] complete commendation of all the
    angels of heaven
And certain home of the chaste ones!
25   As protection for me I take the blessed ones,
Let them give me protection for their part,
[The] protection of the martyrs of God, the eternal noble ones,
[The] protection of him who is humble, [i.e.] just Abel!
Before I suffer [the] death of the evil ones
30   May I have friends from [the] two generous ones,
Michael [and] Gabriel [who are] recommending rewards,
Spiritual and generous companions,
Into the select rule of wise men,
Into the freedom of [the] home of heaven let them escort me:

35   Generously to my soul [let them give] blessings [of the] light,
        In the abundance of [the] light [of heaven] let them place me!

Poem 21 (VII 40)
Hope of salvation

        Let the One who gave us [the] mysteries of speech,
        And utterance and expression,
        [And] who has turned me to sincere confession,
        Turn me to the most virtuous supremacy:
5   To wear away [with tears] the covering of the cheeks,
        To love the true Son of God,
        To do penance against [the] sufferings of hell
        And the effect of sins.
        Alas for [the] man who adheres to false oaths,
10   Alas for [the] robber with his booty in ditches,
        Alas for [the] deceiver who does not give up his deceit,
        Alas for [the] miser because of his wealth [which is] blasphemy,
        Alas for [the] adulterer because of his [way of] behaving during
            his days,
        Alas for [the] proud one on the gibbet of death,
15   Alas for [the] glutton for his gorging himself [on meat] on Fridays,
        Alas for [the] traitor because of his angry thoughts,
        Alas for [the] one who does not attend the fine Masses of Christ
        [On the] cross [of] the agony of [His] wounds,
        Alas for [the] one who offends [his] mother wrongfully ([this] is
            not a lie)
20   Alas for [the] one who offends [his] father ([this] is not the gift of
            the King),
        Alas that he was born, false, [as] a counsellor
        Of envy and its offshoots.
        The sins of the people are [the] seven chief sins [as] sin,
        Their names are in the Bible;
25   About the seven chief sins of the world (this is neither untrue
            nor false),
        The seven prayers of the Lord's Prayer [are the] best practice,
        [The] seven blessed graces, let me know its beginning,
        [The] seven lights, let their names be spoken,
        [The] seven perfect [and] holy words before the pain of death
            [on the] cross
30   Which Christ uttered with His lips.
        Let the five ages of the world consider [their being] lost,
        When the only Son of God went on the best day

To [the] entrance door of [the] hell [of the] evil and captive host
To strike without persuasion, with His cross and His blood,
35   The savage serpent in his mouth.
There were boiling (woe because of the sufferings!)
Seven hundred thousand cauldronfuls of souls,
And sleet and snow, and serpents and lions,
And each one without respite in his agonies,
40   And the multi-spiked nails and the horned devil
And on his heels the sharp-pointed horns,
And the crested rats with snouts of horn,
And the blue iron stone and the trampling-place of arrows,
And the tumult prolonged and evil with the furnace of darkness,
45   And each one with his eye on his paws,
And every sort of vast evil and every bitterness,
And every [type of] ivy on old doors,
And every sort of practice to cause pain [to the] flesh,
And every flesh-hook-thrust with the flesh-hooks,
50   And everyone moaning, and every one crying out,
And every one crying out that death does not kill him.
Tongue cannot describe, mind cannot tell,
Except the Trinity, the best Unity,
The grieving crowd of people in a stifling marsh,
55   The torment of [the] captive and evil host of hell.
I ask a request from my Lord, the wisest Wonder-worker
(I shall not be found valuable without His miracles)
From the bright slopes, from the place where the sun rises,
Let Him not give me to [the] devil, for the sake of His nails,
60   For the sake of His covenant, for the sake of the five wounds,
For the sake of His riven side and His wounds,
For the sake of Absalom's kinsman, because of the pain of His
    breast,
For the sake of the blood of His heart and His bosom bleeding
    from [its] wounds.
I pray to my Father, the Spirit and the Son of Grace
65   [For] a share of His faithful love, as He created me.
Before [going to] the tomb of [the] graveyard, [in order] to
    abandon my sin,
… not mine is drunkenness,
[By] lenient penance, succeeding in reaching
Communion and confession and [the] benefit of the books [of
    the Bible],
70   Oil and [the] last anointing and saying 'Amen',
And peace with my Lord, the best forebear.

Let me not be gluttonous [and] lazy, let me not be feeble [and]
      fearful,
Let me not be a doer of wrongs,
Let me not be accusatory, let me not be quarrelsome,
75   Let me not be hateful, whetting falsehood,
Let not my life be defective because of [any] other [evil] action,
Let me not be a foolish man in the face of death.

Poem 22 (VII 41)
Alas for the Lawyers!

I greet God first, the Most High One who owns
Heaven and earth, and [animals] wild and tame, Lord of spirits,
Sea and depths, Support of kings, essential channel of graces,
And the firmament and the whole present world, [with]
      unceasing gifts,
5   And paradise, He ransomed us, auspicious ransom,
And all peoples, and [that is] no marvel, Lord of sensations.
Jesus, Jesus, who shall be, who was, by virtue of the nails of
      blessing,
He is an authority of great glory, greatest Guarantor,
He understands and knows all sciences.
10   There is not, O King, Lord God, [the] least trace of defect.
Why do not the honourable officials who are holder(s) of offices,
      consider
That they will not be forgotten (death comes to wild and tame),
And that they do not know, because of what diseases they feel
Intensifying anxiety, when their removal [by death] will come,
15   And that the verdict upon the lord of armies with fine strong
      sword will not be better
Than that upon the weakest and least important man in the
      assembly.
They will be fools, they judge them wrong with regard to their
      judgements
Without [having] anything holy from the worldly pomp of the
      laws of the world.
Law of deceit and impeachment (such filthy wrongs!)
20   And injustice without mercy, and unseemly words
And fierceness [in] question and response, affliction [resulting
      from ownership] of property,
And bringing [an] indigent one illegally to extreme afflictions:
The day will come, when not without fear will be the distortion
      of words

Against a weak Christian unlawfully, [cause for] streaming tears;
25   The one who practises them, too great wrongs of excessive
         conflict,
He will not have one arm without more than its load of sins.
Woe to [the] cheat, woe to [the] accuser of the invitations [to
         take part in wrong-doing],
And the proud fellow-banqueter because of the excess of [his]
         rewards of treasure,
When fairly judged in the light of stars and signs of the zodiac
30   Before the Lord and the Seer, there are no denials;
There is no power [that will prevail] against Jesus, nor stupefied
         wrigglings,
Nor excusing nor concealing terror of treacherous thoughts.
Then will be paid (necessary is suppression of deceitful lips)
To every man of guile and [every] maligner [for] their actions.
35   When they will be excluded from the number of [those
         receiving] heaven's rewards
They will fall, for lack of warrant (alas for the souls!),
Into the pit of hell, together with the rabble, [into the] afflictions
         of the swamp,
Where there is sadness and darkness and dirt and lice;
And the devils their receptionists [to] chilly pains:
40   Every criminal, all are fearful of their mouths
Snarling [their] teeth at them, [with] reproaches of wrong,
They will be angry, they will pierce sharply with the flesh-hooks,
[With] bitter reproach [because of their] slovenly appearance in a
         cauldron of sufferings,
And gathering them together to punish them constantly,
         [something] worse than death,
45   And after that behold a change in the damaging occurrences
Of snow, frost and ice and strong tempest and downpour of rain,
And worse too would be suffering fever in pools [of] pus.
The one who does not credit how cruel they are, [these] trials
         [perpetrated by] beasts,
See then, [you who are] the cherisher of pride in prolonged sins,
50   How we will get treated by Lucifer [causing us] anxiety [for our]
         deceits.
It would be better to go to [the] place where one is permitted to
         see [the] light of the
Great feast of the King of the west [and its] splendid rooms,
To enjoy a banquet of great honour [and] songs of freedom
Before God [who is] forever [of] sincere blessings.

Poem 23 (VII 42)
This I have done, what hast thou done?

King of Glory, authoritative in His action,
Neither was deceit nor plague to be had on His part.
If [man] had not done as He commanded it [should be done]
[   ] some, very great pride.
5   Breaking prohibitions and supporting robbers
And oppressing weak ones, I know that it does not benefit you.
Evil in the end will be the deceit of your sin
By pride [in] wealth, arrogance that is not good.
Consider, wicked man, according to what is proclaimed,
10   [That] on God's part there will be no arguing,
Rather, truth and gentle peace
And genuine mercy, as is fitting.
Consider your way of life before going to your grave,
If you have sinned, be not amazed
15   That it is necessary to make retribution before Jesus [for that]:
Where [the] triple host may see, [the sin] will cause [you]
          affliction.
Alas for those who believe, if wrong [it is] that they do,
In the world of deceit [i.e. hell], [the] miserable man disappears,
And does not think of what he has earned to excess,
20   The superabundance he has received does not come to his mind!
Although it is desirable [to receive the] worldly pomp
Of a feast of honour [it only] causes displeasure.
I saw Llywelyn [with his] forces like [those of] Merfyn
And the warriors of Wales [up to its] border in his host.
25   I saw the chieftains of Gwynedd and the South,
Maintainers of armies in an assembly together.
I saw warriors in an army and steeds at muster
And wine and a host and a place of play.
I saw crowds and daily revelry
30   And [their] world prospering [through the] victory of noblemen.
That has passed away like the turn of your hand,
Everyone leaves a life [that is] transitory.
[The] rich one is not granted long years
No more than the beggar who does not quarrel.
35   Let [the rich one] consider while he lives, lest [he suffers]
          grievous pains,
What he should seek [and] what to abhor [in life].
Let every blessed one seek the feast that ceases not
[And] the satisfying joy of a faith that prospers.

Let [a man of] deceit not seek, through unjust complaint,
40   Heaven in its [degree of] beauty, since he will not succeed.
When it is fully considered, [in the] penance of the time of
          reckoning
[For the] wrong of the vain evil wantonness of Eve,
That it was not for His [own] sin that the Lord of heaven went
To [the] wood of suffering ([it was] the end result of pride),
45   Alas for [the one of] sinful action that was not born fortunate,
It will be agony to behold the entirety of the scene!
He will show [His] streams of blood and all His wounds
And His nails and His blood and His cross.
'This I have done, what hast thou done?'
50   Says Christ the Lord and King: it was necessary there
That there be ready purity to meet the Trinity
Against the calamity of sin of destructive nature.
Woe to them [the] misers and the deceitful men
And those of perverted thoughts who do not worship
55   Seeing themselves dispatched because of their transgressions
To the pains of hell, [the] secret place of punishment,
And seeing departing to the glory of heaven
Those found in good disposition,
With the joy of the feast that does not end
60   In [the] eternal, free, gracious assembly.

Poem 24 (VII 43)
Hoc cano spontanee

Alas to the King [of] silent and high privilege,
Generous Father, light of eye and hand,
That the sinner does not believe in his undoing
Until he goes to the pit for a lengthy stay,
5   Nor [in the] punishing [through the] destruction of a false heart,
Nor in Christ's going to the cross on his behalf,
And that he does not securely know of our Lord's [being] done
          to death
And in disgrace being truly abandoned.
If a man were to think and reflect on it,
10   How much agony there was [inflicted] on His hands
From [the] sharp nails lacerating [His] flesh,
He would not commit sin nor desire it;
Were it not for the one day ([the] Lord will come to us!),
Judgement Day ordained to purify us completely

15   And the blood a gift [of righteousness for us] as on the day He
          was crucified,
      And His hands stretched, after being inflamed,
      And the blood in streams around His breasts,
      And all His wounds not anointed,
      And His crown made of thorns and [He] Himself a corpse,
20   And His head bowed after falling [to one side],
      And [the] marks of [the] scourges on His sides
      Causing death and pain to Him,
      For the sake of ransoming mankind from the flaming fire
      From his enemy that was legion,
25   In order to show the world His torture and His tribulation,
      In order to rescue it entirely from the power of [the] wolf.
      And then He will say, He will give a sigh:
      'Where is he [who] is evil from [the time] he was granted life,
      And a false accuser, and a perfidious usurer,
30   And a fraud [who is a] traitor [with] treacherous hands,
      And an impious robber, and a deceitful creature,
      And a glutton, and an idler [on whom] the vengeance of terror
          [will come],
      And a lascivious man with his lie and a false religion?'
      Since they have not faith, let them flee from Him
35   To the fiends, to the depth of hell
      Where there is a swamp crushed underfoot,
      And a beacon of fire, and drops of brimstone,
      And each thunderbolt colliding with each other,
      Because of [the] great force of [the] fire and excessive heat
40   Which caused Barabbas to do penance,
      In order to afflict the flesh, in order to punish sin:
      May the master of evil practice come to it.
      We ask the Spirit, Lord, on Your account,
      To listen to us before [we enter the] earth and [the] grave
45   And [cause us to] receive Extreme Unction, and [hear a reading
          from] Scripture,
      And [be at] peace with our King before we are prepared for
          burial,
      And [have] a heavenly dwelling, and a share of mercy,
      And Christ at the last to lead us to Him.

Poems 25–7
Deathbed Poems

Meilyr Brydydd

Meilyr Brydydd is traditionally regarded as the first of the *Gogynfeirdd*. Knowledge of his floruit is dependent on the internal evidence of his compositions. His 'Cerdd Ddarogan' ('Vaticinatory Poem', CBT I poem 5), which must be *post eventum,* purports to foretell the death of Tra-haearn ap Caradog ap Gruffudd, and suggests that he lost his life as a result of his part in the Battle of Mynydd Carn 1081, in north Pem-brokeshire. If this is historically correct then Meilyr's poetic career may have extended from 1081 to 1137. It is of central importance that Meilyr wrote Gruffudd ap Cynan's elegy in 1137, the year in which his patron died. This floruit of fifty-six years appears to be inordinately long for a poet of that period. We can, however, support the possibility when we recall that the career of Llywarch ap Llywelyn 'Prydydd y Moch' covered at least forty-five years.[15]

It is of interest and importance to bear in mind that Meilyr was the head of a family of poets prominent in the twelfth and thirteenth centur-ies, namely Gwalchmai ap Meilyr, Einion and Meilyr ap Gwalchmai, and Elidir, probably also ap Gwalchmai, whose religious poems have been included already. Only three of Meilyr's own poems have survived and each is in a category of its own—all three are attributed to him in the Hendregadredd MSS: (i) *Marwnad,* Elegy for Gruffudd ap Cynan (ii) *Marwysgafn,* deathbed poem and (iii) *Cerdd Ddarogan,* prophetic poem. For a full discussion on the difference of opinion regarding the authorship of the last-named poem, see CBT I, pp. 61–3.

Poem 25 (I 4)[16]

> King of kings, Chief whom it is easy to praise,
> To my supreme Lord I address a prayer.
> Ruler triumphing over the realm of the most high heavenly
>   circle,
> O noble One, make peace between You and me!
> 5   Feeble, fleeting is the memory of the provoking of Your anger
> Because of me, and repentance for doing so;

---

[15] See the Introduction to CBT V.
[16] For a description of deathbed poems, see Part II, preface to Poems 25, 26 and 27.

I have done wrong in the sight of the Lord God,
Neglecting to perform my proper devotion.
I shall, nonetheless, serve my Lord King
10   Before I become helpless in the earth.
A true prophecy regarding Adam and his children
The prophets have told forth:
Of Jesus being in the womb of Mary (daughter of her King!),
Mary, propitiously she bore her pregnancy!
15   I have amassed a burden of grievous sin,
I have trembled [in fear] because of its tumult.
Universal Lord, how excellent You are to pray to You,
May I pray unto You, may I purify myself before I am punished.
King of all glory who knows me, do not refuse me
20   [Your] mercy because of my sinfulness.
Many a time have I received gold and silk
From transitory monarchs in exchange for praising them,
And after the blessing of inspiration, of more excellent vigour,
Very impoverished is my tongue as I fall silent.
25   I Meilyr the Poet, a pilgrim to Peter,
The door-keeper who weighs fitting virtues,
Whenever the time of our resurrection be,
We who are in the grave, make me ready.
Let me be in the abode, awaiting the call,
30   Of the monastery by which the tide sounds,
And which is a place of retreat of lasting fame,
And encircling its cemetery the bosom of the sea.
Island of fair Mary, holy island of the saints,
Awaiting the resurrection, fine therein it is.
35   Christ of the foretold cross who knows me, [He] will direct me
Past the pain of hell, the lodging set apart:
The Creator who created me will welcome me
Among the holy ones of the community of Enlli.

Cynddelw Brydydd Mawr[17]

Poem 26 (IV 18)

I beg You, O God, for a fitting conversion
To praise my generous and blessed King,
Only Son of Mary who brings into being evening and morning
And strong-flowing estuaries,
5   Who created trees and pasture and exact measure,

---

[17] See the biographical preface to Poem 1 *supra*.

Both crops and gifts, God it is who created them;
Who created grass and groves and heather on mountain,
Who made one man blessed by a just decree
And the other lost because of rejected grace
10   Miserably and angrily.
I ask the Son of God, since it is [He] who will achieve it,
For reconciliation for our sin (sinning is not right)
And a welcome in heaven [which will be] a dwelling-place for us:
To the land [which is the object of our] yearning, we shall go!
15   I beseech, O God, I beseech, an excellent paean
I shall intone in verse;
Thousands extol You, O Supreme One,
From amongst your multitudes in Your farthest borderland.
I myself would desire, my Lord, [to have] Your assent,
20   It is through Your love that I believe in You;
From You, [the] acclaimed One, do I have protection,
Gift[s] distributor, do not leave me in want!
Greater than need was the greatest blessing
Of the Prince of valiant ones defending the boundary [of His
      realm].
25   What I contemplate frightens me,
Because of the sinning that Adam sinned.
I am a foolish exile who jouneys towards your blessed land
With your shining host around me;
They are the poets of the most illustrious Church
30   Their support has been apportioned to me.
Pleasant is my course, I journey to a place,
[My] confidence is in the President of justice, I seek [His]
      friendship,
King of all peoples, spare me,
After roaming the earth, [let there be] a benefit for me.
35   Through the consent of the most regal Father
And the Son and the Spirit, of [the] most resplendent sanctity,
In the light of [His] privilege, I shall be fortunate;
In the habitation of [the] angels pure [and] most gentle,
In the blessed land of the Prince, I ask for heaven.
40   Highest Prince, when You were born
Mercy came to us, redemption came,
The children of Adam emerged from the region of unbelief,
From extensive lawlessness, from captivity;
[Object of] our desire came to visit us,
45   Courage came, wonderful fulfilment,
Christ came in flesh, Proprietor of supremacy,

There came in the womb of Mary the Son of expectation;
Five ages of the world escaped from torturing pain,
Out of deceit, out of the hostile darkness of [their] habitation,
50   From painful maintenance, from unyielding grief,
From the prison of the enemy [they] were released.
And He is our Leader, our perfect refuge
Who will judge our action in the light of our work;
And He, Lord of heaven, peace of [our] destiny,
55   Who, when wounded, brought [us] from total perdition;
And He rises for us, and His blessing comes [to us],
And as King He will not hinder our well-being,
And He the gift that was decreed
Fully, powerfully, [with] limitless authority
60   [And since I am one] who would give to God a tithe [of wealth
          received] from His hand
Not denying Him what is His due,
A poet am I, flawlessly have I been formed,
Under the protection of my Creator, Prince of a multitude;
Me, Cynddelw the singer, may blessing be given to me,
65   May Michael who knows me welcome me!
Highest Prince, when I sang about You
Not a vain composition did I compose;
My song was not lacking in refined traits,
Not a slight is the gift wherever I received [it].
70   The immutable God did not create me
To accomplish inanity, deceit or violence.
Not without religion is he who believes in God,
He will not [have to] suffer from the cause of the pain of a
          wound.
Not to be sleepless [for devotions] did I trouble myself
75   Heaven is not given to whomsoever that seeks it not;
I did not display overmuch zeal
Not too great a reward did I deserve.
Not fitting is [the] pride I have nurtured in my heart,
Nor did I think of enduring penance;
80   In the home of the Lord I have desired
[To win] freedom for my spirit, I have begged for [what is]
          essential [to me].
Highest Prince, deign to accept gladly
Worship in the form of a petition, of a harmonious song:
My faultless address has been made,
85   My song, to extol You, Candle-beacon of a hundred lands.
Since you are Possessor, since you are a great Ruler,

Since you are a Guide, a Lord of Light,
Since yours is a prophet's heart, since You are a Judge,
Since You are a generous King, since you are a Benefactor,
90   Since You are my Mentor do not banish me from Your place,
From Your power, from Your fine kingdom:
Do not deprive me of Your blessing, Creator Lord,
Do not scorn me in abasement among a wicked company,
Do not apportion to me from Your hand an impoverished land,
95   Do not banish me along with the dark, contemptible host.

Bleddyn Fardd

Nothing is known of the life of Bleddyn Fardd except what can be gleaned from a study of his poems, all of which are dedications to secular patrons, apart from the deathbed poem (Poem 27). From a careful analysis of the historical background to the secular compositions, thirteen in all, it has been estimated that his lifespan covers *c.*1220–84/5.[18] This places him at the end of the *Gogynfeirdd* period. He composed an elegy for Dafydd Benfras, who claims to have been *pencerdd* to Llywelyn ap Gruffudd, and who was killed on the battlefield in 1258. From Bleddyn's encomium in this elegy one can readily accept the belief that Dafydd Benfras was his poetic mentor[19] and also the suggestion that, as soldiers, they fought side by side with Llywelyn ap Gruffudd.[20] Dafydd Benfras's influence on Bleddyn's poetry is seen best in his 'Marwnad Tri Mab Gruffudd ap Llywelyn' ('Elegy for the Three Sons of Gruffudd ap Llywelyn'). This was probably inspired by Dafydd Benfras's 'Marwnad Llywelyn ab Iorwerth, Gruffudd ap Llywelyn a Dafydd ap Llywelyn' ('Elegy for Llywelyn ab Iorwerth, Gruffudd ap Llywelyn and Dafydd ap Llywelyn'). In addition to these joint elegies, both poets sang elegies for these same three as separate compositions. Furthermore it has been suggested that, sometime after the death of Dafydd Benfras,[21] Bleddyn Fardd became *pencerdd* to Llywelyn ap Gruffudd.

Poem 27 (VII 57)

Receive me, my King, Lord of the baptized,
The object of worship of noble saints of regal privilege.
You have taken, you have won possession of souls

[18] See CBT VII, pp. 521–2.
[19] See J. Lloyd-Jones, PBA xxxiv (1948), 169.
[20] See J.E.C. Williams in LlyB 66.
[21] For a full discussion on aspects of Bleddyn Fardd's career as poet, see CBT VII, pp. 522–4.

From the devil by means of [the] nails of death.
5   Receiver of [the] five ages through [the] gory cross,
Supreme Sovereign, rightful Ruler of the realm,
Lord Father, do not allow me [to] go to the fierce fire
Where there is burning, an infernal invention,
Where there is immense woe without prayer each for the other,
10   Where there is great loss of [the] mortal soul,
Where enemies extol perversion of the truth,
Where there is fierce punishment every day.
Before leaving the world ([and its] mentality [fanciful] as a
        dream)
As food [for the] fine graveyard, land belonging to corpses,
15   Before life's end [in a] grave of stone, let me make a devout
        confession,
Before I am proven guilty, let me be prayerful.
Since You nurtured the privileged King,
Since things are done according to your word, [O] victorious
        Mary,
20   Whilst mindful on my behalf, make an intercession of peace for
        me
In the Kingdom of heaven of the holy Lord.

Poems 28–30
Incipits, Introductory Greetings to the Godhead

The *pencerdd* 'chief poet' had to satisfy a double legal obligation[22]—that of praising God and eulogizing the king or patron. J.E. Caerwyn Williams suggests that this requirement probably has its origins in a very early period in the development of Welsh civilisation. He shows further that during the course of the centuries the predecessors of the *pencerdd* had replaced praise of the pagan god, and his representative the king, by a gradual move towards praising both the One true God and the earthly king, who, in fact, was himself a representative of God. Thus the poets became partners of the priests in the duty of praising and worshipping Almighty God.[23] In general the poets were content to address God in a laudatory incipit, of perhaps no more than a couplet or two, before proceeding to extol their earthly patron. But three poets, Dafydd Benfras, Elidir Sais, and Bleddyn Fardd, one in an ode to Llywelyn Fawr (*ob.* 1240), the second in an ode edited as 'Mawl i Dduw a Dafydd ab Owain' ('In Praise of God and Dafydd ab Owain') and the third in an Elegy for Llywelyn ap Gruffudd ap Llywelyn (*ob.* 1282), seem to have adhered rigidly to the legal requirement just mentioned. Dafydd Benfras devoted the initial 54 lines of his 92-line poem to God and the rest to his patron. Elidir Sais devoted 24 of his 34 lines to God, and just 10 to Dafydd. Bleddyn Fardd addressed lines 1–12 of his to Christ and the remaining 32 lines to the memory of Llywelyn ap Gruffudd. These lengthy introductory openings are given in Poems 28, 29 and 30.

Dafydd Benfras

According to *Cyfres Beirdd y Tywysogion* VI, pp. 363 ff., Dafydd Benfras was the principal poet in the Court of Gwynedd from the second half of the reign of Llywelyn ab Iorwerth and the early years of the reign of Llywelyn ap Gruffudd. Internal evidence in his poetry suggests *c.*1220–58 as the years of his floruit. Yet over that long period only 804 lines of his poetry survive: they include encomia for Llywelyn ab Iorwerth and his son Dafydd, as well as elegies for both and for Gruffudd ap Llywelyn. He also elegized Ednyfed Fychan who died in 1246. Saunders Lewis ranks

---

[22] See LlB 25.18–20, *Pan yvnho y brenhin waranndaw canueu, canet y pennkerd deu ganu idaw yg kynted y neuad, vn o Duw ac arall o'r brenhined;* and according to the Gwynedd recension of the Laws, *Llyfr Iorwerth,* ed. A.Rh. Wiliam (Cardiff, 1960), 21, *Ef a dele dechreu kerd, en kentaf o Duv, a'r eyl o'r argluyd byeyffo e llys, neu o arall.*
[23] See J.E.C. Williams: CCG 10.

him, with Cynddelw and Llywarch ap Llywelyn 'Prydydd y Moch', as
the three most important of the *Gogynfeirdd*.[24]

Incipit of Poem 28 (VI 24)

Son of God, I am bound to consider You,
Great [and] powerful [One], listen to me.
So meet for me in virtue of the gift which comes to me from
     You,
On my part, [to intone] a meek word without distortion on it.
5   Protector, Lord, Ruler, henceforth
My intention is to seek you.
How wrong it is for man to desire according to his carnal nature
Enslaving sin or to wish for it;
How well [You] can wisely show [the] meaning
10   [Of] morning bustle and late evening quietude,
[And that] presumption for a man of the world, though he has
     wealth,
Is not necessary nor the brag of boasting:
It is the Son of God who bestows it upon him,
And the Son of God [who] withdraws it from him
15   And the Son of God on the Day of Judgement will come to test
     him,
What is his strength in virtue of his wealth.
He will not be united with the Son of God
Whom the wealth of the world endangers.
[The] elect Son of God, Him will I choose,
20   He is the Lord most choice, [may I have] from Him protection!
Confused was the situation of the host [as they were] looking on
The day Christ took up [the] cross as his own,
In the depth of hell, in the grip of a terror-stricken existence
The four ages clashed with each other
25   And a host of animals tearing them
And the fire of the heat of wrath scorching them,
And a court, pointless [it is] to [offer] battle or to battle on its
     behalf
And its host of spirits wreaking havoc.
And utter darkness [for an] evil [one] residing [there],
30   And a legion of demons devastating it
And many wild animals without thinking of any generosity
And much thirst for release throughout it,
And hosts of people each one [of them] falling silent

---

[24] See Saunders Lewis, *Braslun o Hanes Llenyddiaeth Gymraeg I* (Cardiff, 1932), 15.

And lions with a wheel trapping them,
35 And a place where it was piteous, because of the promise of
        Cain,
    For innocent folk to listen to it.
    When the Son of Grace came, there was need for Him,
    To the entrance, [that is the entrance] of our captivity, and
        blessing on Him,
    To [the] dangerous swamp of hell, without leaving it either,
40 On the one morning in order to harrow it,
    Because of the five ages of the world there were in it,
    Fair noble One, short thorns through Him:
    [The] Son of Grace of the exalted Father, lest His right[s] be
        circumvented,
    Woe [to him] who is not just on the day that will come!
45 When[ever] he, Michael, may come to make a stand for him
    Against the devil, announcing tumult,
    And to censure him for [his] forging [of] falsehood,
    And the inevitable coming of death to him:
    Why does the son of man not love God and seek Him?
50 Why does he not earn heaven as his possession?
    If he goes, [that one] has not been born who will not marvel at
        Him,
    The Lord of Glory (seeing [Him] is to hold a feast),
    He in whom no fault was found in anything,
    The One from whom no way to flee from Him can be found.

Elidir Sais[25]

Incipit of Poem 29 (I 16)

    I petition the Father (most generous [is] my King)
    And the Son and the Holy Spirit of excellent purpose.
    That is not perverseness in our thoughts since we are at one
        [with Him / Them],
    [There is] no need for us to doubt the books of learning [the
        books of the Bible].
5   To Christ I sing, according to [the] custom of the law,
    An excellent eulogy with my tongue in a fine song.
    Brilliant is my poetry in Myrddin's style,
    Splendour that was spun from the source of inspiration
        (lit. from the cauldron of the Muse).
    Escaping loftily [from] anger [of judgement] above the angels,

[25] See the biographical preface to Poems 4–8 *supra*.

10   I shall be a poet to God as long as I am a [living] man
        I pray for the protection of the Son of Mary, defence of the
            believer,
        Creator, Emperor, joyful Ruler,
        Against the mob of the cold swamp [in] painful hell,
        [And the] unbearable grip of the abysmal place.
15   Place me, Lord of the illustrious ancient ones,
        (God accomplishes much on behalf of men)
        Ruler of heaven and earth, for fear of the dire wrath of the fire,
        Between Your hands before Your knees.
        You have caused oppression (that does not hold You back)
20   Immense victorious God, because of [the] Jews
        About the tomb of Christ: Creator of heaven, inevitable it is![26]

Bleddyn Fardd[27]

Incipit of Poem 30 (VII 50)

        [O] Christ, mighty generous Lord, I seek a blessing,
        Christ Son of the true God, think of me!
        Christ just [and] bountiful, strongest defence,
        Whose body endured [the] harshest suffering.
5   I shall say [that] which pertains to a man:
        He who may suffer tribulation, let him be most patient;
        He who, by nature, has highest authority,
        Let his thought [of himself] be least.
        Christ came to the world lest Adam
10   And his descendants be in hell, [the] most enchained host,
        [But] might fill heaven, all around [the] exalted Lord
        Which [the] most inept angel lost.

---

[26] The poet seems to make God the Creator responsible for the fall of the Holy City—
surely a rather stark comment. To understand the couplet it is necessary to examine the
historical context of this, especially lines 23–4 which mention Saladin and obviously refer
to his capture of Jerusalem in 1187. All Christendom was shocked and Elidir Sais speaks
of the pain felt at this outrage. The reference to the Jews in this context is problematic;
Elidir Sais may be referring to the success of the Jews in crucifying Christ or perhaps he
identifies them as Turks or Arabs [in Saladin's army]. It is also possible that the word
'Jew' signifies all infidels or pagans.
[27] See the biographical preface to Poem 27 *supra*.

Part II

Commentary on Translated Poems

Commentary on Translated Poems

Cynddelw Brydydd Mawr

Poem 1 (IV 16)

Chronology will be taken as the general norm in establishing a numerical sequence for the following translations with their prefatory notes. This would mean that the 'Awdl i Dduw' ('Ode to God') by Gwalchmai ap Meilyr (CBT I 14) should take precedence over all others as probably the earliest surviving dedication to God by a Welsh court poet. However, in this volume that privilege is accorded to Cynddelw's 'Canu i Dduw' ('Ode to God') (CBT IV 16). Certain reasons have dictated this choice. The poem is in fact nearly contemporaneous with that of Gwalchmai, and, as the longest surviving *Gogynfeirdd* dedication to God, it affords a unique opportunity to study salient thematic and stylistic features of Welsh religious poetry in the twelfth century. Artistically it is skilfully constructed, with subtle word and rhyme balance effecting a pleasing musical harmony which would certainly have met the expectations of the court audience and won the approval of his patron. Its 224 lines are analysed canto by canto.

Preoccupation with sin, penance, repentance, life's end, Judgement Day, heaven and hell suggests that the poem was composed towards the end of the poet's life.[1] However, when we recall how frequently these themes occur in other *Gogynfeirdd* religious poetry, we must accept the possibility that Cynddelw was merely adhering to current poetic practice. A full study of his secular poems reveals him as a confident poet, unhesitating in challenging his patrons to reward his contribution to their success in the court and on the battlefield. The poem is divided into 6 cantos, with cantos 1–5 very nearly equal in length, while canto 6 is shorter with only 29 lines.

Canto 1 as a poetic unit is so carefully constructed that it could stand on its own as a fine composition. In the first six lines God is addressed as the 'One God' *unum Deum* reminiscent of the *Credo*,[2] which the poet would have heard or recited at every Sunday Mass. In language similar to that of the Psalms, outstanding attributes of the Godhead are listed, as the poet proclaims his intention of writing a sacred song of prayer in His honour. Cynddelw addresses God as the mighty Lord, Ruler, the eternal

---

[1] CBT IV, pp. 261–2 is followed in stating that the poem belongs to the later period of Cynddelw's canon.

[2] See *Missal* 802–4.

and merciful One, King, Sovereign and Nobleman. His dealings with the unrepentant sinner when, as 'Lord' and 'Prince of the swamp' He harrows hell, are outlined in the petition for repentance.[3] This concept of Christ's descent into hell after His death on the cross captured the minds of many of the *Gogynfeirdd*. On many occasions we find them describing in gruesome detail the condition of the souls detained in captivity prior to Christ's coming to liberate the faithful ones. Cynddelw speaks of the enslaved spirits approaching God in three groups[4]—the first consists of mottled and quarrelsome souls, the second those full of hatred, while the third are resplendent in holiness and love. The poet himself fears death but cautiously avoids use of that word, preferring descriptive phrases, e.g. being 'consigned to the grassy grave',[5] and he prays for steadfastness in the face of the enemy with pleas for divine mercy. He pleads with God, as King and Judge, that by his learned eloquence he may sing praise to Him in a fitting manner (33–9). The canto ends with a petition that God may avert His anger from he who is merely a sad and passionate intercessor.

Canto 2 opens with an echo-reference to the divine anger. Decline in morality and the evil consequences of treachery, unchristian belief and general infidelity are treated in an objective manner (43–6), and in the same vein the poet philosophizes on the wisdom of working for reward, before the grave claims the 'noble chivalry' and before the powers of the devil embroil it in shameful strife.[6] In commenting on the sacrificial plan of the Son of God, which led Him to His death on the cross and to the harrowing of hell, He is identified with God the Creator,[7] a role which is generally assigned to the Father. God's universal sovereignty places Him

---

[3] This reference to the 'Harrowing of hell' seems to be the earliest example in the works of the *Gogynfeirdd*. In the thirteenth century we find similar references in the poems of Einion ap Gwalchmai, e.g. CBT I 28.33–6; Llywelyn Fardd (II), *ib.*, VI 10.72–3; Dafydd Benfras, *ib.*, VI 24.21–42; Gruffudd ab yr Ynad Coch, *ib.*, VII 40.30–45, 41.35–50; see MWRL 89.

[4] In MWRL 104 we read: 'These hosts are the three *turmae* who appear in a seventh- or eighth-century treatise, *De numero*, ascribed in the Middle Ages to Isidore of Seville. The first is the host of the *nec valde boni, nec valdi mali* who will have been purged by fire before the Last Judgement; the second is the host of the damned, the *valde mali*; and the third is the host of the saints already enjoying heavenly bliss, the *valdi boni'*; see also p. 147, footnote 32 for sources and other examples from medieval Welsh poetry.

[5] In MWRL 100, C. McKenna points out that generally the Gogynfeirdd poets, while preoccupied with the idea of death, avoid direct use of the word and prefer 'kennings for the grave'; see Poem 11 *infra*, where Einion ap Gwalchmai, in a long reflection on death, uses a variety of images for approaching death and then many 'grave' pictures to convey his meaning.

[6] Here is a suggestion of the *sic transit gloria mundi* idea, which occurs so often in medieval poetry; see Intro. under *Themes* and footnote 60.

[7] See Part III 1. 3.

above the nine choirs of angels and the nine shores.[8] There are attractive lines depicting the Son of God as 'our Chief in joyful leadership', a blessed Gift-giver who, when He comes, will be strong and loving; but the poet reminds us that we, too, must be gift-givers. Gloomy and depressing is the picture of Judgement Day when the Redeemer will be the unrelenting Judge of 'the free and the slave' and where all is manifest and clearly visible to Him who 'watches over us with foresight' (69–74).[9] In the following couplet we gain a glimpse of the adroit Cynddelw who states the obvious and yet introduces a note of subtle irony. In fact these two lines are quite enigmatic and can leave us wondering if it is true that God loves excellence? Certainly the poet, or friend of poetry, does not love meanness but the difficulty arises when the preferences of the poet and those of God are juxtaposed. The canto closes with a comment on the importance of generosity.

Canto 3 introduces a joyful note. The poet depicts the bliss and peace of heaven where he will have calm for his troubled spirit in the company of his Ruler or Guide, trustfully rejoicing in the idea of God's rewarding goodness. Under His monarchical titles of King and Prince,[10] God's mercy is invoked lest he, straying in wantonness, be driven away.[11] While the poet admits his guilt he traces the root of his own sins, and that of all sinfulness, to Eve's greed in eating the apple.[12] There follow some general comments on the dangers of greed and sinful indulgence in food before the scene is flashed back to the 'Prince of heaven' honouring Adam by placing him in the garden of Paradise with its wealth of blessings.[13] The canto concludes as the poet, praising and glorifying the Saviour, pleads for his own salvation.

---

[8] Note the comments in MWRL 74 on numerology in Gogynfeirdd poems and the listings of examples on pp. 57, 69–70, 72–3, 74 and 90; see also ThU 164–5; on 'celestial hierarchies' and their division into choirs, see ODCC 51 s.n. 'angel'; also Wesley Carr, *Angels and Principalities* (Cambridge, 1981).

[9] See Part III 1. 6.

[10] See Part III 1. 10.

[11] These lines are redolent of the words of the *Salve Regina*, which is an ancient hymn to Our Lady sung in solemn chant by the Cistercian monks each evening after the conclusion of Compline. See ODCC 1210.

[12] Gn 2 gives an account of the Fall, but no reference is made to the eating of an apple; Scripture merely mentions the forbidden fruit; and Dict s.n. points out that the identification of the apple with the fruit of Paradise is without foundation and furthermore it is not certain that the apple was cultivated in ancient Palestine. *A Dictionary of Biblical Tradition in English Literature*, ed. D.L. Jeffrey (Grand Rapids, Michigan, 1992), lists the OE 'Genesis' poem as having a reference to the apple; see C.W. Kennedy, *The Caedmon Poems*, 28. Mr D. Huws wonders if this early reference may not have come to Northumbria from Ireland. Jeffrey also cites a reference from the *Homilies of Aelfric*, ed. Thorpe, 2.240–1.

[13] See Gn 2.

Canto 4 picks up the word of 'praise' and in a double couplet acclaims the value of praising God while decrying those who fail to do so; the poet states his own delight in praising Jesus, which he believes is purifying for the soul (121). In a litany-style sequence Cynddelw begs for deliverance from, or protection against, the powers of evil, hell's torments and the horror of familiarity with sin (124–36). But he does seek to be 'perfectly at ease in mind and wisdom', enjoying the privileges of familiarity with the blessed saints. Some of the situations mentioned beg further comment, e.g. 'in the urgency of [the] labour of book producers'. Does this suggest that poems were written down during the lifetime of these medieval Welsh poets? (143).[14] Cynddelw's expectation of heaven appears to be an extension of all that is best and happiest in this life (137–44). Mention of the 'fine choirs' may refer to the poets as singers or may echo words of the 'Preface', a stylized prayer of praise recited or sung on celebratory occasions at Mass.[15] But the excellence of these singers is only beneficial to the singer if it secures the necessary graces, when he comes before the anger of the judges on Judgement Day. In the closing lines of the canto the poet refers again to the meeting of the three groups,[16] and their encounter with Christ as He entered hell after His crucifixion. Now they stand before the judgement seat to receive their deserts. In the final couplet the poet asks again for a place in the company of the blessed ones of heaven 'as befits wise ones'.

Canto 5 opens with the link word 'unwise' and contrasts such a miserable one, unwilling to seek help and preferring to remain sad in lonely isolation, with the fortunate one who is contented with his lot; here again the poet emphasizes the value of repentance. These comments have a homiletic ring and the philosophic element brings to mind some biblical aphorisms as found in the Wisdom literature.[17] The poet prays that Christ may come to meet him and grant his request for help so that he can abandon his evil ways and pursue the path of goodness (161). With mention of the journey, he recalls once more those good souls who have travelled the narrow way of perfection, those whom Christ after His passion and death has rescued in their five ages.[18] Twice in this canto we

[14] See Daniel Huws, *Medieval Welsh Manuscripts* (Cardiff, 2000), 193–226.

[15] See *Missal* 814, 'It is truly fitting and proper, right and profitable to salvation, that we should always and everywhere give thanks to You, Lord, holy Father, almighty and ever-lasting God, through Christ our Lord. Through whom the angels praise your majesty, the Dominions worship You, the Powers are in awe before You. The heavens and the heavenly Hosts and the blessed Seraphim join together in a hymn of praise …'. On the history of the Missal, see NCE 9; pp. 897–9; see also *op.cit.* 414–28, on the developments and changes in the rituals of the Mass down the centuries.

[16] See lines 15–20 and footnote 4 *supra*.

[17] See Qo 7–8.

[18] Here we have reference to the Ages of the World. In several of the *Gogynfeirdd* poems these are mentioned and, depending on the rhythmic or other requirements of the

are challenged to seek and act in accordance with God's will. We learn, too, of the poet's own appreciation of the importance of such a moral response (175, 187–8). Recourse to penance is the natural corollary, and Cynddelw resolves to make amends for his past misdemeanours and failures. His prayer for help and support is based on trust in Christ who died on the cross (181–2), on God's saving of Noah[19] and his family from the flood, and on the rescue of the Three Youths, Sadrach, Mesach and Abednego, from the fiery furnace (184–6).[20] In the last line of the canto, Cynddelw refers to himself by name.[21]

Canto 6 begins with a reminder that God plans our transient life span and the poet calls on His mercy before being committed to the grave. God in His excellence, wisdom and faithfulness is described as the One, who knowing us has redeemed us from the fate of the 'five ages of the world through the baptism of John'. This surprises us until we recall that in announcing Christ, the Messiah, John the Baptist was seen as instrumental in bringing about our redemption.[22] On Judgement Day Christ is the One who will protect us against the anger[23] of God by virtue of having died on the Cross. In lines 207–14 there is a vivid and startling description of the horrors which will throw all nature into confusion as the wrath of God erupts on the world. Cynddelw switches from this gloom and doom to depict court feasting and largesse on New Year's

context, the reference may be to four, five or six ages; see 'Difregwawd Taliesin' in Bl BGCC 352–9, esp. lines 31–9; for exx. see Intro. under *Themes* and footnote 59. See CBT IV, p. 294, n. 170, where Gogynfeirdd references to the Five Ages of the World are listed; also MWRL 89–90 on the historic background to this usage in medieval poetry. For a full-scale treatment on the subject of the Ages of the World, see D. Ó Cróinín, *The Irish Sex Aetates Mundi* (Dublin, 1983); H. Tristram, *Sex Aetates Mundi* (Heidelberg, 1985).

[19] See Gn 7, and 8.

[20] See Dn 3:8–41.

[21] For a discussion on the name Cynddelw, see the Introduction to CBT III. Note a similar practice by Irish court poets, e.g. Tadhg Óg Ó hUiginn names himself in the closing couplet of poem V (pp. 8–10) of *Dán Dé* (ed. McKenna): *Saor ó bhréig an bheatha ché . go raibh Tadhg tráth an fhínné / gurab é a chríoch re ndol dé . síoth Dé re for a bhuighbhe.*

[22] See Mk 1:4–13 for an account of John the Baptist preaching and the baptism of Christ. John's preparation for Christ's coming used to be recalled at the end of every Mass, in what became known liturgically as 'The last Gospel' and which was, of course, recited in Latin. This was *In Principio*, from Jn 1:1–14. Cynddelw would have heard time after time the words *Fuit homo missus a Deo, cui nomen erat Joannes, Hic venit in testimonium ut testimonium perhiberet de lumine, ut omnes crederent per illum. Non erat ille lux, sed ut testimonium perhiberet de lumine* (Vulgate version). With the passage of time the *In Principio* gained an importance and popularity to the point where it was regarded as having miraculous and even magical powers. In his article 'Pre-Reformation Welsh Versions of the Scriptures', NLWJ iv (1946), 105–6, T. Jones asserts that the *In Principio* could have been translated into Welsh by the twelfth century; the oldest version of this translation is in *The White Book of Rhydderch*, now in the National Library of Wales, Aberystwyth.

[23] See Part III 1.9.

Day (215), evoking memories of grandeur and pomp in former times as 'payment [as reliable] as the proclamation of John' was assured.[24] When judgement comes, with all its mayhem, Cynddelw will have no fear because of the skill and excellence of his poetry. The poem ends with a prayer that he may be at God's right hand.[25]

This Cynddelw composition is perhaps the most sophisticated and stylized of all *Gogynfeirdd* poems. Its six cantos concatenate according to norms of the period, effecting a pleasant cohesive unit in what might otherwise have resulted in a dreary and boring repetition of overworked religious clichés. The recurrent use of certain themes seem to fit the poet's desire to emphasize points of particular interest to himself or his audience. Translation cannot convey the linguistic subtleties of this poem. It is too rich in flawless syntactic and grammatical expression, and in its variety of poetic technique and careful choice of individual phrasing. The mere understanding of lines and couplets can on occasion challenge the expertise of even the most learned medieval Welsh scholars.

Poem 2 (IV 17)

This is a shorter poem divided into cantos similar in structure to those of Poem 1. This ode, while possessing a certain elegance expected in a Cynddelw composition, lacks the stylistic finesse of his previous dedication to God (CBT IV 16). Here the religious reflections are deeper but are expressed in a more laboured, and sometimes turgid, manner, with longer lines and movement from one idea to another less skilfully handled. Syntax, too, is more difficult and many nominal sentences occur, in which it is not always easy to establish which is the subject, which the predicate, e.g. line 63.[26] Even a cursory reading will show that it has many of the themes which Cynddelw used in Poem 1 above. These will be obvious to the reader and so the following remarks and comments concern ideas and themes which are new and quite different.

The poem opens with a reference to the 'Lord of the ten grades' and ends with a prayer for refuge in the 'nine heavens',[27] before the poet

---

[24] Probably a reference to the *In Principio*; see footnote 22 *supra*.

[25] This was a prayer of many of the Welsh Court Poets and it seems to be based on Mt 25:34: 'Then the King will say to those on his right hand, "Come, you whom my Father has blessed, take for your heritage the kingdom prepared for you since the foundation of the world ... " '.

[26] See CBT IV, pp. 299–300, where the authorship of the poem is discussed and where the editors come down squarely on the side of accepting Cynddelw rather than Llywarch ap Llywelyn 'Prydydd y Moch' as its author. In this they follow the opinion of D. Myrddin Lloyd, *Rhai Agweddau ar Ddysg y Gogynfeirdd* (Caerdydd, 1997), 10–11; *id.* in *A Guide to Welsh Literature*, i, ed. A.O.H. Jarman and G.R. Hughes (Swansea, 1976), 171.

[27] See R 1235.40 (Casnodyn) for a similar reference to the ten orders of heaven; reference to nine grades is more usual as in l.142 *infra*.

moves on to consider the action of the 'Strong God of justice'.[28] Mention of and comment on, the Trinity occurs at three stages in this poem. Cynddelw asserts that the Trinity will receive perfect praise in language appropriate to such an august subject and this raises the question whether the poet was in fact considering this poem as a paean to the Blessed Trinity (11–14). He claims that he will extol the Three in accordance with his maturity, presumably meaning poetic maturity (95), and again he prays that he may contemplate the Trinity with rightful homage (105–6).[29] Staying with heaven, 'the home of Adam',[30] we find references to a host of angels (139) and the poet makes a petition to Mary for peace before death (135). It is interesting that he turns to Mary for help lest his merriment and fun rob him of the chances of salvation.

Besides the Trinity the poem has a summary of other truths of the Christian Faith—Creation, Incarnation and the Redemption achieved through the action of Christ who, by His five wounds, led the five ages from captivity.[31] The theme of God's greatness and man's insignificance is developed (63–82) with a meditation on the theme of *ubi sunt*? The fate of Arthur, Julius Caesar, Fflur, Brân son of Llŷr, Hercules, Greiddur, Madog and Alexander[32] should be a warning to us of the transience of all earthly prestige and that the one who reaches the pinnacle may be doomed to fall if he turns his back on the Lord, the One who is the fulfilment of Scripture. There is a hint of his fear of dying without a priest and not receiving the Last Sacraments (28).[33]

---

[28] See Part III 1. 8.

[29] See Part III 5.

[30] See Poem 3 *infra* for a similar reference to heaven as *addef Adda* 'the home of Adam'.

[31] Here we have an example of the use of numbers to link Christian belief with other religious traditions, see 'The Five Wounds of Our Lord', *Notes and Queries* 208 (1963), 50–1, 82–9, 127–34, 163–68; MWRL 43, commenting on the foregoing references, notes that devotion to 'the five wounds' of Christ derives from a popularized version of St Bernard's spirituality. See also J. O'Reilly, 'Early medieval text and image: the wounded and exalted Christ', in *Peritia,* 6–7 (1987–8), 72–111. On the 'Ages of the World', see footnote 18 *supra*.

[32] For oft-used medieval theme *sic transit gloria mundi*, see Intro. footnote 60, also E.R. Curtius, *European Literature* ... 80–1, where he deals with the idea that 'all must die', and on the brevity of human life; see *id.* 353n, 487–94. The heroic characters Arthur, Julius Caesar, Hercules and Alexander are well known; of Fflur nothing is known save the mention here in l. 69, which seems to suggest that she was one whom Julius Caesar wooed in vain during his invasion of Britain in 54 or 55 BC; Brân son of Llŷr is a mythological figure well known in Welsh medieval sagas and referred to in poems by Cynddelw and Llywarch ap Llywelyn 'Prydydd y Moch'; beyond this reference in l. 74 nothing is known of Greiddur; from the note in CBT IV, p. 321, Madog may refer to Cynddelw's first patron but mention of a twelfth-century character seems strange in this context.

[33] This refers to Penance, Extreme Unction and Viaticum or Holy Communion, often referred to as the last Sacraments. For a discussion of these, see Ott 325 ff.

On several occasions throughout the poem Cynddelw refers to his poetry asking for 'support for my verse' so that as God's friend he may be a 'bard' unto Him. He asserts that God not only understands his poetry but that it is He who has inspired it (101–2). He vows to worship and extol the Three and hopes for 'a place of refuge' in virtue of his 'excellence' (95–7). In describing the horrors of hell it is referred to as the dwelling-place of Cain.[34]

Gwalchmai ap Meilyr

Poem 3 (I 14)

All allusions and themes of this poem are contingent on its central focus, which is prayer for repentance and forgiveness. Admission of his sinfulness occurs time and time again throughout and Gwalchmai seems to rely on God as Trinity[35] and Unity (19, 24, 54, 110) as well as on Mary (37–47),[36] the apostles (51–2) and the archangels (21) for help to overcome his evil inclinations and sinful desires (11, 28–9, 58, 61, 99 101, 106). It is difficult to distinguish between the metaphorical and the literal in his travel (71–2), pilgrim and exile (12, 74) references. He may be referring to visiting the Holy Land (67–9, 85) and treading in the footsteps of Christ Himself. Mention of the Epiphany[37] and the baptism of Our Lord by John[38] (32–6) could provide a clue either to the time of composition or to the delivery of the poem. The reference to the Lord of heaven, as 'a physician' (99) may echo Luke 4:23, *Medice cura teipsum: quanta audivimus facta in Capharnaum, fac et hic in patria tua.*

---

[34] See Gn 4 for an account of the Cain biblical tradition and also BibT 307–8 for biblical references and a concise and interesting account of the background to Cain's crime and his punishment. Scripture does not state that he went to hell, but in 'Book of the Resurrection of Christ', ANT 183, read 'Jesus rose from the dead, and Abbaton (Death) and Pestilence came back to Amente (underworld) to protect it, but they found it wholly desolate, only three souls were left in it (those of Herod, Cain, and Judas …)'.

[35] This poem has quite a trinitarian dimension and references to the Trinity suggest that Gwalchmai was one person, at least, in the twelfth century who expresses a human relationship with the Trinity or the Three in One. In this connection, see Trin *passim,* and especially p. 15, and also Poems 2 and 3 in Bl BGCC 17–29.

[36] Here we find an outline of Mary's role in the Redemption in her threefold relationship with the Godhead, as 'mother', 'daughter' and 'sister'. See P. O'Dwyer, *Mary: a History of Devotion in Ireland* (Dublin, 1988), for similar examples from Irish sources.

[37] See ODCC 457 and J. Fisher, 'The Welsh Calendar', THSC, 1894–5, 111, for remarks on this feast, which was celebrated on January 6, see also G.G. Willis, *A History of Early Roman Liturgy* (London, 1994).

[38] For accounts of Christ's baptism by John, see Mt 3:11–17; Mk 1:7–11; Lk 3:15–16, 21–2.

It is 'as a sincere Welshman in exile'[39] (12) that Gwalchmai proposes to sing the praises of God, 'in perfect structure', now that he has been brought to recognize his sinfulness. Through references to hardships by land and sea he declares his need of repentance and his readiness to do penance. To God's benevolence he attributes his poetic inspiration (57). Mention of a fortress in (72) is probably a reference to the city of Jerusalem,[40] where Christ suffered. In line 46 there is a reference to the eight sins. This is a variant on the number of deadly or cardinal sins. The more usual number is seven: pride, covetousness, lust, anger, gluttony, envy and sloth. Other listings include murder and sadness. C. McKenna discusses *Gogynfeirdd* interest in these lists, explaining that the sevenfold scheme of cardinal sins was first set forth by Gregory the Great in his *Moralia*.[41]

Elidir Sais

The poetry of Elidir Sais includes five dedications to God and with these we move into the thirteenth century. However, it is not impossible that he could have composed in the late twelfth century, although the emphasis on the ideas of the grave and death in the poems suggests that they were composed towards the end of his life, and possibly when he was a member of a monastic order.[42] These five poems reveal a certain homogeneity, but each has its own particular manner of expression and style which adds to the interest of the whole canon. Either as preacher or spiritual counsellor, the poet in these compositions emerges as a deeply reflective person with an ability to propound the teaching and doctrine of the Church in a gentle and unthreatening way. One wonders if the copyist, in making his selection of what poems should be preserved, chose these five in order to highlight Elidir Sais's particular approach and style as a religious poet. Poem 30 *infra* is an address to God forms the *Incipit* to a historical poem.

---

[39] The poet's mention of 'exile' may refer to his being away from Wales, having been sent away, or even banished, and the reference to the Holy Land gives support to this. On the other hand, the word 'exile' may be seen as a well-known Christian metaphor for the world as a place of banishment. See footnote 11 *supra* on the *Salve Regina*.

[40] The phrase *caerfa urddyn* refers to the city of Jerusalem which, towards the end of the twelfth century, was of great importance because of the Crusades, whose intention was to protect it against, or win it back from, the enemies of Christianity under the leadership of Saladin.

[41] See MWRL 116–17; also footnotes 87 and 88 *infra* and the major study by Ll. Morgan, 'Y Saith Pechod Marwol yng nghanu Beirdd yr Uchelwyr' (Ph.D., Cymru [Aberystwyth], 1989), *passim*.

[42] See CBT I, pp. 322–3.

Poem 4 (I 21)

The particular style and emphasis, expressed in a lyrical and gentle manner, sets this poem apart. Elidir's composition is obviously the result of
contemplating God the 'mighty warrior', whose gift to us came in the
form of Jesus, Son of Mary—He the all-knowing One.[43] The poet
reflects further on the Creator who fashioned the world with its
marvels[44] before entering Mary's womb. He takes up the theme of
Christ's adherence to the Divine plan and the plotting of those who tried
to divert Him from His purpose. In speaking of sin the poet likens our
effort to conceal evil actions to that of Adam and Eve after the fall.

Poem 5 (I 22)

The emphasis in Poem 5 is on a prayer for repentance, and the poet
petitions by virtue of his baptism[45] that the God and Prophet, the noble
King, will place him among 'the baptized host'. Unlike his previous
poem the poet touches on his fear of hell with just a couplet commenting on its horrors. The Virgin *Morwyn* and the Apostles Peter, Maria[46]
and Paul are invoked for help on Judgement Day when, as a hero, Christ
will come to 'free the peoples of the world'. Elidir contrasts the lot of the
good and evil ones on that fateful day. The immediate duty of the poet is
to use his talent to extol in appropriate language the Ruler and 'undis-
puted Lord', whom he petitions as 'Master of the heavenly temple' to
attend to his prayer. In the closing couplet there is an imaginative reference to the Blessed Trinity which concludes with the request to be
'where You are praised / [In the] land of the Spirit of our spiritual
Father'.

---

[43] See Part III 1. 6.

[44] As already noted in Cynddelw's 'Awdl i Dduw' ('Ode to God') Jesus is sometimes
regarded as being the creator of the world; see Part III 7. 1.

[45] This may refer to the Sacrament of baptism, which is necessary for salvation, im-
printing 'a character or spiritual mark' on the recipient; see Ott 355 ff.

[46] The Latin version of Mary's name, connected here with those of Peter and Paul,
probably reflects Liturgical influence, and could echo something of the Litany of the
Saints. On the other hand, Elidir may have introduced Peter and Paul as exemplars of
repentant sinners and may have linked Mary Magdalen as 'Maria' with them in his
petition.

Poem 6 (I 23)

Poem 6 opens with a triple couplet which may be a veiled reference to the poet's leaving behind the attractions of the world in order to enter the Religious Life. The third couplet has a beautiful expression of trust in the saving action of the Trinity. Central to the following eight lines (7–14) is the theme of Judgement Day and the three ways in which souls will come to it. The first way, *gwyry achaws gwirionedd* 'virginity for the sake of truth', may refer to the vow of celibacy; the second, *priawd enw pruddedd* 'chief source of wisdom', may mean 'submission' in the sense of obedience; the third is *adaw* and this form is open to different interpretations, one being 'leaving' / 'abandoning' / 'bequeathing', which may be seen as leaving all things and thus possibly suggesting the vow of 'poverty'.[47] Besides the reference to Eve and the apple[48] there is a rather strange reference to 'Joseph's discourse'. It is unlikely that the Joseph in question is the spouse of Mary, since Scripture records no word of his. Traditionally, Joseph of Arimathea was connected with Glastonbury, and he may therefore be a possibility. However it is likely that Joseph, son of Jacob is meant, since he has often been represented as prefiguring Christ the Redeemer.[49]

Poem 7 (I 24)

Whether or not Elidir had entered a monastery, we certainly find him in this poem delivering a lenten homily. It moves in exhortative mode from Shrove Tuesday, the day appointed for confessing to a priest[50] and receiving absolution from sin, right through to Easter Sunday. The poet reminds us of Christ's forty days without food,[51] which he refers to as

---

[47] See Célí 106–10, where O'Dwyer deals with the Religious Vows, taking each vow in turn, 'Chastity, Poverty, Obedience', showing the strictness of the observance required by the Tallagh monks. Aspects of this may have come across to Wales and also the strict Cistercian rule with regard to the vows. There remains the possibility that Elidir was influenced by the Grey Friars, who were well established in Gwynedd during his lifetime. See Intro. for an outline of the coming of the Franciscans to Wales.

[48] See footnote 12 *supra*.

[49] See Gn 37:1–50:26 and especially 41:55, where the starving people of Egypt turned to Pharaoh asking for food and were told *Ite ad Joseph, et quidquid ipse vobis dixerit, facite;* this brings to mind Jn 2:5 when Mary at the Wedding Feast at Cana says to the servants, 'Do whatever he [Jesus] tells you'. In connection with the suggestion that the reference may be to Joseph of Arimathea, see 'The Narrative of the Assumption' attributed to him in ANT 216–18.

[50] See ODCC 1252.

[51] See Mt 4:1–11; Mk 1:12–13; Lk 4:1–13; see Eger 71–3 for an account of Lent and its special services, and also for a day-to-day description of services in the Great Week, i.e. the week preceding Easter Sunday, also *ib.* 73–6.

'God's fast'. The picture of the sufferings of Holy Week, with particular reference to Wednesday, Thursday, Friday,[52] Saturday and Sunday, is so graphic that it might be an eye-witness account. Perhaps Elidir, either as a member of the audience or as an actor, had been present on some occasion for a dramatic presentation of each day's events. In several European countries passion plays were a means of instructing people in the story of our Redemption in a monastery or a parish church, and Wales may have had a similar practice. Delighting in the marvel of the Resurrection, the poet notes that in all these events Christ showed Himself as the fulfilment of His plan of Redemption. In a brief account of the harrowing of hell in lines 29–34 and in line 35 pride is mentioned as chief of the eight[53] deadly sins. The poet's own repentance finds a place in the poem, which ends with a resolution to amend his ways and a prayer that he may be in the company of the blessed with God.

Poem 8 (I 20)

To validate the acceptance of this poem as the work of Elidir Sais, we must consider its early manuscript tradition. Without title or attribution it remains in the final folios of the Hendregadredd MS (c.1325–50),[54] and appears again in the Red Book of Hergerst (c.1400),[55] but this time at the end of the section headed Elidir Sais ai cant 'Elidir Sais sang it' (cols. 1143–6), where Elidir's other religious poems occur. Following on immediately in R are the poems of Meilyr ap Gwalchmai (see Poems 12–15 infra). Therefore, it seems reasonable to accept that the copyist of the Red Book of Hergest regarded this poem as part of Elidir Sais's canon, and it has been accepted as such in the editing of Cyfres Beirdd y Tywysogion I, and located before Elidir's other dedications to God. This poem merits a place since it lauds the Godhead and addresses and petitions the Divinity under a variety of titles other than God—King,

---

[52] Here we have reference to 'the cross / crucifixion of our Father', which seems rather strange since it was Christ, the second person of the Blessed Trinity, who suffered and died on the Cross. There are other examples from the Middle Ages of God, or God the Father, being cast in the redemptive role. In Peritia, 6–7 (1987–8), 52–3, Éamonn Ó Carragáin cites the opening line of the Ruthwell crucifixion poem 'Almighty God stripped himself. When he willed to mount the gallows' and shows that the phrase God Almeztig translates the Latin Deus Omnipotens, which taken on its own almost always refers to God the Father as in the opening phrase of the Apostles' Creed. Ó Carragáin further draws our attention to the Antiphonary of Bangor where, in describing Christ ascending the Cross He is referred to as 'Almighty God'; E. Okasha translates 'God almighty stripped himself, when he wanted to ascend the cross, brave before men—' in Hand-list of Anglo-Saxon non-runic inscriptions (Cambridge, 1971), 111.
[53] See footnote 41 supra.
[54] See H 322.
[55] See R col. 1146.

Seer, Ruler, Lord, Generous One, Father, Supreme Power, Leader, Defender, Guarantor, and the word Christ occurs once. Thematically the poem accords with parts of Elidir's other religious compositions. Henry Lewis entitles it *Erchi Trugaredd*, 'A plea for mercy', and suggests that it could possibly be seen as a 'deathbed poem'.[56] Could the poet have been experimenting with the *inominabile* dilemma?[57]

Einion ap Gwalchmai

As has been shown above, Einion ap Gwalchmai sang to lay patrons as well as dedicating three compositions to God, Poems 9, 10 and 11. These three vary in length and, to some degree, in thematic content and poetic expression. Each has a verve and lustre of its own. In Poem 9, which contains 110 lines, Einion ap Gwalchmai frequently used medieval religious themes, but also included references which are specifically Welsh in character (92–4). Poems 10 and 11 are much shorter and may have been delivered to a monastic audience familiar with the general caveats and warnings expressed in these compositions. However, Poem 11 eases into a rather sentimental memento of the joys of the poet's former warrior life, while in the closing line we gain the impression that at last he has chosen the better part. Could this poem be a reflection on 'The Rich Young Man' in Mt. 19:16–22?

Poem 9 (I 27)

This poem is edited in three cantos—canto 1 concentrates on the poet's own spiritual condition and needs; canto 2 contemplates Christ's suffering and the poet's response in faith; canto 3 begins cheerfully but swiftly moves into the *mea culpa* and petition mode. Unlike many other *Gogynfeirdd* poems, the cantos here are not determined by end-line rhyme, which remains in *-eu* throughout. The distinguishing mark of the ornate capital letter, at the start of the poem and also at lines 37 and 69, in the Hendregadredd Manuscript (*c.*1300) influenced the editors in presenting the poem in cantos.

The connecting theme throughout Poem 9 is a cry for forgiveness and peace before death. Einion laments his many private and personal faults as well as those committed in the course of his official duties (80). He seems to envy the monks and the clergy (51) and resolves to go and live in a monastery before death overtakes him (67–8).

---

[56] See HG Cref 71–2 (poem XXVII).
[57] See Part III 8 for the alternative names of God in the Gogynfeirdd poems, both secular and religious.

The poem opens with a prayer to God, 'supreme prophet of miracles', for blessings but the poet also mentions his own gifts as a 'talented man', and enumerates his virtues and vices in his plea for mercy. Tears of repentance, he hopes, will win pardon before he has to render an account of his life and actions; 'the foul sin of [desecrating] Sundays' (24) probably refers to a violation of the third commandment of the decalogue *Memento ut diem sabbati sanctifices*,[58] but the rather difficult language and syntax obscure the poet's precise meaning. He strikes an unusual and original note when he refers to transgressions as 'words of wantonness' and excessive eloquence. For these and all other sins he resolves to make atonement doing penance on the banks of the Jordan (31–6). Furthermore, he is ready to endure the hardship of *Mynydd Mynnau*, the Alps, in order to reach the place where God is.[59] It is worth noting that there is mention of both the five (37) and the six ages of the world (48).[60] Having reflected on the Feast of the Ascension and the Son of God going to heaven to sit on the right hand on Thursday (61–6),[61] the poet hopes that he himself may retire to Bardsey Island[62] until it is time for him to go to heaven.

In a contrite attitude the poet lists his errors covering many of the 'do nots' of the decalogue (69–82).[63] This examination of conscience moves him to pray for repentance and thus win a place in Paradise (83–6).[64] He hopes that Peter,[65] heaven's doorkeeper, may not exclude him and asks

[58] See Ex 20:8, also Part III 1. 23.
[59] See *supra* where Gwalchmai (Poem 3.69–70) speaks of the Holy Land and may be referring to a visit there. This reference to the Jordan supports the idea of a pilgrimage of penance as does the resolve to endure the hardships of the Alps en route; see CBT I, pp. 456–7 and D. Stephenson: GG 208, where we see King Henry III granting Ednyfed Fychan (seneschal to Llywelyn ab Iorwerth *ob.* 1240) and his retinue safe conduct through England on their way to the Holy Land in 1235. See also RC xliii (1925), where J. Loth interprets the phrase *Mynydd Mynnau* as a reference to the Mount of Olives, but in the light of the article by I. Williams, 'Mynydd Mynnau', B xvii (1956–8), 96–8, we accept it as meaning the Alps.
[60] Reference to five ages may connect with the five wounds in the following line; for further references see Intro. footnote 59.
[61] Ascension Thursday is a solemn feast celebrated forty days after Easter; for NT accounts of Christ's ascension see Mt 24:30–1, Mk 16:14–20; Acts 1:9–11.
[62] On Bardsey Island, which is situated to the west of the Llŷn peninsula, there was a famous monastic settlement; traditions survive in the Book of Llandaff and 'The life of Llawddog' suggesting that anyone buried there would be immune from hell's punishment. Furthermore, it records that three pilgrimages to the island were the equivalent of one to Rome. See C.N. John, 'The Celtic Monasteries of North Wales', TCHSG xxi (1960), 14–41.
[63] See Ex. 20:2–17.
[64] See footnote 13 *supra*.
[65] See Mt 10:2, 16, 17, 26:33–5, 69–74; Jn 20: 2–10, 21:1–23. The Mt accounts tell of Simon's call as an apostle, his declaration of faith in Christ and his election as leader of the

that Michael[66] will come to his aid in the manner of Cwyfan, Elfodd and Cenau.[67] He also turns to Mary, the four Evangelists, St Silin[68] and St Marthin,[69] not omitting Paul, for their assistance at the hour of death. The hierarchies of heaven[70] are invoked as he prays for inspiration to praise the Trinity 'with gentle thoughts'. On his decision to eschew the use of arms[71] and 'God's treasures' he stakes his hopes for pardon, and with a petition for rest from his labours before 'lying down in the grave' the poem ends.

Alliteration, consonantal and verbal, features throughout the ode, which concludes with an *englyn* or quatrain.

Poem 10 (I 28)

The centre of this poem (5–42) is cast in an exhortative and homiletic style, where Einion deplores the ills of society and the need for penance, almsgiving and other good works, while the opening couplets and the final six lines are his own personal petitions, initially for poetic inspiration and finally for a place in the company of the ninefold host with the One God in His Unity. No proper names occur and the poem is sparse on thematic references of the type noted in Poem 9, and other *Gogynfeirdd* compositions already discussed.

Poem 11 (I 29)

In his plea for repentance Einion ap Gwalchmai remarks that the loss of a man of sixty years is a grievous matter (23), then in an 8-line sequence

---

apostles and his change of name to Peter. John records Peter's denial of Christ and finally his reinstatement as leader.

[66] On Michael the archangel in Gogynfeirdd poems, see MWRL 127–8.

[67] See CBT I, p. 471, notes 92, 93, 94 (on Cwynfan, Elfodd and Cenau).

[68] St Giles (?8th century), see ODCC 558.

[69] Marthin (a Breton name) figures as a co-worker with St Patrick, but he has often been confused with Martin of Tours (LBS iii, 439–40); on the latter, see ODCC 864; the use of the form Marthin may be an example of consonantal accommodation to the *-th-* in Mathau, also occurring in CBT I 27.95.

[70] See footnote 15 *supra*.

[71] We have evidence that the Gogynfeirdd poets fought in battles side by side with their patrons. See CBT VI, p. 369, where it is shown, from near contemporary evidence, that Dafydd Benfras probably died while fighting alongside Llywelyn ap Gruffudd. See also ByT 33–4, for a discussion on poets in battle in Ireland and elsewhere, but note that J. Carney, 'Society and the bardic poet' in *Studies*, 62 (1973), p. 235, argues that poets did not fight in battles; see also PWP 27–8.

(25–34) he casts his eye around the pleasant things of life[72] with sensitive lyrical emotion, but concludes that more pleasant and noble still is the praising of the Lord of magnanimity. This reference to delight in praising God may indicate that Einion has in fact left behind the delights of the world, which he has just enumerated, and is now a monk in Bardsey, and there fully committed to his *opus Dei*[73] or the praising of God in the Divine Office. However, we have evidence that the laity in medieval Wales may have participated in some at least of the Canonical Hours, perhaps along with a monastic community.[74] Could it be that this poem is an exhortation to his fellow worshippers, either laity or monks?

Meilyr ap Gwalchmai

Meilyr ap Gwalchmai, setting his sights on the bliss of heaven, tends to be cheerful and hopeful. As he covers many themes in the *laud* mode his allusions and references are wide-ranging; however, when in homily style, he inveighs strongly against the dangers and evils of riches. The shortness and fragility of human life can at times fire Meilyr ap Gwalch-mai to emphasize the need for constant vigilance in avoiding the occa-sions of sin. For his own personal transgressions he is truly sorry, and resolves to set his foot on the road to penitence lest he be assigned to the company of Cain and Satan for all eternity. Exhortation and prayer, sometimes as petition, sometimes as praise, alternate within his composi-tions.

Poem 12 (I 30)

Petition is the salient feature of this poem. Meilyr begs for many of the Christian virtues and asserts his faith and trust in God under a multiplicity of titles: He is the Creator, the Ruler, the Counsellor, the Lover, the King of heaven while Christ is described as the blessed teacher and Lord. (Note the Latin version *Christus* in line 22, a very rare form in medieval Welsh poetry.) The poet begs that with 'God the Creator and Ruler' as 'guide' he may be sinless until the Day of Judgement. This has been

---

[72] Line 26 has a reference to *pall* which presents a difficulty in the context; see CBT I, p. 491.

[73] See RB for an account of the evolution, development and continuation of the use of the *Psalterium Romanum*, which has remained virtually untouched since St Jerome cor-rected it in 383 A.D.

[74] See the closing triplet of the series in Bl BGCC 289, which suggests that a Christian can best find forgiveness through 'rising in time for the morning service, and remaining awake at night, in prayer to the saints'. *Pilgeint*, 'cock-crow' meaning 'dawn', is the word generally used for the early morning Hours of the Divine Office; usually a summary of the life of the saint, whose feast day was being celebrated, was read.

described as a covenant poem, and entitled *Erchi carennydd Duw* in HG Cref 57.[75] The poet on his part promises to live according to the norms of the Christian ethic, and prays that Christ will honour His side of the covenant and grant him the freedom to live daily in the 'friendship of God' (31–42). It is in acknowledging God's supremacy that he resolves to amend his life.

The poem is particularly stylized and as in his other poems the poetic device known in Welsh as *cymeriad,* which links lines by the repetition of the same initial letter, word or syllable, features in this composition.

Poem 13 (I 31)

Here we have a praise poem written in a very positive and hopeful style. Rather than dwelling on the Last Judgement, the poet emphasizes the blessings of heaven where the children of Adam, in the company of the hosts of Christendom, will shine in light with God. Mary first and then fair Michael are named as pre-eminent advocates of those souls in distress (11–14). The passage on believers may be understood as referring to monks, and this could support the idea of Meilyr ap Gwalchmai himself as a member of such a community. They abide in the blessedness of the Trinity, he claims, as a reward for their chanting the praises of God.[76] To be in Paradise is the poet's great ambition and he hopes to arrive there and take up his abode in the company of the saintly souls already enjoying their reward (15–22). In virtue of his reconciliation, achieved through their intervention, the archangels Gabriel and Raphael[77] will 'in wisdom' honour him, standing as his advocates on the Day of Judgement. They will lead him to eternal blessedness and the throne of the Lord God (23–32).

[75] See CBT I, p. 510. *Carennydd* is given as 'kindred, kinship, relationship, descent, affinity; friendship, reconciliation; kinsman, relation' in GPC 436. Thomas Charles-Edwards in 'The Date of the Four Branches of the Mabinogi', THSC, 1970, 278–9, states that *carennydd* is a formal, legal relationship and not just personal. *Tangnefedd* and *carennydd* indicate a state of legal peace between two parties when outstanding claims between them have been satisfied. E.P. Hamp in B xxix (1980–1), 683, explains why *carennydd* could come to mean not 'friendship' or 'kinship' but 'legal or political non-aggression'. See also MWRL 34, 89, for comments on its use in medieval Welsh religious poetry.

[76] This probably refers to the Canonical Hours of the Divine Office, which may have been recited or sung in Gregorian or Plain Chant, as was the practice at that period.

[77] See ODCC 534 and 1338.

Poem 14 (I 32)

Thematically the poem seems to fall into three sections. Lines 1–10 dwell on the obligation to love God,[78] an unusual and new idea in the poetry of the *Gogynfeirdd*. Normally the poets describe a fear-inspiring God with the power to punish the sinner. The omnipotent God is envisaged as One to be appeased and placated lest He cast us into hell. The second section (11–23) reflects on the attributes and divine actions of God. Here we have a clear statement on the Trinity in its three persons, including one of the rare mentions of the Holy Spirit[79] in *Gogynfeirdd* poetry. Section three (24–34) concentrates on the virtue of faith. The poet highlights different aspects of this virtue and states his own position in this regard. God, being 'credible' (29),[80] inspires him to trust in the Divine intention. In the final couplet the poet prays that mutual faith and trust may exist between God and himself.

This is a very carefully constructed poem, regular in its metrical style and interesting in that the three main themes are clearly visible, each having its own particular *cymeriad* or linear uniformity of initial letter, word or phrase.

Poem 15 (I 33)

Here we come to the longest of Meilyr's religious poems, with 103 lines presented in seven cantos, each one of different length, and each with its own particular end rhyme. Six of these cantos are cleverly interlinked with the preceding canto. Line 8 refers to lost souls as *maledicti,* one of the rare Latin words occurring in *Gogynfeirdd* poems.

Henry Lewis has aptly called this poem 'A Prayer against hell'.[81] But what an unusual sort of prayer! By and large it seems rather gloomy and threatening, with a few flashes of relief when the petition is for a place in heaven with the blessed. It is a reflection cast in the mould of a homily and includes many of the usual *Gogynfeirdd* religious ideas and aspirations. A few of these deserve mention. The reference to David is interesting in its ambiguity and, following the interpretation of *Cyfres Beirdd y Tywysogion*, it is taken it to mean St David, whom the poet calls upon as his supporting patron (18–19).[82] Meilyr also enlists the aid of St Peter, St

---

[78] See Deut 6:5 and Lv 19:18 as well as the many NT references to the great commandment of love.

[79] For further references see Part III 4.

[80] See CBT I, p. 527.

[81] See HG Cref 61.

[82] The *pont Dewi* is difficult and J. Lloyd-Jones (PBA xxxiv), who understands it as referring to St David, is followed here, but Henry Lewis in HG Cref 209 suggests a different interpretation by introducing an emendation and other possible readings.

Ezechias[83] and Mary the 'mother of her Father'. To her he turns asking that she 'pray to her Boy' to obtain that he, Meilyr, may not go to the abode of Judas[84] and so suffer the fate of Cain and Satan.[85] In lines 23–4 and 48–51 the poet rails against the dangers of wealth, and, dwelling upon the cognate idea of our transience, he admonishes us concerning 'transient honour' (18) and reminds us of our mortality, 'He who was long-lived yesterday, today is no more' (58), warning us that there is '... but a short period of penance in the world' (73).

Llywelyn Fardd (II)

The poet reveals himself in his two religious compositions as an accomplished and confident artist and craftsman. Because of its length the second allows greater scope for variety in subject matter and style. Both poems deal with sin and its punishment, while stressing the need for repentance. In addition to this, Poem 17 reflects contemporary devotional practices, while Old Testament characters and traditions are mentioned. References also show an acquaintance with the cults of some of the better known saints.

Poem 16 (VI 9)

In this poem of just 16 lines we find a list of six sins which require atonement before death. This number is a variant on listings of seven and eight,[86] and elsewhere we find evidence of this same inconsistency.[87] Listing of sins has a scriptural basis as we see in Eph 5:3–4 and Col 3:8–9.[88] Inconsistency in numbering these sins is found when they are mentioned by other Welsh poets. In *Llyfr Du Caerfyrddin*, for example, there are two different lists.[89] The origin of this enumerating in Wales is unknown, but it seems that the practice of listing and categorizing theological and devotional material is more characteristic of thirteenth- than

---

[83] See CBT I, p. 550, note 96 referring to ThU 393 n1, where Ezechias is identified with Heseciah (2 K 18:1–20, 21–2).

[84] See footnote 34 *supra*.

[85] See *ib*.

[86] On the listing of sins, see M.W. Bloomfield, *The Seven Deadly Sins ...*, and for the list of six sins, see *Visio Sancti Pauli*, ed. Theodore Silverstein (London, 1953), 73, 121.

[87] PG xxxiv, 609–10. In Homily XV of Marcarius of Egypt, for example, the sins to be avoided are listed as *voluptas, avaritia, vana gloria, fastu, aemulatione et ira*; and in PL ii, 1020, we find that Tertullian in his 'De pudicitia' gives as the most lethal sins *homicidium, idololatria, fraus, negatio, blasphemia* and *moechia et fornicatio*.

[88] *Ib*. 39, 1812, in a homily attributed to Caesarius of Arles, the six main sins are *concupiscentia vel fornicationis spiritus, furor, tristitia, desidiae tepor vel negligentiae, cupiditas* and *invidia*.

[89] LlDC 58 (27.16–17, 19–21).

of twelfth-century Welsh poets. Therefore this poem is attributed to Llywelyn Fardd (II) and placed in *Cyfres Beirdd y Tywysogion* VI with other thirteenth-century poems.[90] In the concluding couplets the poet prays to the Lord of joy and purity, the One who created 'a variety of seeds, and birds'. He prays that he himself may be just at all times 'with the Son of Grace', and that he be a servant of God before he goes to the grave. Here, taking the phrase literally, *gwas Duw* is translated as 'servant of God'; it could perhaps be understood metaphorically as 'hermit' or 'anchorite'.[91]

Poem 17 (VI 10)

This is a longer poem whose 96 lines have been presented in three cantos, of varying length. Llywelyn Fardd (II) dwells on the necessity for conversion and repentance as he calls upon the help of David and relies on the intervention of Peter (23) when he meets Mary and Michael. Heaven, he asserts, cannot be won by human effort—by eloquence, arrogance or anger—but by morning and evening prayer with intercession to the saints and the petitions of the Lord's Prayer.[92] In contemplating the transience of life he reflects on his own sinfulness, focusing on the folly of amassing rich gifts with the risk of a spiritual downfall. Pride is condemned as the greatest evil. The scene of the Last Judgement is set on the Mount of Olives, with Michael present.[93] Paul is mentioned in the context of God's redeeming of all peoples (56), and in subsequent lines the poet lingers on the Saviour's redemptive action, referring to Him as the 'God of Israel' (58).[94] In an unusual line (59) the poet expresses his desire for companionship with God, pledging to devote his poetic gift to Him, but proceeds to warn against the fate of one who neglects to do so.

---

[90] See MWRL 41–80, 116–18.

[91] See CBT VI, p. 131 and GPC 2448.

[92] Could it be that prayers of the *Libellus sacrum precum* had become available in Wales by the thirteenth century? This book of private prayers included intercessions and hymns of Hilary, Ambrose, Augustine, Jerome and other Fathers; the litany also is included, see PL 101.1383–1416. See also NCE, 11, p. 680 on 'Books of Private Prayers'. MWRL 72 says that the seven petitions of the Lord's Prayer are listed in *Pwyll y Pader o Ddull Hu Sant* which is preserved in Peniarth MSS 16.

[93] This reference to Michael is based on Rv 12:7; at the Last Judgement his duty will be to assess the merits or otherwise of the souls. See S.G.F. Brandon, *The Judgement of the Dead* (London, 1967), 119–29; B.G. Lane, 'The Beaune Last Judgement and the Mass of the Dead', *Simiolus*, xix (1989), 167–80. For other references to Michael in this poem, see line 11, which refers to his receiving souls immediately after death, and 91, where the poet looks forward to Michael welcoming him to heaven; see also footnote 66 *supra* and the 'Gospel of Bartholomew', ANT 175–6.

[94] See Poem 6.19 *supra*.

Many of the usual *Gogynfeirdd* themes occur throughout the poem, and the explanatory and didactic attitude of the poet (15–22, 31–52) strongly suggests a composition for public proclamation.

Madog ap Gwallter

A freshness and vibrancy characterizes Madog ap Gwallter's work. He shows confidence in the use of scriptural and moral references which bespeak a knowledge of Christian teaching of the kind expected from an educated priest towards the middle or end of the thirteenth century.

Poem 18 (VII 32)

This poem is certainly addressed to the Godhead, but with a change in emphasis, which now focuses on God the Son as the addressee. It is in fact a paean on the Incarnation with the narrative of Christ's Nativity, according to St Luke,[95] interwoven throughout. The 'city of David' is mentioned and the Gloria sung by the angels bears the good news of Christ's birth to the shepherds, as they look after their sheep on the hillside outside that city, which we know as Bethlehem (24–32). Madog elaborates on the coming of the 'three kings' as they follow the sign that leads them to Jerusalem and on to Bethlehem (29–50).[96] Continuing the Gospel account, Herod's frustration and the massacre of the Holy Innocents leads to a pious comment on the reward of martyrdom. The couplet (59–60) mentions Christmas with an encouragement to be happy. There is a unique reference to the Son as the 'Lord of all priests, who owns everything' (62). Does this suggest that priests should not own property or wealth since all things belong to God alone? Or might it reflect the Franciscan emphasis on the practice of vowed poverty? The poet mentions Our Lady and her role in our salvation in the concluding couplet, which calls to mind another couplet from a thirteenth-century English lyric: 'Lady, pray for us to your son who bought us dear, / and defend us from the hateful house made for a fiend'.[97]

In view of the suggestion that Madog ap Gwallter was a Franciscan it seems reasonable to assume that he could have been in one of the monasteries of that Order in Wales and that he addressed this poem-homily

---

[95] See Lk 2.
[96] See Mt 2.
[97] See 'The penitent hopes in Mary' in *Medieval English Lyrics,* ed. R.T. Davies (3rd ed., London, 1971), 69; P. O'Dwyer, *op.cit.*; D.M. Lloyd, 'Y Brawd Fadawg ap Gwallter a'i Gân i'r Geni', *Y Tyst,* 25 Rhagfyr 1947, 6–7; A. Breeze, 'Madog ap Gwallter', YB xiii (1985), 93–100, also P. O'Dwyer, *Mary: a history of devotion in Ireland* (Dublin, 1988), 73, 76, 80, 109–10 *et passim.*

either at a community celebration on Christmas Day or on the Feast of the Epiphany.

Gruffudd ab yr Ynad Coch

Here is a versatile poet who displays a great facility with a variety of poetic ornament in different metres and this, conjoined with an adroit control in the use of vocabulary, can produce a pleasing effect. With a carefully chosen word and phrase he paints graphic images, which at times are blood-curdling in the detail of their horror. However, he is more than a sensationalist. He is a serious poet whose reflective runs can be deeply moving and inspiring. As his five religious poems show he experiments with different forms and subject-matter.

Poem 19 (VII 38)

With ardour and vehemence the poet questions the lot of one who, disregarding the certainty of death, does not repent of his sins. Miserable is such a one in his lack of faith in God and his lack of concern for the punishments prepared for him by Lucifer.[98] The world is content to ignore the consequences of Judgement Day when the crucified Christ will proclaim aloud all the sins of each one,[99] and when His five wounds will announce blessings for faithful souls, who will be marked with a sign on their forehead. Of particular interest is the listing of the 'Ages of Man' (22–43), giving stark descriptions of advancing age and a horrific portrayal of man's final dissolution.[100] The reference to the white-spotted hand (41) is enigmatic and may possibly suggest leprosy.[101]

Poem 20 (VII 39)

This ode is a good example of the combination of ecclesiastical *refugium* and Welsh *nawdd*, words which are virtually synonymous, expressing a similar usage in both traditions. The poem is a formal call for the protection of God, the angels and the saints, where the term *nawdd,* and its

---

[98] References to Lucifer occur also in lines 17 and 40 *infra,* Poems 17.6 *supra,* and 22.50 *infra.*

[99] See NCE 2, pp. 697–8, for a discussion on the Book of Life also Rv 20:12, which echoes many references found throughout Scripture, e.g. Ex 32:32–3, Pss 69:28, 139:16; Is 4:3; Dn 7:10 and in the NT Lk 10:20.

[100] On both these topics, the 'Ages of Man' and the 'Signs of Age', see MWRL 51; see also J.W. Jones, *Archaeologia,* xxxv (1853), 167–89, and compare Gwalchmai's couplet in Poem 3.91–4 *supra,* where he speaks of the difficulties of life's beginning and end.

[101] At the initial stages leprosy manifests itself in white blotches on the skin. MWRL sees the words merely as a reference to skin discolouration in old age.

derivative *nodet,* occurs eighteen times. Seeking *nawdd* from powerful secular patrons was part of the legal and social system of Wales in the Middle Ages and was also a central feature in poet-patron relations.[102] Transferring this idea to religious usage was an easy step for Gruffudd, who regularly called on similar language in praising God or his earthly patron.

The poem echoes the style of Church litanies and particularly that of the Litany of the Saints, which was sung in Paschal Time and on the Rogation Days, as well as during processions or pilgrimages. It was also sung or recited on the Feast of St Mark (April 25).[103]

Poem 21 (VII 40)

Points central to Christian belief and religious practice at the time—the seven deadly sins, the seven petitions of the Our Father, the seven gifts of the Holy Spirit, the seven spiritual works of mercy and the Beatitudes— are given prominence in this ode.[104] Noteworthy, too, are the horrific descriptions of hell and the torture and sufferings of captive souls who await Christ's coming to liberate them. The availability of 'Purdan Padrig'[105] may account for some of these descriptions, but by the time of Gruffudd ab yr Ynad Coch so much on the 'harrowing of hell' had been heard in Welsh court poetry that it had become almost indispensable for any exhortative religious composition. Could it be that Gruffudd ab yr Ynad Coch had heard these infernal details from the lips of an over-zealous preacher? All that was then required was for his lively imagination to enlarge on the frightening scenario and depict a state of suffering appalling in its realism.[106] Very interesting here is the inclusion of some of the less agreeable aspects of Welsh weather and environment: fogs and swamps intensify the torments of hell (54–5). In requesting to be spared from the clutches of Satan, the poet makes intercession in virtue of the love of Absalom (62).[107] He also asks for the grace of the last rites of the church—the Sacraments of Penance, Holy Communion and Extreme Unction.[108] The closing six lines, each beginning with a *Ni bwyf* ('Let me

---

[102] See WLW 49–50; H. Pryce, *Native Law and the Church in Medieval Wales* (Oxford, 1993), 163–74; P.K. Ford, 'Welsh *Asswynaw* and Celtic Legal Idiom', B xxvi (1974–6), 147–53.

[103] See ODCC 1038–9 *s.n.* The Litany of the Saints and *ib.* 1405 *s.n.* Rogation Days.

[104] For a fuller discussion on these heptads, see MWRL 72–3, where C. McKenna notes that an indirect source may have been *Pwyll y Pader o Ddull Huw Sant,* see footnote 92 *supra* and also DrOC 4–7.

[105] See J.E. Caerwyn Williams, 'Purdan Padrig', NLWJ iii (1943–4), 102–6.

[106] See Intro. footnote 61.

[107] On Absalom, his death and David's reaction to the news, see 2 S 13–18 and 19:1–2.

[108] MWRL 117 takes the references to the Sacraments as an indication that the decrees of Lateran IV (1215) were being implemented in the Welsh Church. See also footnote 33 *supra.*

not') plea, reflect, perhaps, some familiarity with the Litany of the Saints and its 'ab omni ... ' intercessions and 'libera nos, Domine' responses.[109]

Poem 22 (VII 41)

Henry Lewis named this poem 'Rhybudd rhag Barn' ('A Warning before Judgement') and, in view of its main emphasis, this seems an appropriate title. Having completed the opening formalities, the poet assumes a homiletic stance and rails against the abuse of riches and power, directing his most mordant invective at lawyers as being particularly culpable in this regard. He details the deceit and oppression of members of the legal profession, who do not scorn to fill their coffers at the expense of the weaker and poorer sectors of society. This obsession with riches renders lawyers unwilling and incapable of giving thought to the next life.

   Much of the language of this poem has legal connotations, e.g. Jesus is a Gwarant, 'Guarantor', and words like barn, 'verdict', cyfraith hoced a chuhudded, 'law of deceit and impeachment', gwylltineb hawl ac ateb, 'fierceness in question and response' may suggest that Gruffudd was familiar with law court language and perhaps experienced in its practice too. We know that he belonged to a family of lawyers and may himself have been a member of that profession. The whole purpose of his vilification of lawyers is to draw attention to the inevitability of meeting on the Day of Judgement a God of justice, to whom an account must be rendered. If then the balance swings against the defendant, Lucifer will be empowered to mete out his punishments (36–50). In the concluding lines the poet gently recommends an alternative option, which is to accept God's graces, in order to enjoy the heavenly feast, with the freedom for song and celebration. A reference to the signs of the zodiac (29)[110] emphasizes God's universal openness and knowledge of all that is in heaven and on earth.

Poem 23 (VII 42)

This poem may be regarded as one of the most incisive, if not the most incisive, of all Welsh religious court poems. It is a fine example of the theme sic transit gloria mundi[111]—all must die, even the most illustrious, as did Llywelyn ap Gruffudd, last native prince of Wales, who was cruelly

---

[109] See Missal 1820, and for a discussion see MWRL 54, 58–9.

[110] See The New Shorter Oxford English Dictionary (Oxford, 1993), which explains the word zodiac as 'a belt of the celestial sphere extending about 8 or 9 degrees on each side of the ecliptic, within which the apparent motions of the sun, moon, and principal planets take place, and which is usu[ally] divided into twelve signs'.

[111] See footnote 32 supra.

done to death in 1282, and for whom Gruffudd composed one of the finest and most poignant of all Welsh elegies.[112] Perhaps it was this great personal loss and the realization of the inevitability of death that enabled the poet to speak in such precise and sensitive language. Many of the themes found in previous compositions occur here again.

Note some unusual lines as when the poet refers to 'the vain evil wantonness of Eve' being responsible for the Lord's going to the 'wood of suffering' (42). But perhaps we have something which is unique in *Gogynfeirdd* poetry but common in medieval literature, when Christ speaks out clearly and asks, 'That I have done, what hast thou done?' (49)[113] In the closing lines the poet contrasts the lot of the unrepentant ones, doomed to go to '[the] secret place of punishment', with those found in good dispositions on their way to the 'joy of the feast that does not end / In [the] eternal free, gracious assembly'.

Poem 24 (VII 43)

This poem is a meditative comment on the Last Judgement, with Christ portrayed as the 'Suffering Servant', a theme which appears often in European art and literature of the Middle Ages. In references to Christ the image presented in twelfth-century *Gogynfeirdd* poetry differs from that seen here and in other thirteenth-century compositions.[114] The poem opens with annoyance at the indifference of the sinner, who does not believe in hell until it is too late; if he contemplated the sufferings of Christ he would not sin. There follows a detailed description of Christ coming on the Last Day in His crucified body, its flesh marked by wounds 'not anointed', and head crowned with thorns. The Passion of Christ was to ransom souls from the legions of hell, 'from the power of [the] wolf' (13–26). In a dramatic address to the assembly, the Lord asks who are those unrepentant sinners—the usurer, the robber, the glutton, the profligate and unbeliever—and the poet declares that such perfidious ones should flee from the presence of Christ, and betake themselves to the depths of hell (27–36). A stark and gruesome description follows (37–42). In line 40 there is a strange reference to Barabbas's repentance.[115] In

---

[112] See CBT VII, pp. 414 ff.

[113] See *The Anglo-Norman Lyric,* ed. D.L. Jeffrey and B.J. Levy (Toronto, 1990), 152–4, where we find a similar plea in an Anglo-Norman poem *Vous ke me veez,* translated 'You see me dying on the cross / and for love of you suffering so terrible a death / ... make just this effort for love of me, / and for the rest of your days keep from sin', also **5. 1. 22** *infra.*

[114] For a fuller discussion on Christ in Gogynfeirdd poetry, see MWRL 86–94; also Part III 6 *infra.*

[115] See Mt 27:15–22, Jn 18:40 for Barabbas, the brigand, being released by Pilate. But there is no mention of his repentance in the NT, nor in the apocryphal account of the

the closing couplets the poet prays that peace with 'our King' may be ensured through the Sacrament of Extreme Unction and the words of Scripture. He further prays that Christ in His mercy may lead us at last to Himself in heaven.

Deathbed Poems

In essence the deathbed poem is a poem of repentance. The Welsh word *marwysgafn* is a compound of *marw* = 'death' and *ysgafn* < L. *scamnum* = 'bench' or 'bed', so we get the meaning 'bench / bed of death' and with the passage of time there developed the idea of a 'song on one's death-bed'. Following the Lateran Council of 1215 greater stress was laid on the confessing of sin in the Sacrament of Penance, and since this was preached to the faithful the practice of confessing one's sins before death became a general practice. This is perhaps what is reflected in the *marwysgafnau* under discussion. In a way we can equate the deathbed song, or plea for forgiveness from God, with the *dadolwch*,[116] which is also a petition for reconciliation with a secular patron. Similar repentance poems are to be found in Irish e.g. '*Aithreachas an Bhráthar Bhoicht*' ('The Repentance of the Poor Brother').[117]

Meilyr Brydydd

Poem 25 (I 4)

Each of the 38 lines of this short poem is pregnant with meaning and beauty. Directness of petition and resolve is one of its marked character-istics. The poet's request is for peace and reconciliation with the Sover-eign Ruler, King of kings before he 'becomes helpless in the earth'. Again and again Meilyr confesses his negligence and sinfulness, which has provoked God's anger; now he resolves to mend his ways and henceforth serve God worthily. The double couplet (11–14) recalls the prophesies of

same incident in the 'Acts of Pilate', see M.R. James, 103. *Baraban* is the actual word in the poem and in the note, CBT VII, p. 498, the readings *bâr aban* or *bara ban* are suggested, meaning '[one causing] disturbance [because of his] anger', and '[one] noisy [in his] anger'. In the context these interpretations seem impossible.

[116] See Intro. footnotes 23, 24, 25.

[117] Énri Ó Muirgheasa, *Dánta Diadha Uladh* (Dublin, 1936), 131–3 and a short com-mentary on 134; for other exx. of repentance poems in Irish, see *Dánta do chum Aonghus Fionn Ó Dálaigh*, ed. L. McKenna (Dublin, 1919), nos. xxiii, xxiv, xxxix. Bl BGCC poems 17, 18, 19, and 20, all deal with repentance before death; on pp. 283–6, there is poem 27, 'Sut i ennill maddeuant' ('How to gain forgiveness'), which reflects characteris-tics of the *marwysgafn*.

redemption for all the children of Adam[118] to be fulfilled through Mary's willingness to bear a son, Jesus, in her womb.[119] Meilyr names himself as poet (25) and, recalling the rewards received from kings for his verse, declares that it was God's inspiration which enabled him to compose. He now realizes that the time of his earthly pilgrimage is coming to an end and that he is on his way towards Peter,[120] who will weigh his merit. In referring to the resurrection of the body,[121] and his hope for assistance from those who are already in the grave (27–8), the poet echoes part of the Apostles' Creed, where we have a direct reference to the doctrine of the Communion of Saints.[122] As he prays for a resting place in the monastery of Enlli or Bardsey Island, which lies off the coast of the Llŷn peninsula, he paints a pleasant picture of the sea embracing the cemetery of this 'Island of Fair Mary, holy island of the saints'. There in that great company he will await the resurrection and 'Christ of the foretold cross' will lead him 'past the pain of hell', the (g)wahan westi, 'lodging set apart',[123] and the Creator will welcome him into the holy company of the saints of Enlli.[124] We can assume that Meilyr hoped to spend the rest of his life in the peace and quiet of Enlli. Burial in a monastic cemetery assured one of everlasting life in heaven according to traditional belief.

Cynddelw Brydydd Mawr

Poem 26 (IV 18)

This, the longest of the three surviving Gogynfeirdd deathbed poems, is presented in five cantos. The poem begins with a plea for forgiveness in order to praise God, the blessed King, and only Son of Mary. He is lauded as creator of certain natural features of the countryside, with which Cynddelw would have been familiar. The canto closes with a prayer to the Son of God for reconciliation and a safe home in heaven (11–14).

---

[118] See, e.g., Is 7:14, 30:30, 33:22 and 35:4, all of which appear in the liturgy of Advent Masses.

[119] See Lk 2:26–39.

[120] See Mt 16:18: 'You are Peter and on this rock I will build my Church. And the gates of the underworld can never hold out against it. I will give you the keys of the kingdom of heaven ...'

[121] See Credo: Et expecto resurrectionem mortuorum.

[122] See Missal 1857.

[123] This seems to be a reference to Purgatory. See J. Le Goff, The Birth of Purgatory (London, 1984). The use of the noun Purgatorium appears to go back to the Cistercian writers, and it occurs in a sermon by St Bernard of Clairvaux. But it was among the Paris theologians of the late twelfth and early thirteenth centuries that the concept was clarified. See Colin Morris, Papal Monarchy (Oxford, 1989), 490.

[124] See footnote 62 supra.

Conscious that he is eulogizing God in verse, the poet relies on the support and help of all those other poets who praised God in the past, and are now among the 'shining hosts'. As an exile, foolish in his sinfulness, he yet retains confidence in 'the Leader of justice' to obtain peace and happiness for him and to secure him a place with the angels in 'the blessed land of the Prince'. This idea resonates with that of the secular appeasement poems, where the poet in exile pleads to be taken back once more to the court of the patron from whom he has been alienated.[125] Some reference is made to his own sinning as resembling that of Adam (26), but the poet asserts that, through the bidding of the Blessed Trinity, he will gain the reward of heaven at his life's end. It is interesting to note the number of *Gogynfeirdd* praise terms and descriptions of God which appear in this composition—*Modrydaf* 'the Supreme One' (17);[126] *Ced wallaw* 'the Gift distributor' (22);[127] *Gwledig* (39–40, 66), *Llywiawdr* 'Prince' (63); *Rhi, Rhiau* (2, 57), *Udd* (89) 'King'; *Penrhaith* 'President' (32); *Llyw* 'Leader' (52);[128] *Priawd* 'Proprietor' (46).

A brief summary of the Incarnation and Redemption[129] follows an address to the 'Highest Prince' (40–59). Many of the themes, which we have already noted in Poem 1 (IV 16) *supra,* recur here, e.g. the 'children of Adam', the 'womb of Mary', the 'five ages of the world'. Again God is addressed as the 'Possessor of victory',[130] 'the Leader and our perfect refuge', 'Lord of heaven', and still other descriptive names of God, as in so many of Cynddelw's poems. There is a reference to the Resurrection (56) and, continuing in Psalm-like encomium, the poet resolves to pay a tithe to God and not deprive Him of His due. Without a blush the poet boasts of his own excellence and, calling himself 'Cynddelw the poet', prays for benediction and Michael's[131] welcome.

With a reminder to the 'Highest Prince' of the poet's excellent praise of Him, Cynddelw claims that God did not create him for inanities or worse. He recommends belief in God and refers to his own lack of devotional zeal, which kept him from meriting a worthy reward.[132]

---

[125] See *Salve Regina*, etc., *supra* footnote 11 and see e.g. CBT VI, pp. 433 ff., where Dafydd Benfras seems to be away from Wales and begs to be brought home to the court of Dafydd ap Llywelyn.

[126] See Part III 1. 7.

[127] See *ib*. 1. 15.

[128] See *ib*. 1. 10.

[129] See *ib*. preface to 1. 19.

[130] In *ib*. 8; the word *priawd* literally means 'owner, possessor, chief owner' and occurs several times in the secular poems of Cynddelw, but there is only one other instance of it as a description of God and that is in the mid-thirteenth century, i.e. Poem 13.

[131] See footnote 66 *supra*.

[132] This seems like a conscious juxtaposing of the care and attention the poet gives to his professional pursuits with the lack of care he devotes to his spiritual life, the one gaining worldly reward and the other depriving him of merit.

However, despite his defects, he now prays for repentance and every necessary grace. In another address to the 'Highest Prince' the poet renews his resolution to make his requests in a mature song of reparation. This leads into a swift run of praises pronounced in high-flown terms, which recognize God's unlimited title to supreme power (85–91); relying upon all this the poet again asks that he may not be excluded from the Kingdom. In the closing double couplet there is a rather abject plea that he be not rejected by God and abandoned to the company of the 'dark, contemptible crowd'.

The profuse style and richness of language and expression in this deathbed poem contrasts somewhat with that of Meilyr Brydydd.

Bleddyn Fardd

Poem 27 (VII 57)

This constitutes the third and final deathbed poem which dates from the second half of the thirteenth century, perhaps as late as 1284 or possibly 1285, if we assume that it is the final composition by Bleddyn Fardd. A mere 21 lines, it affords a typical example of the poet's conciseness. Thematically, it encapsulates the same style of address to God and general sentiments seen in the two previous poems which date from the twelfth century. Bleddyn Fardd is a master of the artistic phrase and skilful in his use of traditional metres and other features of *Gogynfeirdd* composition; note his use of *cymeriad* or alliterative line initials (8–12). His intercession to Mary (18–21) is reminiscent of the deathbed poems of Meilyr and Cynddelw.

Incipits, Introductory Greetings to the Godhead

See Part I *supra* for a note on poetic *Incipits,* which are Introductory Greetings to the Godhead.

Dafydd Benfras

Poem 28 (VI 24)

Of all the *Gogynfeirdd* poems, this is the composition which conforms most closely to the legal requirement that the *pencerdd* should sing first to God and then to king or prince.[133] Here we deal with the 54-line *incipit,* which could validly be regarded as a complete poem of dedication to the

---

[133] For the exact words in the legal tract see Part I footnote 21.

Godhead. It opens with a 6-line address to God the Son and then in homiletic style proceeds (7–20) to deplore the futility and wrong of the pursuit of wealth. Here we may possibly catch echoes of the parable of Dives and Lazarus in Lk 16:31, or perhaps other warnings characteristic of Luke on the danger of riches which should be distributed in alms; the couplet (18–20) carries the poet's avowal of his own resolution of adherence to the Son of God.[134] Next follows an extended account (21–48) of Christ's harrowing of hell. He, wearing His crown of thorns, is much needed when He arrives at the door of hell to claim His rights. Rather unusual is the reference to *pedeiroes*, 'four ages' of the world, covering the period from Moses to David the Prophet (24); much more common is that of *pymoes* in line 41.[135] Dafydd Benfras sees Cain as the one responsible for the hosts held captive in hell's torment (35). However, Michael,[136] the archangel, will also be at hand to oppose the devil, whose reign will then be at an end (45). The *incipit* concludes with an exhortation to love God, from whose dominion no one can escape (49–54).

Dafydd Benfras displays great art in these lines, employing many of the usual *Gogynfeirdd* skills and compositional techniques of alliterative linear sequences, adroit internal rhyme and a happy choice of vocabulary. His style is generally clear and concise, verbiage does not blunt the edge of his caveat or exhortation.

As already suggested these 54 lines, taken on their own, might well form a complete dedication to God, but in the original Welsh version it is obvious that they link very skilfully with the second section. Two lines achieve this transition (55–6); for the poet, God is the first and greatest One, but Llywelyn is a good second. As it stands, this poem of 92 lines remains a prime example of the poet's ability to produce a unified encomium for his dual patrons, God and Llywelyn ab Iorwerth.

Elidir Sais[137]

Poem 29 (I 16)

Entitled 'Mawl i Dduw a Dafydd ab Owain' ('In Praise of God and Dafydd ab Owain') this poem of 34 lines has a 21-line *incipit*. The three persons of the Blessed Trinity are addressed in the opening couplet, and Elidir sees himself as being at one with Them. There may be a direct ref-

---

[134] See Ps. 49:16–17 *Ne timueris cum dives factus fuerit homo ... Quoniam, cum interierit, non sumet omnia*; Lk 3:11, 11:41; 14:14; 16:9; 18:25; 19:8.
[135] See footnote 18 *supra* and Intro. *Themes*.
[136] See footnote 93 *supra*.
[137] See the biographical preface in Part I to Poems 4–8.

erence in line 5 to the legal requirement already described which could account for this long *incipit*. However, the phrase *ar fraint canon* 'according to law' may be understood as referring to the *llyfrau lleen* 'books of the Bible' in the previous line. A comment is made on the excellence of his Myrddin-style composition inspired by the Muse (7–8) and the poet resolves to devote all this talent to praising God as an assurance against the wrath of Judgement Day. To the Son of Mary he turns for protection from the horrors of hell. A strange note is struck in lines 19–21 where God seems to be blamed for the events 'about the tomb of Christ'. On the difficulty of this passage within the context of lines 20–4, see CBT I, p. 340.

Bleddyn Fardd

Poem 30 (VII 50)

Like Dafydd Benfras, his teacher and mentor, Bleddyn Fardd adheres to the legal requirement that a *pencerdd* should preface his eulogy or elegy for a secular prince with a eulogy on the Godhead; in this case Llywelyn ap Gruffudd is the patron being elegized. In the 12-line *incipit* Christ is the subject of laud and the One who, by virtue of His sufferings, is addressed with petitions for grace and protection. Lines 5–8 strike a homiletic note in a certain proverb-like style. Then some aspects of the Incarnation and Redemption follow, with Christ's coming to redeem the children of Adam from infernal enslavement, and bring them to the freedom of heaven, which had been lost through the incompetence of an angel (9–12).

Stylistically this resembles Dafydd Benfras's *incipit*.

Part III

Study of References to the Godhead

1. *Duw* God
2. *Tad* Father
3. *Mab* Son
4. *Yr Ysbryd Glân* The Holy Spirit
5. *Y Drindod* The Trinity
6. *Crist* Christ
7. *Iesu* Jesus
8. *Alternative names for God*

Study of References to the Godhead

As shown in the Introduction, much of the religious poetry of the *Gogynfeirdd* displays both an Old Testament and New Testament approach to God; this has been noted also in commenting on the poems in Part II. It seems reasonable, therefore, to preface Part III with a brief overview of what appears to be this understanding of God. Although the *Gogynfeirdd* may not have known a great deal about Patristic writing or the concept of God as discussed by these Early Fathers of the Church, a reading of their poetry, and especially their dedications to God, has many echoes of Augustine, who addresses God in a manner which highlights the multiplicity of His attributes: 'What art Thou then, my God—Most high, most good, most potent, most omnipotent; most merciful, yet most just, ... most hidden, ... most beautiful, yet most strong; ...'[1] The *Gogynfeirdd* would have acquired their knowledge of the Divine Being, and consequent moral responsibility, from experience and teaching within the Welsh church context. This assimilated knowledge is expressed in carefully selected language, suitable to describe God and His attributes and so capture aspects of His infinite diversity. Most of their references are certainly within the norms of contemporary Christian thinking and practice based on certain sections of Scripture, both Old Testament and New Testament. Moral comment which occurs in these references provides evidence that they were aware of the import of the Decalogue and the Commandments of the Church. In line with the Psalms, God is addressed under a multiplicity of names, and He is portrayed in His dealings with people as One who has sight and hearing, is subject to anger, can appear to change His mind, and at times avenge Himself.

In God the poets saw an exemplar of the noblest of human qualities and these they attribute to Him in language similar to that in which they address their earthly patrons. However, they understood that certain attributes pertained to the Godhead alone. References to these will occupy sections 1–7 of this study and in the brief prefaces to these sections account will be taken, as seems appropriate, of Church teaching promulgated prior to, and during, the period of the *Gogynfeirdd*.

Compiling the list of references to God in the *Gogynfeirdd* poetry meant that a wide variety of titles for God and the Godhead were marshalled and a certain degree of homogeneity established. Therefore, Part III is presented under separate title-headings, beginning with the

---

[1] See C. Journet, *The Dark Knowledge of God*, translated by J.F. Anderson (London, 1948), 1 ff.

great theological beliefs of one true God, as eternal, and as the Creator—first cause and last end—etc., before dealing with those titles which have a more anthropomorphical connotation, and where human values and experiences, which have coloured the idea of God, are reflected in petition, praise or comment about Him.

In the different sections, all Welsh references are cited first in modernized spelling and then translated literally into English. In general, examples are numbered according to the order in which they appear in the volumes of *Cyfres Beirdd y Tywysogion*. Name of the poet-author, title of the poem, the volume, poem and line references are appended. The titles are translations of those given in the edited versions of the poems; but it should be noted that poem titles do not appear as such in the manuscripts from which they have been taken.

The method of presenting these references to God is that each section contains a brief commentary, with examples of the particular usage given in the Appendix. Citations are numbered in bold type, but in the prose introductions a bracketed number will indicate a reference, e.g. (2) is the second example in any given section.

1. 1
True God

The paucity of references to the 'true God' in the *Gogynfeirdd* poems does not suggest that they ever doubted that 'the One God is ... the True God' any more than the authors of the Old and New Testaments, where few references to Him in these words occur.

An examination of the three examples cited below shows that the *Gogynfeirdd* associated this attribute 'One true God' with other divine attributes, e.g. *cywiraf* 'the most faithful One' (1) or again the *dewrwir* 'strong and true' (2), but this description of God as *dewrwir* may be translated as 'brave truth' or 'wise truth', which somehow identifies God as the one who dispenses justice. The first two references are from dedication poems to God, while the third is from a secular poem where Llywelyn ap Gruffudd is addressed in an appeal for the release of his brother Owain, whom he had imprisoned after he had won back the inheritance of the kingdom of Gwynedd. We have here a poet exerting his right to rebuke his patron who is failing in his moral duty. In lines 29–33 of the same poem, the question is asked 'if God has suffered and yet has forgiven those who crucified Him, why can a brother not forgive his brother, since to God alone belongs the right to disinherit another person'.

1. 2
Eternal God

The epithets *tragywyddawl* and *tragywydd* 'eternal' describe God in two of the following examples. Neither of these words are particularly poetic or musical, nor do they fit happily into *Gogynfeirdd* metres. This linguistic limitation may account for the small number of examples of *Tragywydd-awl Dduw* or *Duw tragywydd,* which occur in Welsh court poetry. It may also be worth noting that the word 'eternal' as applied to God does not occur in the Creeds, though it may be implied in the phrase *ante omnia saecula* 'before all ages' when speaking of God the Son as born of the Father. Example (1) is from Gwalchmai's dedication to God unlike (2) and (3) which are from a secular appeasement poem. The poet, Gwilym Rhyfel, has obviously incurred the disfavour of his patron and in a series of *englynion* indicates his unhappiness because of this breach in their relationship. In the final quatrain, from which (2) and (3) are drawn, the poet moralizes on the twofold aspect of perfect love—that of loving the eternal God and secondly loving the other person, in this case Dafydd ab Owain, the patron, in order to attain 'certain peace' with God. The expression used is *cerennydd* meaning 'friendship' or 'kinship' which was a term to describe 'the state of legal peace between two parties when outstanding claims between them have been justified'. From Cynddelw's poem to the Welsh St Tysilio comes (4). Here there is not a direct reference to God as *tragywydd, -awl,* but the sense of the line implies that divine attribute.

1. 3
God the Creator

From the examples cited in this section, it is abundantly clear that the *Gogynfeirdd* believed implicitly in God as universal creator of 'All things in heaven and all things on earth' *pace* St Paul. This concept of God formed part of the poets' thinking and their view of life in Gwynedd, Powys or Deheubarth during the twelfth and thirteenth centuries. They would certainly have known the words of the Apostles' Creed which professes that God is 'Creator of heaven and earth', while the Nicene Creed, recited or sung at Mass on Sundays and big feasts, includes 'all that is seen and unseen'. All created things, therefore, are good.[2] Indeed, they have their own rightful autonomy and are not simply means to some spiritual end. This teaching is clearly set out in the *firmiter* document of the Fourth Lateran Council (1215).[3] All material and spiritual

---

[2] See J. Fitzgerald, 'Aquinas on the good', *Downside Review,* cv (1987), *passim.*
[3] See PapM, 447, 451, 494.

realities come from the creative hand of God: 'God saw all that He had made and indeed it was very good'.[4]

In dealing with creation references in this section, cognizance is taken of the hierarchal order of nature, with human beings as both distinct from nature (humans alone know that they know) and at one with it.

God as creator of heaven: Heaven, the abode of purely spiritual beings, must be at the apex of that hierarchical pyramid, but in fact there are only three references to God as the creator of heaven. Example (1) occurs in a secular poem to a patron where the 21-line *incipit* is a good example of the poet adhering to the legal requirement of praising God before he eulogizes his patron. The full translation of this *incipit* appears in Poem 29 *supra*. God is spoken of as *Gorfawr Dduw* 'immense victorious' and the line goes on to mention Christ as Creator. The inclusion of *Crist* here may have been dictated by its alliterating with *Creawdr*. In section 6. 1 *infra* this example is examined further. Examples (2) and (3) are from a dedication poem to God and here the reference is to the creation of *Rhodd bêr paradwys* 'the fine gift of Paradise', which left us *heb ddim eisau* 'without any need'.[5]

God as creator of human beings: These references are presented in two categories. The first category merely states that God is the creator of a particular person or persons, as in (4) which refers to the St Cadfan's *Llan* and the two elders for whom it was made are Cadfan and Morfran, Abbot of the Church of Tywyn.[6]

God as creator of the unique individual: Ten examples occur in this second category, all of which accord with the literary device called '*topos* of inexpressibility' by E. Curtius in his discussion on medieval literary forms.[7] Each poet sees God as having created his patron as an unmatched person. This is evocative of the *non similis* of the Psalmist—'Yahweh, who can compare with You' (Ps 35.10); 'Yahweh, God of Sabaoth, who is like You?' (Ps 89.8) In Gwalchmai ap Meilyr's 'Exaltation of Owain Gwynedd', (7), Owain is described as *yn orau dyn Duw rhy'i creas* 'the best of mortals whom God has created'. This and the two examples which follow occur in twelfth-century compositions. Gwilym Rhyfel, in appeasing Dafydd ab Owain, asserts in (8) that 'God made you of the valour of Benlli the Giant' and there was 'no other king like you'. In (9) Owain Gwynedd is described in the words *Ni wnaeth Duw neb dyn*

---

[4] See Gn 1:31: *Viditque Deus cuncta quae fecerat, et erant valde bona.*

[5] Note that Paradise is considered as a gift with light abiding and for an account of paradise see Gn 2.

[6] See CBT II, p. 29 (notes 60 and 62).

[7] See E. Curtius, *European Literature and the Latin Middle Ages,* trans. by W.R. Trask (London, 1953), 159–62.

dwywawl ffydd, 'God did not make any man [with] holy faith [like him]' as the poet mourns his loss. Whether the references from Llywarch ap Llywelyn emanate from the twelfth or the thirteenth century, it is quite obvious that he favours this style to express the high esteem in which he hopes his patron will be regarded by those present at the declamation of his poem. Note that in each one of these examples: (10), (11), 12), (13) and (14), mention is made of different gifts, e.g. *hael* 'noble' / 'generous', which are unique to the recipient, who is also an unconquerable 'warrior'. Dafydd Benfras, probably Llywarch's poet-pupil, and definitely his successor as *pencerdd* in the court of Gwynedd, has two examples. Since these occur in eulogies to Llywelyn ab Iorwerth, who died in 1240, we can say that all references to God, as creator of a unique person, are found in *Gogynfeirdd* poetry composed before the middle of the thirteenth century, with Llywelyn ab Iorwerth as the *non pareil* in five of them.

God as creator of plants and animals: All material comes from the creative hand of God. 'All things in heaven and all things on earth'. The Scriptural expression *heaven and earth* means all that exists, creation in its entirety.

In (17) and (18) Meilyr ap Gwalchmai speaks of God's creating *o'i ddefnyddiau* 'from His materials' (perhaps meaning His divine essence or resources) *lles llyseuau* 'the virtue of plants'. Could Meilyr be thinking not only of the food and aesthetic advantage of plants but also of their possible healing and medicinal properties? In the same 'Ode to God' the poet in (19), reflecting on the creation of *ffryd a ffrwythau* 'streams and fruits', laments the harmful effect of Original Sin on the inanimate world, which he claims would otherwise have been *dinam* 'without blemish'. Llywelyn Fardd (I)[8] in writing 'Signs before Judgement Day' joins in a tradition which, through different literary media, records the portents due to appear during the fifteen days before Doomsday. These imaginary warnings, whose origin is obscure, had been widespread throughout Europe from the end of the eleventh century. In (20) the poet refers to the twelfth day before Judgement when God makes the sea animals act in a threatening manner to give a sign of the impending doom. In (19) the reference may not be to God as Creator but rather to Him as continually caring for the created world; *ffrwythau a doniau* 'fruits and gifts' (or taking *ffrwyth* meaning 'strength' or 'virtue') are what Cynddelw in (21) mentions as a facet of God's creative action, while Madog ap Gwallter

---

[8] See W.W. Heist, *The Fifteen Signs before Doomsday* (Michigan, 1952); *id.,* 'Welsh Prose Versions of the Fifteen Signs Before Doomsday', *Speculum,* xix (1944), 421–32; *De novissimis et Antichristo,* cap. IV, 'Signa praecedentia judicii diem ex S. Hieronymi sententia' by Peter Damien (*c.* 1050–72) in PL cxlv, col. 840–2 and also C.A. McKenna, 'Welsh Versions of the Fifteen Signs before Doomsday Reconsidered' (1983).

(22) speaks of His creating 'creatures' which could, of course, be interpreted as embracing humankind as well as animalkind.

God the Creator until judgement: The following example is a petition to God the Creator for guidance until the end of time. References to Judgement Day are frequent in the dedications to God, and the phrase *hyd Frawd* 'until Judgement' could merely indicate an extended period of time. It often occurs in medieval poetry, where Judgement is seen as a terrifying possibility.[9]

1. 4
God of heaven

Heaven is regarded as God's own place—'Our Father in heaven'—and consequently as meaning eschatological glory. The word heaven can also refer to the abode of the saints and angels, who surround God, Pss 115:15–16; 19:2.[10] It is taken that those who die in God's grace and friendship and are perfectly purified live for ever in heaven with Christ.[11]

Heaven on high or above: In the opening line of his poem (1) Llywarch ap Llywelyn addresses God as *nefawl Dad celi* 'heavenly Father on high', *celi* or *fry* 'on high' being substitute phrases for heaven. In (2) the same poet prays that Rhys Gryg will enjoy *hendref* 'winter' and *hafod* 'summer' dwellings in heaven in *teÿrnas Duw uchod* 'the kingdom of God on high'. It is interesting that the *hendref* was located in the valley to which the family and its stock returned after spending the summer months in the *hafod* 'on the mountain', so that there is an idea of heaven as the best above and below for a Welshman. *Hendref* can also mean 'permanent residence' and that interpretation cannot be disregarded in this instance. In the other examples *fry* 'on high' is the phrase used for heaven. Going up generally means going towards God, towards heaven. Because example (3) occurs in an appeasement poem, we are not surprised that the poet pledges to make recompense or satisfaction to God on high. The argument runs: since God on high accepts recompense, so should Rhys Gryg. This may be a reference to one of the conditions required for a sincere reception of the Sacrament of Penance—the four conditions being Contrition, Confession, Satisfaction and Absolution.[12] Since neither the word fortress nor one of its synonyms appears in the

[9] See Intro. footnote 63.
[10] See Mt 5:16: '… your light must shine in the sight of men, so that, seeing your good works, they may give the praise to your Father in heaven'.
[11] These souls are destined to become like unto God for ever, for they 'see Him as He is', face to face: 1 Jn 3:2; 1 Cr 13:12; Rv 22:14.
[12] See Ott 426–36.

text of (4) and, because 'God on high' does, it is given a place here rather than in the next subsection 'Heaven as refuge'.

Heaven as refuge: This notion of the fortresses of heaven may sound rather strange today but for medieval man, and especially the poets, the image of God was often that of a military magnate, and for a poet in Wales, a land frequently under siege, a fortress represented safety and possibly comfort and happiness. In (5) Einion ap Gwalchmai receives God's love *i mywn caerau nef* 'within the battlements of heaven'. In examples (6) and (7) it is not easy to say whether *noddfa* 'refuge' and *dinas* 'fortress' refer to heaven or to God, but in (8) there is no doubt that Dafydd Benfras has *noddfa* as 'refuge'.

Abodes of heaven: In (9) Einion ap Gwalchmai seems to confer on Peter, doorkeeper of heaven, the power of excluding a soul from heaven, a right which in fact belongs to God alone. This may be an echo of the image of Peter holding the keys of the Gate (Mt 16:19). Compare *Mi, Feilyr Brydydd, berierin i Bedr, / Porthawr a gymedr gymes deithi*, 'I Meilyr Brydydd, a pilgrim to Peter, / The door-keeper who weighs fitting virtues'.[13] Within the Abodes of heaven the examples of **Light of heaven** and **Throne of God** will be included. Meilyr ap Gwalchmai in (11) speaks of *Duw yn lleufer* 'God in light' in describing heaven and the verb *llewychant* 'shine', applied to the faithful Christians, sustains the metaphor. The *lleithig* 'throne' (a seat for a sovereign or a bishop) in (12) substitutes for heaven. Throne in general signified the maintenance of law and authority since judgement was pronounced from it.

Banquet in heaven: The idea of a feast in heaven would have a distinct appeal for the *Gogynfeirdd* who knew scarcity of food, if not full-scale famine, particularly during military engagements and war. For like reasons and in a similar context, the banquet image of heaven captured the imagination of the Hebrews and as a substitute for heaven the word 'banquet' occurs again and again in Scripture.[14] It is rather surprising that the poetry of the *Gogynfeirdd* contains only one example (13) of a heavenly banquet connected with the word *Duw* and this occurs in an elegy from the first half of the thirteenth century—*yn y wenwledd, fry yn y wenwlad* 'in the blessed banquet, in the blessed land on high'.

---

[13] See Part I, Poem 25, 'Marwysgafn Meilyr' ('Deathbed Poem of Meilyr Brydydd') (I 4.25–6).

[14] See Is 25:6: 'Yahweh Sabaoth will prepare for all peoples a banquet of rich food...'. The Jews, basing their ideas on this text, often described the joyous messianic era as a banquet and this imagery carries over into the NT period, so we find in Lk 14:15: 'Happy the man who will be at the feast in the Kingdom of God' and in Rv 19:9: 'Happy are those who are invited to the wedding feast of the Lamb'.

General references to heaven: In each of the four examples cited the phrase *Duw nef* 'God of heaven' or *Duw o nef* 'God from heaven' occurs.

1. 5
God is Holy

Direct references to God as holy in *Gogynfeirdd* poems are few, even though the words of Is 6:3 *Sanctus, sanctus, sanctus Dominus, Deus Sabaoth* ... 'Holy, holy holy, Lord God of Sabaoth ...' were recited or sung at every Mass they ever attended. Furthermore, the credal phrase *Tu solus sanctus* 'You alone are holy', again sung or recited, could hardly have eluded them.

The translation in (1) takes *gwyn* as meaning 'holy' but perhaps the meaning could be 'blessed'; as a description of God there is little difference between the two adjectives. Actually *gwyn* could have been chosen to alliterate with the *gwy-* in *gwybod* and thus satisfy the metrical requirement of the line. In example (2) the word *llen* is difficult. In her note M.E. Owen gives *croglen* as the modern Welsh equivalent and, following GPC 2151, sees the meaning as either 'mantle' or 'veil / curtain' in a figurative sense, e.g. 'dividing this world from the next' or, possibly, dividing the world inside the monastery from the world outside. If it means 'curtain', it could refer to the apocryphal idea of earth and heaven being separated by a veil depicting the whole of human history.[15] Could *llen falchwen* refer to the architectural feature known as the 'Rood Screen'? Difficulty arises when we consider the reference to old age and youth in the following line.

1. 6
God is All-knowing

God does not only possess knowledge, but is Himself knowledge.[16] God's knowledge is universal as to space and time, which presupposes His omnipresence, an idea clearly conceived and beautifully expressed in Ps 139:7–10.

A brief consideration of the seven examples shows that the *Gogynfeirdd* were aware of this attribute of God. It is of interest to note that three of the examples (1), (2), (3) come from Elidir Sais. This may be due to his use of the verb *gwybod* 'to know' in its different tenses which occurs in two of the three examples. *Cyfarwydd* 'well-informed, familiar, expert,

---

[15] See *The Old Testament Pseudepigrapha, i*, ed. J.H. Charlesworth (London, 1983), 240.
[16] See 2 Ch 16:9; in Ac 15:8 and 17:24–8 we read that God is the ever-present Creator who knows hearts. In a word, all things stand bare before his eyes.

proficient' (GPC 685) is the adjective he uses in (2) to describe God's conscious familiarity with his grief for the death of Hywel ab Arthen. In this example he also expresses confidence in the sympathetic support of God during this time of trouble and mourning. The example from Cynddelw (7) may, perhaps, refer to a joyful God.

1. 7
Almighty / Supreme God

The *Gogynfeirdd* employ different words to express this supreme attribute, all emphasizing the transcendence of God. Sources for these can be traced to similar expressions in the Psalms and the prophetic works; Jb 34:13–15 states that without God 'things of the flesh would perish all together, and man would return to dust'. Nothing is impossible to God: Lk 1:37 and Mt 19:26. The Apostles' Creed professes: *Credo in Deum Patrem omnipotentem* and the Fathers of the Church repeatedly ascribe to God the attribute 'Almighty'.

In his appeasement poem (1) Einion Wan harks back to the time when *o gysgawd* 'through the protection' of his tongue he could rely on the help of the *un Duw mawr yn ei undawd* 'One great God in His Unity'. Is example (2) a reference to the poet's earlier poetic accomplishment, or is it a reference to the poet reciting his own poetry under divine inspiration? It seems to echo the opening words of the Divine Office, *Domine labia mea aperies et os meum annuntiabit laudem tuam*, 'Lord open my lips and my mouth shall declare your praise'. In (3) The 'great Lord' is spoken of as *deg Wawr dewaint* 'fair Lord of midnight darkness' but we must realize that *gwawr*, literally meaning 'dawn', has become an alternative word for whatever is good and beautiful, and that here it stands for 'Lord'. There is probably a conscious use of antithesis in the juxtaposing of God as Lord of both light and darkness. Here, too, is an interesting reference to the protection of a multitude of saints. The *nawdd naw mil* textual combination fits happily into the couplet to give a satisfactory metrical reading. In using such an inflated number the poet depicts a vast multitude *o saint* 'of saints' or 'the blessed' and his belief in their intercessory power. Deliberately, or inadvertently, he is affirming belief in the 'Communion of Saints', a doctrine expressed clearly in the Apostles' Creed. In the final example (4), which comes from an *incipit,* the poet makes his petition to God under the title of 'Emperor of men'.[17] Influenced by their experience of Empires and Emperors—Roman, Merovingian and Carolingian—all medieval kings throughout Europe coveted this rank and title of pre-eminence. It is not surprising, therefore, that the *Gogynfeirdd* bestowed this prestigious royal title on God just as they did on their secular patrons.

---

[17] For a discussion on this emperor title, see J.E.C. Williams: CCG 23.

1. 8
God is Just in His Judging

This attribute of God as attested in numerous passages of Scripture, in the Old Testament and the New Testament, exemplify His justice working harmoniously with His goodness and mercy and this will be seen again in section 1. 14 *infra*.

In example (1) note the occurrence of 'throne' as dealt with in section 4 above. Here God's mercy for all without exception is evident. St Paul tells us that God has no favourites and does not prefer strong to weak; He is an impartial Judge. Llywarch ap Llywelyn in (2), addressing Hywel ap Gruffudd in high encomia, assures him of God's rewarding welcome to the abode of gracious hospitality amongst the blessed ones. Here we have a warm picture of the heavenly happiness awaiting the deceased patron and a clear instance of the poet's reliance on God. In the final quatrain of this elegiac series the poet prays that in His merciful justice God will place Hywel at the right hand of the Lord, 'in the abode of the Archangel Michael'. Example (3) also comes from an elegy, this time that of Gruffydd (*ob.* 1244), whose *llarydad* 'generous father' was Llywelyn ab Iorwerth. The line is part of a rather involved triple couplet where the poet seeks help from the *Duw deg gyfreithiau* 'God of just laws' in eulogizing Gruffydd. The laws here probably refer to the Decalogue. See Dt 5.

1. 9
An Angry God

Scripture connects anger with the punitive justice of God and shows that He is master of His anger as of His justice, and Dt 32:19–22 shows a vehement expression of this anger which was not arbitrary, but avenged the covenant broken by sin.[18] Both God's saving justice and His anger culminate in the passion of His Son.

Very few references to God's anger occur in *Gogynfeirdd* poems and to claim that it is anthropomorphic is an inadequate description as far as they are concerned. Certainly Meilyr ap Gwalchmai (1), believing that human actions can make God angry, deplores such conduct in his *Gwae a goddwy Duw*, 'Woe to the one who may anger God'. Cynddelw (2), likewise realizing that God's anger has to be respected, prays to placate Him. Example (3), outlining the avenging consequences of an angry God, occurs in the same poem. In (4) a couplet is taken from Llywarch ap Llywelyn's 'Ode of the Hot Iron', which deals with a cruel medieval

---

[18] See Dt 9:8: 'At Horeb you provoked Yahweh and God was so angry with you that he was ready to destroy you'. In times of disaster public fasting and public prayer were proclaimed to placate God and to discover the fault that had provoked his anger.

device used to force a defendant to tell the truth. The poet implores the iron to vindicate his innocence, and voices his wish for God's good pleasure and [a chance] of fleeing His anger. Reminiscent of the *Ab ira Tua libera nos, Domine*, 'From Your wrath O Lord, deliver us!' petition of the Litany of the Saints (see *Missal* 1222) is (5) from the couplet pleading for deliverance from God's anger in Phylip Brydydd's appeasement poem. The idea of God 'as a friend patronizing poetry' introduces a gentle element to what could otherwise reflect a fear-filled relationship with God.

1. 10
God as King

In this section, sixteen *Gogynfeirdd* references to the divine Kingship are listed. This seems a very small number but it must be borne in mind that only lines or couplets with the word *Duw* can be included. The examples which follow reveal that the sovereignty of God is expressed by the usual translations of King, *Rhi, Brenin*, and then different synonyms imply God's kingship—*Dofydd* Lord, *Gwledig* Ruler (given as King in GPC, 1682), *Naf* Lord, *Rhwyf* Lord, Ruler, *Pennaeth* Head, Chieftain.

The *Gogynfeirdd* would certainly have been familiar with the idea of God as king and of Him as Sovereign Lord, a religious concept which dates from Old Testament times. They would also be in tune with the petition *Adveniat regnum tuum*, 'Thy kingdom come', from the *Pater Noster,* originally addressed by Christ Himself to the Father, and becoming in time the most revered prayer of the Church, having been incorporated into the liturgical prayers of the Church from the beginning. The model of God as king was developed systematically, both in Jewish thought (God as Lord and King of the Universe), and in medieval Christian thought (with its emphasis on divine omnipotence).[19]

Brenin: There are five references to God as *Brenin* or to His *brenhiniaeth* 'kingship'. In (1) He is *Breienin breinawl* 'noble King' and Cynddelw (2) speaks of *Duw fry freenhiniaeth!* 'Kingdom above'. For Llywarch ap Llywelyn (3) He is *(G)werthefin Freienin fry* 'the supreme King on high'. In (4) Y Prydydd Bychan refers to ... *Brenin coeth* 'illustrious King' and

---

[19] To the Israelites, God was eternally King and as such is often portrayed in the Psalms, e.g. 97, 99. It is worth remembering that the first personal confession of faith noted in St John's gospel links royalty with the dignity of Sonship: Jn 1:49: 'Rabbi, you are the Son of God, you are the King of Israel'. Note, too, that I.G. Barbour, *Myths, Models and Paradigms: A Comparative Study in Science and Religion* (New York, 1974), 156, holds that the Christian movement never abandoned the royal metaphor for God and God's relation to the world; see also 'Scripture and Tradition' in *Christian Theology: An Introduction to its Traditions and Tasks* (Philadelphia, 1985), 68, where eds. P.C. Hodgson and R.H. King support this idea.

Gruffudd ab yr Ynad Coch in (5) addresses God as *Frenin,* 'O King', qualifying with the Latin *Deus Domin* 'Lord God'.

Rhi: From Cynddelw comes the only example of the combination of *Duw* and *Rhi.* Referring to the Irish prayer practice An tAth, Diarmaid Ó Laoghaire S.J. comments: 'There is no commoner term for God or Christ in ancient times than *Rí,* King. However, the king was one of the people, and was related in kinship to many of them'. Certainly his words cannot be applied with equal validity to medieval Wales if we are to judge by *Gogynfeirdd* references. However, we find *Rhi* as an alternative word for God occurring seventeen times and not combined with the word *Duw.*

Rhwyf: Again Cynddelw's (7) is the only example of *Rhwyf* in combination with *Duw* being used in a royal sense. Like *Rhi,* it is well attested as an alternative word for God, with twenty-seven examples casting God in the role of 'Ruler, Prince or Chief'.

Dofydd: *Duw Dofydd* 'God the Ruler' comes from Seisyll Bryffwrch in the twelfth century (8) and Cynddelw's *Dëws Ddofydd* (9) is translated as 'Lord King'. As an alternative word for God, *Dofydd* occurs thirty-seven times in *Gogynfeirdd* poems.

Gwledig: There is only one example from Cynddelw (10) where *Gwledig* is translated as 'King'. As an alternative word for God, there are twelve instances of this form.

Naf: This form for Sovereign in (11) appears to have been chosen by Einion ap Gwalchmai to rhyme with the verb *[g]wnaf,* which occurs earlier in the same line. Throughout the *Gogynfeirdd* poems there are thirteen instances of *Naf* as an alternative word for God

Meddu translated in GPC 2394 as 'to rule, control, have authority (over), prevail, have a right (to), be able (to) possess, enjoy'. This verb *meddu* 'to rule' or 'govern' implying kingship or sovereignty occurs in five examples, four of which are in the third person singular present tense. Elidir Sais in an elegy from the twelfth century (12) asserts that *Duw a fedd* 'God governs' *o'i fuddugoliaeth* 'by virtue of His victory' meaning by His conquest of Satan in dying on the cross. The same poet in (13) refers to a human being, Moses, making God's will known but points out that it is God who sees to the fulfilment of that divine ruling. This is a reference to the Decalogue.[20] Hywel ab Owain Gwynedd (14) asserts that God achieves the plan as shown in a dream. From the same century Gwynfardd Brycheiniog, in his dedication to St David, states

---

[20] See Ex 20.

Duw a fedd 'it is God who governs' (15). In (16) Cynddelw, lamenting the warband of Powys, comments on the futility of contemplating conquest unless it comes from God's willing it.

1. 11
God of Life and Death

An examination of the twenty-nine examples in this section shows that they fall naturally into two categories—those which refer to the poet himself and those which deal with the death of a patron. By virtue of His Divine omnipotence God has supreme dominion and all life depends utterly on Him. This right of lordship belongs to Him by virtue of His being creator of the world and Redeemer of mankind. See Pss 23:1–2, 4; 88:11–12; 144:11–13; 1 Co 6:20; 1 Tm 6:15. Certainly the *Gogynfeirdd* saw God as the One who held supreme dominion over every aspect of His creation and this had to embrace His right to decide the length and term of each person's life span. The references to God as exerting this prerogative are shown below in two categories.

References to the death of patrons: Nineteen of the twenty references listed under this heading come from elegies. In these the poets reproach God for their patron's death, and from some of the language used we gain a sense of anger at God's action. Therefore, the highlighting of relevant verbs and nouns may help to clarify the poet's response to the loss of a patron.

Gallael: This verb has two sets of meanings in GPC: (1) 'to be able to, have power to, to be able to accomplish', (2) 'to take, take away, steal; cause'. In the two examples which follow, the past tense of the verb is understood as *cipiodd* and so translated as 'snatched away' or 'taken away with violence'. The word *trais* 'violence' used by Bleddyn Fardd (2) for God's action seems rather shocking, but it must be kept in mind that it alliterates well with *trist* 'sad' in the same line. The poet is obviously blaming *trais Duw* the 'violence of God' for the death in battle of Dafydd Benfras, his friend and mentor, and the circumstances of the tragedy may account for the use of such a strong expression.

Dwyn: 'take, take away', in its different tenses, is the verb most used, and where it occurs there is an associated sadness and regret that God has caused personal or national loss, depriving the poet of a friend and benefactor, and Wales of a champion of its cause and culture. Of the nine examples listed in the Appendix, two deserve special mention: Cynddelw's (3) is from the twelfth and (5) Gwernen ap Clydno's is from the thirteenth century. In importance Cynddelw, with his remarkable skill as a poet, evidenced in his canon of 3,852 lines, is ranked as the greatest of all the *Gogynfeirdd*. Ap Clydno, at the opposite end of the scale, owes his mention among the court poets to the survival of a mere four-quatrain dedication to an unknown patron. In example (6) Dafydd Benfras, complaining of God's 'taking away' Llywelyn ab Iorwerth, uses a legal term *diebryd*—given in GPC as 'unpaid or unsettled debt, property withheld from owner'—claiming ownership of his patron, a right which he now seems to regard as being infringed by God's act. (See CBT VI, p. 440 note 59 for citations from Welsh law.)

Lladd: 'strike, kill' evokes the 'reaper' or 'leveller' image of death. The verb appears in its past tense, *lladdawdd,* and in the two examples combines with the other verb *dwyn,* in its different tenses, giving the image of God taking life away.

Trais: The most vehement accusation directed at God occurs in the use of *trais,* a noun which can mean 'violence', 'oppression' or 'rape'; it is translated by the word 'violence' in examples (14), (15) and (16). In **1. 10. 4** *supra* note that many poets are described as raging against [*y B*]*renin coeth* 'the illustrious King' because of the death of Rhys ap Llywelyn. In (16) the poet speaks of death as causing him *angau angen* 'oppression of loss' and blames God for 'saddening and punishing him' with this *necessitas leti.*

Prayers: There are two instances of prayers for a worthy manner of death, one of which occurs not in an elegy but in a praise poem (18); here, too, there is a petition for a *di-fefl hebrwng* 'a perfect [funeral] cortege'.

Extreme grief: Poets express what appears to be genuine grief. Dafydd Benfras, having suffered the loss of three patrons, grieves for them (20). *Peri* 'to cause' is the verb he uses in assigning the cause of death to God.

Throughout these examples there runs a pervasive sense of fear, but also a thinly-veiled resentment which is manifest in the constant reproaching of God, the One seen as responsible for the death of each patron.

General references: Five of these references come from dedications to God, one from a secular poem and finally one from 'Lament of the Pilgrim'. Gwalchmai ap Meilyr in (21) hopes that God will reward him for his repentance and penance and release him from the hardships of this world. His son Meilyr ap Gwalchmai hints at God taking man from the fears of this life (22). The same Meilyr consciously gives salutary advice in one section of his poem and the example given below occurs within this exhortation. It is of interest that he addresses the recipient in the second person singular. Should this lead us to regard Meilyr as a counsellor or spiritual director, perhaps in a role akin to that of the Irish *anamcarae*?[21] These two poets, and also Hywel Foel ap Griffri (28), frame their observations in the inevitability of death context. In a line from his 'Ode to God' (Poem 1 *IV 16*), Cynddelw comments on the transience of life. The last example (29) claims that *dwg Duw bawb yn y diwedd* 'God finally will take everyone'.

1. 12
Wise God

The *Gogynfeirdd* seem to have accepted that God alone is wise. In the presence of false human wisdom, the Wisdom of God was unable to impose itself upon mankind, and we find St Paul contrasting human wisdom with that of God, showing that the only true wisdom finds its consummation in Christ. Many facets of God's wisdom are presented both in the Old Testament and the New Testament, eg. in Ws 9:10, 10:1–2; Pss 2:10 ff., 119 *passim*. In the New Testament God adopted a new way, that of the foolishness of the Cross of Christ, as seen in Rm 1:19–25, 1 Co 1:21–5 and the *locus classicus* Rm 16:25–7.

These poets have not left many references to *Duw* as *doeth* 'wise'. Two of these come from poems by Einion ap Gwalchmai, (1) from his elegy for Nest, where, praying that she be received into the happiness of heaven, he speaks of *Duw ddoeth Ei ddetholi* 'God, whose choosing is wise'. In (2), which is from a dedication to God, he comments on the power of intercessory prayer but qualifies with the reservation, 'Where it befits Your powers, [O] wise God'. In example (3) Llywelyn Fardd (I) prays to God *dewrddoeth* 'wise and courageous' that He may protect the kingdom of Cadfan. This and the final example are both from the twelfth century. In (4), Cynddelw's 'Poem to St Tysilio', the poet speaks of God *doeth i deithi* 'wise with [the] attributes' of kings.

1. 13
Faithful, Strong, Supporting God

An examination of the thirteen references to the reliable and faithful God as recorded in this section will demonstrate their affinity with both Old Testament and New Testament accounts of the Godhead. Scripture shows that the salvific power of God guaranteed the fulfilment of all His promises and associated them with the themes of pardon and conversion. In poetic images the Psalmist expressed these divine qualities, e.g. 31:1

---

[21] See DIL *s.v.* anmcharae (ainim(m) + carae 'soul-friend, confessor, spiritual director), and on Confession in the context of the Célí Dé 9th–10th century reform movement in Ireland see P. Ó'Dwyer, *Célí Dé* (Dublin, 1981), 90–5.

'In You, Yahweh, I take refuge'; 91:2 Yahweh 'My refuge, my fortress, my God in whom I trust!' In the New Testament the incarnate God spoke of Himself as 'the same yesterday, today and forever'.

The examples cited are drawn from twelfth- and thirteenth-century compositions. Of these, one is a vision or dream poem, five are extracts from dedications to God, five from secular poems and two from hagiographical compositions. Example (1) occurs in Gwalchmai's dream poem. This, though not classed as such, is in fact a religious poem. Now, as an old man, and deeply affected by the deaths of Madog (*ob.* 1160), Goronwy and, most of all, by the loss of his wife Genilles, he repents and, turning in supplication to God, resolves to keep His laws until death comes to him. In this reference from the penultimate couplet he prays to God recalling *bod Duw i'm diau gadwyd* 'that God is certainly saving me'. In (2) Gwalchmai's trust is repeated, but in this instance it is God who *diwyd arbed* 'will faithfully rescue' him from the Judgement of the Trinity! This may seem rather strange but it exemplifies two aspects of *Gogynfeirdd* composition—exaggeration and the limiting effect of metric and rhythmic demands. Maintaining an *-ed* end rhyme over 28 lines could have forced the poet to resort to unexpected word combinations. The audience, accustomed to a grand finale, are not disappointed when the General Judgement threat is sounded. In example (3) Elidir Sais connects God's steadfastness with the repentance of the sinner, while in (4) the 'faithful God' redeems his children from plague and sadness. Plague constituted a particular fear for the *Gogynfeirdd* as it did for peoples everywhere during the Middle Ages. Plague was often used as a synonym for 'misery', 'great suffering' or 'torment' and occurs as such in *Gogynfeirdd* poems of the twelfth and thirteenth centuries. Meilyr ap Gwalchmai (5) trusts in a faithful God and in (6) describes Him as *terwyn* 'steadfast'. Examples (7) and (9) are from dedications to St Cadfan and St David. In (7) *Cedwis Duw urddas* 'God defended the dignity' as man and as youth the son of Eneas (that is, Cadfan). Example (9) is merely a statement on God's supporting help for St David. In number (10) Phylip Brydydd has an indirect reference to the enduring quality of God's grace. Dafydd Benfras in (11) says that the *trais* 'force' of God is irresistible, and in (12) expresses reliance on the *Duw a'i nertha* on the 'God [who] will strengthen him' in referring to his patron, Llywelyn ap Gruffudd. The final citation is from Bleddyn Fardd, who composed very close to the end of the *Gogynfeirdd* period. In it he prays to God for *nawdd* 'protection' *rhag tawdd tanllachar uffern* 'against the fiery molten state of hell'.

1. 14
Loving and Merciful God

The *Gogynfeirdd* express their reliance on God's love and mercy in very many examples which in this section are subdivided under appropriate headings. They appreciated God as being infinitely merciful and Scripture testifies to this quality more than to any other attribute of God. See e.g., Ps 103:8: 'Yahweh is tender and compassionate, slow to anger, and most merciful'; 117:1, 4; 135, 145:9: 'Yahweh's tenderness embraces all his creatures'; also Ws 11:24 ff. The harmonious association of God's mercy with His justice is magnificently shown in the death of Jesus Christ on the cross, see Jn 3:16, Rm 3:25 ff.

God as loving friend: In general the *Gogynfeirdd* do not dwell on a personal relationship with God but in the four references in this sub-section their idea of a loving God is quite clear. Gwalchmai in (1) reflects the Johannine emphasis summed up in 'God is love' (1 Jn 4:9). It is as a 'Friend' that he turns to God for pardon and reconciliation. Here the term *cerennydd*,[22] used of the relationship between poet and patron, is applied to God. In (2) Cynddelw refers to God as taking a repentant sinner as *yn brifgar* 'a best friend'; thus also in (1) and (2) God is described as *câr* 'friend' reminiscent of Jn 14:14–15: 'You are my friends if you do what I command you ...'. Llywarch ap Llywelyn (3) speaks of God loving his patron as a *byd-ohen Gymro* 'Welshman seeking out all the world', poetic exaggeration since Gruffudd ap Cynan's world lay within the confines of Wales and Ireland. Reference (4) is the final quatrain in this same series, where the poet prays that God, *Duw dy Dad* 'God your Father', *a'th garo* 'may love you'.

God of mercy: In the six references to mercy we find explicit evidence of the awareness of the *Gogynfeirdd* of this divine attribute. As humans who realized their sinfulness they were in touch with their need for God's love and mercy in the same manner as the Israelites of old had been.

Meilyr ap Gwalchmai (5) simply prays to God for mercy, and in (6) Gwynfardd Brycheiniog asserts that St David will welcome us *Ar drugar-edd Duw, ar Drugarawg* to 'God's mercy, to the merciful One'. Note the alliterative combination *ar drugaredd ... ar Drugarawg* in this example and also in (7) and (9). In (7) Llywarch ap Llywelyn prays that his patron 'may have the mercy of the merciful Lord' and in (9) Llygad Gŵr does likewise. An anonymous poet in (8) addresses God as being *gwaredd gwirion* 'clemency for the innocent'. Gruffudd ab yr Ynad Coch states in

---

[22] See section 1. 2 *supra* and the comment on **1. 2. 2/3**; also Part II footnote 75.

(10) that with God there is truth, peace and *gwir drugaredd* 'genuine mercy'. Note the metrical aspects of the combination *gwâr dangnefedd / gwir drugaredd*.

God as refuge: A repeated pattern of favour, fall, punishment, repentance and forgiveness is recorded in the historical and prophetic books of the Old Testament. This cycle of events reveals the God of mercy, and the God that does not change. Example (11) echoes this cycle where the poet Cynddelw, as did the Israelites of old, makes his plea for protection to a forgiving God.

Mercy implied: Gruffudd ap Gwrgenau (12) implies divine mercy for his deceased friend by stating that 'God will not let him suffer perdition', while Cynddelw (13) reflects the loving mercy and kindness of God in bestowing His *golwg* '[affectionate] gaze' upon one who is meek, faithful and just. In (14) Hywel ap Griffri pleads for the liberation of his patron with the reminder that God waived His right to seek justice for the death inflicted upon Him. This forgiving is the supreme example of His divine mercy. (Compare **5. 1. 20** *infra* and see the footnote.)

1. 15
God the Giver

God's benignity or benevolence reveals itself through His bestowing on created things countless gifts in the natural and supernatural order, and permitting them to participate in His goodness (creation, preservation, providence, redemption, sanctification). See Ps 145:15 ff; Mt 6:26 ff; Jn 3:16; Rm 8:32. In a word all comes from God.

The examples cited show that the *Gogynfeirdd* make their requests for gifts and blessings to God in the same terms and language as those they address to their earthly patrons; references are presented in subsections.

Benevolence of God: The first four examples may be classed as general expressions of their understanding of the benevolent God. Gwalchmai in (1) points out that God would not belittle him with a *digfryd oseb* 'a gift of angry intent', though this phrase is somewhat puzzling. In CBT I 25.8–9, footnote 11, the form *gosseb* (*goseb*) is discussed showing that it could mean *preswyl* 'abode' as well as *rhodd* 'gift' to give the inter-pretation: 'Not homely for me would be God with an angry abode or dwelling-place'. However, this seems contrary to *Gogynfeirdd* understand-ing of God and so *rhodd* 'gift' is the preferred translation. Einion ap Gwalchmai (2) addresses God as *Rhegofydd* 'Gift-giver' while *Gwerthefin* 'Giver of benefit' is how Seisyll Bryffwrch in (3) speaks to the Godhead in the *incipit* to his elegy for Owain Gwynedd. Then in a very human way Gruffudd ap Gwrgenau (4), in the closing couplet of the elegy for

Gruffudd ap Cynan, pleads with God not to be *cyfyng* 'miserly' or 'tight-fisted' towards the deceased. Thus all four poets make direct or indirect comment on God's reliability as a Giver. In the valedictory couplet of his praise of Llywelyn ab Iorwerth (5) Llywarch ap Llywelyn prays that his patron be holy 'through the bestowal of the Lord God'.

Dawn: Under this heading there are four references in which the word *dawn* 'gift' is attributed to God. The first is in Cynddelw's 'Appeasement of the Lord Rhys' (6) where the poet, begging God's protection, mentions His *diamau ... ddawn* 'unquestionable gift'; in the second example (7), taken from a dedication to God, the same poet remarks on the divine *dawn ehelaeth* 'abundant bounty'. From an unusual *Gogynfeirdd* type of poem, a bardic contention,[23] comes (8) with the poet, Phylip Brydydd, claiming that 'man cannot dishonour a gift of God'. In (9) Dafydd Benfras, commenting on *cedawl Dduw* 'generous God', moves on to assert that *Ei ddawn a iolir* 'His favour is requested'.

Rhoddi: In this subsection there are nine examples of the verb *rhoddi* 'to give, to bestow' in its different tenses and one in the nominal form *rhodd* 'a gift'. *Cyngweiniant* 'Remorse of conscience' is what Meilyr ap Gwalchmai in (10) records as having received, while a place on the *bryn llewenydd* 'hill of happiness' in Brefi is God's gift to St David, as recorded by Gwynfardd Brycheiniog in (11). Gwilym Rhyfel notes in (12) that God gave to Dafydd ab Owain, with whom the poet is seeking reconciliation, the 'gift of oppressing of the enemy' and in (13), which is from the same series of quatrains, adds to this *tri dawn i drinwychydd* 'three gifts to the lord brave in battle'. In TYP² 122–8, there is a triad on the three gifts bestowed by God, namely the strength of Hector, the wisdom of Solomon and the comeliness of Adam. In example (14) Cynddelw asserts that God made Llywelyn ab Iorwerth without defect and in (15) points out that this was *yn rhodd Duw a'i ganiad* 'through God's gift and consent', while Llywarch ap Llywelyn (16) speaks of the Lord God who will give him *cymwynas* 'a gift'. In (17) Einion Wan boasts that God has bestowed power on his patron, Madog ap Gruffudd, and in (18) that he received a *llafn waedlif* 'bloodstained spear'. Finally, Llygad Gŵr states in (19) that God does not withdraw a gift once given.

Rhannu: In the four examples which follow, God is seen as distributing or sharing out His gifts. In (20) Gwynfardd Brycheiniog mentions the *mad rad* 'good gift' shared with the Lord Rhys. In quatrains to Dafydd ab Owain (21), Gwilym Rhyfel declares that in virtue of the gift received

[23] See CBT VI, pp. 195–216.

from 'God who exalts noblemen' he may have *dawn gaffael fal Turn* 'prosperity ... like that of Turn'[24] and 'tribute like that of Israel'. The reference to Turn is probably to presage success in battle for his patron and perhaps the reference to Israeli tribute suggests that Dafydd, bearing the same name as the King of Israel, may, like him, attain success and prestige. In (22) we see the prodigality of God in distributing *donion anghymwys* 'innumerable gifts' and Dafydd Benfras refers to God (23) as *hael reiniad* 'generous giver'.

1. 16
God of Joy

In the *Gogynfeirdd* poems direct references to a joyful God are scarce. Yet much of their yearning and intercessory prayers for the blessedness and bliss of heaven bespeaks a firm confidence in God, who will welcome them to an abode of kindness and happiness. God's attribute of blessedness is often affirmed in Scripture and there are many references to the delight which God takes in His people. From the following texts it is clear that He desires their happiness and well-being: Zeph 3:14–17; Is 9:2–6; 66:10–14; Pss 72:28, 119:12: *Benedictus es, Domine* 'How blessed are You, Yahweh!' (JB), and 149:1–4 may suggest a well-pleased, smiling God. However, it is above all in Lk 1:68 ff., the Canticle of Zacharias, which became known as the *Benedictus*, that we see this quality of happiness or blessedness best expressed. This Canticle was, and still is, recited or chanted each day at the end of Lauds or Morning Prayer and may have been familiar to the *Gogynfeirdd*. Other references to the joy and happiness of God occur in the work of the *Gogynfeirdd*, e.g. in CBT I 14.39, I 16.12 and IV 16.82.

1. 17
God the Miracle-worker

In the context of God's exerting authority and dominion over every aspect of creation, Scripture speaks of Him as working marvels or miracles 'beyond our understanding'.[25] A study of *Gogynfeirdd* poetry shows clearly that these poets had implicit faith in God's miraculous interventions, but

[24] Perhaps Turn can be identified with Turnus the son of Daunus, King of the Rutuli; see CBT II, p. 504 note 1, also Virgil's Aeneid Bk VII.

[25] See Jb 9:10: *Qui fecit magna, et incomprehensibilia, et mirabilia, quorum non est numerus,* also 1 Kg 19:1–8, where Elijah is miraculously fed and saved from dying of hunger, and in 2 K 4:38–44 we have the 'nine miracles', *Nova Elisei miracula,* the last of which is the 'multiplication of loaves', prefiguring the miraculous feeding of multitudes as recorded in Mt 14:13–21, 15:32–8 and Jn 6:13. Ps 74:12–16 dwells on God's power over the universe and His interventions on behalf of certain aspects of the endangered natural world.

finding examples of this for this particular section is difficult because of the norm of adhering to a strict *Duw* reference. The term *Dewin* 'prophet, seer, or wonder-worker' occurs seven times as an alternative word for God.

In the five examples given below we note that *Dewin* as an epithet describes God and *gwyrthau* 'miracles' is applied to His actions. *Dewin* is translated by GPC 941, as 'wizard, magician, sorcerer, charmer, fortune-teller, conjurer, enchanter, diviner, soothsayer, prophet, seer, sage', none of which would accord exactly with the general understanding of God seen in the works of these poets. 'Miracle-worker' is the preferred translation of *Dewin* in this study but 'Seer', 'Prophet', 'Wonder-worker' or even 'Magician' may, in fact, be more suitable in certain instances.

Example (1) is from an appeasement poem and, not unexpectedly, Elidir Sais employs language similar to that of his religious poems. He prays that Llywelyn ab Iorwerth may have mercy 'through loving God [the] Miracle-worker'. In (2) Einion ap Gwalchmai refers to God as the 'supreme Wonder-worker of miracles' and similar to (1) and (2) is the reference from Llywelyn Fardd (I)'s 'Song to Cadfan' (3). In 'Signs before Judgement Day' (4) the same poet comments that during the fifteen days preceding Doomsday 'God's marvels' will be manifest. 'Faithful Prophet' is how Gruffudd ab yr Ynad Coch speaks of God in (5). Perhaps it is reasonable to see all five examples as coming from compositions which are either by name or intent religious in character.

1. 18
The Rewarding God

It is curious that references by the *Gogynfeirdd* to a rewarding God are so few in number. Perhaps their petitions for a 'home in heaven' and for 'happiness along with the saints' and such other hopes imply rather than express their awareness of this divine attribute. Phrases such as *golwg Duw* 'the gaze of God'; *teÿrnged* 'tribute'; *bodd* 'benevolence'; *yng ngleindid* 'in [an abode] of sanctity' may suggest that these are rewards from God. For what is one being rewarded? This brings us face to face with the question of our co-operation with the graces, free gifts or blessings which we receive from Him. See the eight beatitudes, Mt 5:3–10, which are a formula for the good life, and promise a heavenly reward. In Rm 2:6, St Paul, citing the Old Testament prophets, admonishes us that God 'will repay each as his works deserve'.

Einion ap Gwalchmai (1) maintains that God will not give a reward unless a prescribed service is performed. He mentions the *braint dewaint* 'midnight [service] prerogative', which presumably means attendance at Matins, the first hour of the Divine Office. In (2) Meilyr ap Gwalchmai believes that God will accept us because *Ef a'n gorug ac a'n gweryd* 'He who made us and will save us', and in (3) a steadfast man was honoured by God. This refers to Cynddelw's patron, Owain Gwynedd. In (4) the same poet relies on God to reward him for his *o'm rheiddun ofan* 'gift of craftsmanship' and also because of his *(g)waith y winllan* 'labour in the vineyard'. This sounds quite biblical as Christ mentions 'labourers in the vineyard' and, as an image, vineyard is often used of the Church. Llywarch ap Llywelyn in (5) and again in (6) expects reward for his *dlid* 'endowment [as a poet]' and that the *caniad Duw* 'consent of God' is a help before preparing for death. The latter probably refers to Christ's freeing mankind from the grip of evil due to original sin.

1. 19
God the Saviour

It is not surprising that this section contains references by the *Gogynfeirdd* to fear of hell and its torments, mention of the sufferings on the Cross as well as straightforward ejaculatory prayers where the poet prays that he himself or his patron may be saved. In the Old Testament, Yahweh the redeemer is seen as avenger, saviour and rescuer of his servants from death, e.g. in Ps 49:15: 'God will redeem my life from the grasp of Sheol, and will receive me'. Further discussion on Christ as Redeemer follows in section 6 *infra*.

In (1) Einion ap Gwalchmai trusts God who will hear his anxious cry, and in (2) he prays to God to be rescued from the *ffrawdd* 'fierceness' of the *oerfel ... uffern ... ffrawddus ffrydiau* 'cold of hell's fierce currents'. In Meilyr ap Gwalchmai's reference (3) he refers to *Duw ... brynwys Ei garant O'r poenau a'r pechawd a wnaethant* 'God who ransomed His friends from the pains and sin they had committed'. This *prynu* is often used to describe the redeeming act of God. In the lines of this poem which follow, the poet states that these friends were the descendants of Adam. Here and in the next example (4) we find a departure from the usual assignment of roles to the persons of the Trinity; normally the Son is the One accredited with effecting the redemption of humankind. Cynddelw (5) affirms his trust and belief that God will bring him to the happiness of heaven and later in the same poem states that God *dug yng ngwynfyd* 'brought us to happiness'; in (6) he refers to our being saved by means of the Cross. Llywarch ap Llywelyn in the poem of threat addressed to Dafydd ab Owain (7) makes a confident statement that God will not withdraw His goodness to him because of *Ei ddaioni* 'His grace'. In (8) the same poet states that God *a'n gwares* 'has redeemed us'. Example (9) does not really refer to God as a spiritual Saviour but rather acclaims Him as having caused the poet's patron, Owain ap Gruffudd ap Gwenwynwyn, to restore lands to their rightful owner in Powys, i.e. to Gruffudd ap Gwynwyn *c.*1277–8. Phylip

Brydydd (10) prays that God will save him *mal gwirion* 'as an innocent one'. Finally, in praying to God for protection through *nawdd y Grog* 'through the Cross', Gruffudd ab yr Ynad Coch (11) reminds Him that He has undertaken it, *er Dy ddynion* 'for the sake of your people'. Again the Cross is connected with God rather than with any one person of the Trinity.

1. 20
Will of God

In this section on the will of God there are sixteen references drawn from poems of the twelfth and thirteenth centuries. Clearly these *Gogynfeirdd* poets accepted the importance of this divine prerogative. Certainly they would have been familiar with the prayer 'Thy will be done on earth as it is in heaven', the third petition of the Lord's Prayer which was sung or recited audibly in Latin at every Mass. They may also have heard something of the Old Testament belief on the subject of God's free will where it was taken as the basis of world-order; see Ps 134:6: 'In the heavens, on earth, in the ocean, in the depths, Yahweh's will is sovereign'. Scripture further accepts it as the supreme norm of morality as pronounced in Is 46:10.[26] In the New Testament Jn 6:38–40 speaks of being ruled only by the will of God and in Ep 1:3–14 St Paul outlines His plan of salvation.

In this section examples will be examined and presented under different synonym forms which express the concept of God's will.

Mynnu: GPC, 2537, lists the following translations for this verb: 'to want, desire, will, be willing; obtain, procure, get, claim, demand, insist upon; seek, maintain'. In example (1) Llywelyn Fardd (I) concretizes the effect of God's plan *Ar a fynnwy Duw* for 'the one whom God wishes'. Such a person would not be presumptuous in daring to scale the heights of Snowdon, since God can accomplish whatever He wills. In (2) Gwynfardd Brycheiniog states that *a fyn Duw* 'whatever God ordains' will redound to His glory, and in the same poem the poet notes (3) that it was God's will that St David be established with metropolitan rights in Mynyw. Llywarch ap Llywelyn talks in (4) of *Duw, na fyn fy niddawl* 'God, who does not wish to see me impoverished' and Dafydd Benfras in (5) sees God's will as inexorable, *wrth a fynno Duw, dim ni ellir* 'against what God wishes, nothing can be done'.

Bodd Duw: There are three examples of *Gogynfeirdd* use of *bodd* to indicate God's will, one from the twelfth century and the other two from the thirteenth. Cynddelw in (6) sees St Tysilio *Can fodd Duw ... 'n ei ddilen*

---

[26] *Consilium meum stabit. Et omnes voluntas mea fiet.* 'My purpose shall last; I will do whatever I choose.'

being 'according to God's pleasure … in his withdrawal'; this may be a euphemism for his death. In (7) there is the use of *Gŵr* as an alternative word for God and in this case it substitutes for the Son of God who performs the miracle at the wedding feast at Cana in Galilee and does so *gan fodd Duw* 'according to God's will'. For a Gospel account of this miracle, see Jn 2:1–11, and compare CBT VI 29.56–7, where there is another reference to this miracle by the same author. In (8) Hywel Foel refers to Christ's death on the cross as being *bodd Celi* 'the will of God'.

Llunio: The two twelfth-century examples (9) and (10) are both from Llywelyn Fardd (I) and speak of events being in accord with God's plan and design.

Miscellaneous examples of God's will: Six examples have been assembled because of their heterogeneous nature. However, certain elements, isolated from within the references, can throw some light on *Gogynfeirdd* thinking with regard to God's plan in dealing with his creatures as mentioned. In (11) Cynddelw allots right to God (*iawn i Dduw*) to stand by His decision, while in (12) and (13) he attributes to God forms of the word *dewis* 'to choose' reasoning that as God 'made a choice' of Rhirid Flaidd for special privilege so now in this elegy the poet accords to Him the right to 'choose' and 'take him to Himself'. Perhaps this example would fit equally well into Section 11 *supra, God of Life and Death*. Llywarch ap Llywelyn in (14), an elegy, speaks of God 'granting permission' using the verb *caniad*. The same poet in (15) uses the verb *adwneud* 'to undo' to comment on God adhering to what He has ordained. Dafydd Benfras, in (16), refers to God using the verb *gadu* twice, once in the past tense meaning 'permitted' and then in the present/future, impersonal, 'will be allowed to remain'.

1. 21
God Source of Inspiration

The Welsh word for inspiration is *awen*, but throughout the *Gogynfeirdd* poems we find words like *dawn*, which in particular cases means 'talent, genius, intellectual gift' (note its Irish cognate *dán* which in Modern Irish means 'poem'); *rhodd*, 'gift', meaning the gift of inspiration, also occurs. In the following examples it will become abundantly clear that the poets depended on God for their inspiration. The statement *Inspirat omnia, / Vivificat omnia … Spiritus Sanctus inflat in eis* shows that the Irish author of the poem 'Deus Meus' placed his trust in God and the Holy Spirit for inspiration.[27] Much later in the sixteenth century we find Fear Flatha Ó

---

[27] See James Carney, *Early Irish Lyrics* (Dublin, 1967), 4–6.

Gnímh greeting his patron Ó Fearghal Óg, *Cuimseach sin, a Fhearghail Óig, fuarois tiodhloicthi ón Tríonóitt;* 'This is comfortable, O Fearghal Óg: thou hast gotten gifts from the Trinity'.[28]

Awen: As mentioned in 'Awen y Cynfeirdd a'r Gogynfeirdd',[29] the Welsh poets had recourse to the pre-Christian oracle or seer, Ceridwen,[30] as well as to God, as a source of poetic inspiration. Only two *Gogynfeirdd* examples have been traced where the word God occurs together with *awen*: (1) is in the *incipit* of an anonymous twelfth-century eulogy, where the poet asks for inspiration to compose his poem; very interesting is the fact that in the following couplet he mentions Ceridwen's *urddas* 'dignity' or, perhaps, her 'standing' as a source of inspiration. Obviously, the poet requires all possible support, both Christian and pre-Christian. The word he uses for God *Dëws* is dissyllabic deriving its form from the Latin *Deus*. Two other interesting forms appear at the end of the line *amen, ffiad*, the first coming originally from the Hebrew, the second from the third person, singular, imperative mood of the Latin verb *fieri* 'to be done', which gives the meaning 'let it be done'. In Christian parlance this *fiat* became the symbolic term for submission to God's will. The two main scriptural instances are Mary's *fiat* in response to the angel's request that she consent to be Mother of God (Lk 1:38); the second is that of Jesus, when He consents to submit to the sufferings of the Passion. It is spoken in the Agony in the Garden: 'Not my will but Thine be done', Mt 26.42. As in the example under discussion, *amen* and *fiat* are often conjoined, the *fiat* as it were clenching the proposition with a firm 'so be it'. On the history and development of 'amen' meanings see *The Prayers of Jesus,* 111–15.[31]

Dawn: Six examples of *dawn* 'grace', 'gift' or 'talent' appear in *Gogynfeirdd* poems. In Gwalchmai's (3) there is a petition to God of His *dawn* to grant that he may compose an *awdl ffrwythlawn* 'a powerful ode' for his patron Madog ap Maredudd; in (4) the same poet this time resolves to sing about his patron Rhodri ab Owain for as long as God endows him with His *dawn ardderchawg* 'excellent gift'. Cynddelw in (5) prays for *cyfarchddawn* 'intercessory talent' to eulogize the hosts of Powys and in (6) petitions for a *dawn cyflawn* 'perfect gift', without blemish in order to produce a 'faultless poem' to Hywel ab Owain Gwynedd. Example (7), from the same poet and poem, is a similar request. Llywarch ap Llywelyn

---

[28] See O. Bergin, *Irish Bardic Poetry* (2nd ed., Dublin, 1974), 118 and 265.
[29] See BaTh 34.
[30] For an account of the tradition of Ceridwen and her activities, see TYP[2] 308–9.
[31] See J. Jeremias, *The Prayers of Jesus* in *Studies in Biblical Theology,* 2nd series, 6 (1967–74), 111–15. See Mary's *fiat* 'yes' at the Annunciation, Lk 1:38, and Christ's in the Agony in the Garden, Mt 26:43.

(8) in an *incipit* to a eulogy for his patron, Llywelyn ab Iorwerth, seems to use the word *dawn* as meaning 'power'. *Dawn* as instanced in the examples just cited is clear evidence that for the *Gogynfeirdd* it implied 'inspiration as a gift' from God.

Rhoddi: There is just one example of inspiration which is connected with the verb *rhoddi* 'to give'; it dates from the twelfth century.

Parablu: 'to speak', **prifiaith** 'fine language', **ceinfolawd** 'excellent paean' are the key words in the five remaining examples. In (10) and (11) Einion ap Gwalchmai makes a request to God for speech, in order to *parablu* 'speak' about Him. Seisyll Bryffwrch (12) implores God, the Trinity, for *prifiaith* 'fine language' to elegize his patron, Owain Gwynedd. Cynddelw's request (13) for a *ceinfolawd* 'a fine paean' occurs in a deathbed poem, which in reality is a repentance poem. From towards the end of the *Gogynfeirdd* period comes Llygad Gŵr's request (14) for the gift of *moliant* 'praise' in order to *clodfori* 'extol' the last Prince of Wales, Llywelyn ap Gruffudd.

Human Attitudes and Response to God

1. 22
Response in Prayer

The *Gogynfeirdd*, through homilies or instructions, would have known of the scriptural emphasis on prayer and they seem to have taken to heart Jm 5:13–18: 'If any one of you is in trouble he should pray; if any of you is happy he should sing a Psalm … pray for one another'. They would certainly have been familiar with the *Pater Noster,* a perfect model of intercessory prayer, as taught and prayed by Jesus.[32] In the examples which follow, these poets show consciousness of the power of prayer and of the injunction of Christ to pray always. Of the fifty-four citations listed, all are prayers of petition and are classed under separate headings according to their particular emphasis.

Poet prays on behalf of a living patron: From the twenty-one references cited below, certain features of composition and certain points, which describe the patron's need or his qualities, are isolated which led the poet to make intercession on his behalf. Example (1) merits recognition as being the very first line of *Gogynfeirdd* poetry edited in *Cyfres Beirdd y Tywysogion.* For his patron, Hywel ap Goronwy, the poet prays that God be 'a succour, a strength, a support, a help'. Llywelyn Fardd (I),

[32] Jesus at prayer to His Father is seen in Lk. 5:16, 6:12, 9:18, 28–9 and 22:41; Luke also emphasizes the value of intercessory prayer in the parable of the importunate friend, 11:5–13.

in his dedication to Cadfan (2), prays that God be with the nobles of Merioneth so that they in turn can help us. This seems a rather self-interested prayer and may be an example of the *Laudo ut des* tradition. Poets, on the whole, were never slow in expressing their own needs. The same poet in (3) pleads that God's *bodd* 'favour' may be with Owain Gwynedd and in (4) he prays *As dewiso Duw y diweiriaf* 'may God choose the most faithful' of men. And still with Llywelyn Fardd (I), but now in a totally different mood (5) we hear him call upon God *am arglais* 'concerning the anger' of his patron, Owain Fychan, with whom he obviously has had relationship difficulties. However, further on in the same poem (6) he prays that Owain's men may have the 'protection of God'. Note that these warriors are clad in *calchdöed* 'coloured armour'. In (7) Llywarch Llaety trusts that God will accompany Llywelyn ap Madog on his course. In (8) Cynddelw prays that Owain Gwynedd may have *hawddamor* 'good fortune'. A cheerful note is struck by Llywarch ap Llywelyn (9) in asking that God protect *cadr heddwch* 'the fair peace' for Dafydd ab Owain Gwynedd, who was *hyddyn am winllad* 'a person ready with a gift of wine', and in (10) he asks that the Triune God abide with his *trugarddawn* 'merciful gift-giver', Gruffudd ap Cynan. In (11) the same poet prays that God may permit his patron to remain for *tair oes byd* 'three ages of the world'. This is clearly hyperbolic! Is Llywelyn ab Iorwerth expected to live for the duration of the first three ages, a period extending from Adam and Eve right up to Moses when the fourth age begins?[33] There is a suggestion of bargaining with God in (12)—if He is prepared to accept *difwyn ynni dyn* 'man's unprofitable energy' then He should have no hesitation in accepting Llywelyn *llyw cadeithi* 'the war leader'. Evidently war and successful warring were reckoned a virtue by the *Gogynfeirdd*. Compare (14) where the same patron is recommended as terror of enemies and a ruler of *ongyr aelaw* 'many spear strikes'. In (13) there is a petition for the recovery of Madog ap Gruffudd Maelor.

Blessings: Two examples may be classed as 'Blessings'. Note that in (15) Cadfan is described as *dwywawl* 'godly' and also as a 'servant'. Cynddelw in (16) invokes God's blessing on the princes of Powys.

Sefyll: Both examples in this subsection show two poets of the twelfth century who are fully aware of their patrons' reliance on God's supporting help. In (17) there is a play on the verb *sefyll* 'to stand' or 'survive', 'fulfil one's role' and then God is asked that he may 'support' or 'stand by' Madog, heir to Cedifor. Llywarch Llaety (18) points out that his patron Llywelyn ap Madog is strong *dra safo Duw ganthaw* 'as long as God supports him'.

---

[33] For a note on the 'three ages of the world' see CBT V, p. 209 note 36; also MWRL 89–90, and the footnote for sources.

Ejaculations: Examples of this type of instant intercessory prayer come from Gwalchmai ap Meilyr in the twelfth century and from Llygad Gŵr towards the end of the *Gogynfeirdd* period (19–22).

The poet prays for himself: Because of the many examples of poets praying for themselves, several subsections indicate particular aspects of these intercessions.

Help of God's special friends: Both examples (23–4) come from Cynddelw in the twelfth century. God's *porthwyr* 'assistants' may be understood as the supernatural beings, angels and archangels, and also the saints who have already earned and received a place in heaven.

Conversion: In view of the general mentality of the *Gogynfeirdd*, it comes as no surprise to find eight examples of individual poets praying for conversion and an amendment of their lives. Einion ap Gwalchmai has a series of petitions which directly or indirectly refer to his desire for conversion. In (27) he implores God for grace to avoid the 'sin of [desecrating] Sunday'. This may refer to a violation of the third commandment of the Decalogue, 'Remember that thou keep holy the Sabbath day', which by this period would have been applied to Sunday. In the early centuries of the Church, Sunday was chosen for the celebration of the Eucharist because of Christ's rising from the dead on that day. With the merging of the Hebrew Sabbath and the Christian Sunday, the strict laws of observance were transferred to Sunday, which became a day of rest from manual works rather than Saturday. Violation of that Sunday or Sabbath rest constituted a grave sin.[34] Cynddelw, in (30), asks to be converted from the *dewredd byd* 'splendour of the world'. The three great evils were the world, with all its attractions, the flesh and the devil. Compare (36) *infra*. In (31) Llywelyn Fardd (II) prays that he be a *gwas Duw* 'servant of God' before being consigned to the grave; then in (32) his request is that God may turn him from his *trasalwder* 'great wickedness'.

Special favours: In asking for the fulfilment of his *anian* 'nature', Llywelyn Fardd (I) is really referring to his poetic talent and need for learning as is clear from the next line of the poem. Example (34) is from Cynddelw's elegy for his son Dygynnelw, but it comes as a surprise to hear him suggest that with God this need be no *cwyn ddielw* '[an occasion of] unprofitable grief'. Then, naming himself, he prays for a happy death.

---

[34] On the development of Sunday worship and observance see H. Dumaine on 'Dimanche' in *Dictionnaire d'archéologie chrétienne et de liturgie*, IV (1921), 858–994; also Máire Herbert's article, *Dlíthe an Domhnaigh in Éirinn, 600–750 AD*, in *Cothú an Dúchais*, ed. Máirtín Mac Conmara and Éilís Ní Thiarnaigh (Dublin, 1997), 60–9; see also V. Ryan OSB, *The Shaping of Sunday (Sunday and Eucharist in the Irish Tradition)* (Dublin, 1997).

Llywelyn Fardd (II) in (35) prays for two favours *un ffydd â chrefydd, a chred* 'one faith with religion, and belief'. In (36) Madog ap Gwallter asks God to defend him against *tri gelyn dyn* 'the three enemies of man'. These enemies would be understood as the world, the flesh and the devil, see (30) *supra*.

Nawdd: All three examples seek God's *nawdd* 'protection'. Both (37) and (38) are from religious poems of Elidir Sais. In (39) Gruffudd ab yr Ynad Coch seeks not only the protection of God, but also that of all the saints and angels. See Part I Poem 20.

'God be with' prayers: Here are four examples of short intercessions (40) from Seisyll Bryffwch and (41) is Cynddelw's cry 'God deliver me'. Einion Wan prays in a similar fashion for his patron in (42) and (43) from Llywelyn Fardd (II) is in a like vein.

The poet prays for deceased patrons and others: All the examples in this subsection are taken from elegies for patrons. Four come from Cynddelw and two—(46) and (47)—from the elegy for Cadwallon ap Madog ab Idnerth. They are pleas to God to be mindful of the deceased. In (46) the plea might be understood as a veiled threat to God *Nis ddiddolwy Duw o'i deÿrnles* 'Let not God keep him from his kingly bene-fit'. It suggests that Cadwallon is still in death entitled to regal privilege by virtue of his royal rank while on earth. A Welsh version *Dëws* of the Latin *Deus* is combined with *Dominus* to introduce (47). In (48) Cyn-ddelw, grieving for his own son, Dygynnelw, tells him how hard it is to be without him and asks God to be with him. In the remaining citations there is a petition for happiness and peace in the end, presumably a synonym for heaven. Bleddyn Fardd, in (52), asks that God, who is *Llywiawdr braint y saint* 'guardian of the saints' privilege', may take care of his patron Llywelyn ap Gruffudd. Is the poet suggesting that Llywelyn is a saint and so deserving God's special guardianship?

1. 23
Response in Praise

Gogynfeirdd praises of God can at times resonate with much that we find in Scripture, Pss 35:18, 69:30, 109:30; Ezr 3:11, where God is revealed as worthy of praise and thanksgiving in all His benefactions. Less obvious is their exterior manifestation of joy, a reaction which Scripture suggests as coming from praise, thanksgiving and especially from a confession of the greatness of God. (See Is 42:12; Ps 22:24, 50:23; 1 Ch 16:4; Lk 17:15–18; Ac 11:18; Ep 1:6.) It is mainly in a suppliant mood that the Welsh poets praise God, expressing a great variety of sentiments and aspirations and asking for a continuance of divine largesse. The *do ut des*[35] idea can be synonymous with *laudo ut des* in that *laudo* is an important way of giving. The *des* element is often thinly veiled if not open and manifest. We note something similar in the Psalms of praise, celebrating God's majestic attributes—His power as Creator manifested in the visible creation, or in thanksgiving Psalms, which can be either individual or collective in character. A good example of mixed types can be seen in Ps 85. The poets would have heard these *laud* Psalms at church services and the refrains would have lingered with them, e.g. Ps 67: 'Let the nations praise you O God, Let all the nations praise you' and in the *Benedicite* hymn of Lk 1:67–79 there is a fine example of corporate community praise. The Cistercian choirs sang this every day, and the poets may have heard it and also Ps 94, often intoned at the start of the day's Divine Office, as an exhortation to praise, thanksgiving, and petition to God, as has been mentioned *supra*.[36]

Prayers of praise: There are eleven examples of *Gogynfeirdd* prayer as a response in praise to God. In (3) God is described as *un diffyniad ysydd* 'the sole protector there is' by Llywelyn Fardd (I). Praise combined with intercession in (4) and (5) exemplifies the *do ut des* idea. Cynddelw (6) adds to his own praise of God *molaf a'i dywaid* 'I extol those who proclaim it'. An example of numerical exaggeration occurs in an anonymous thirteenth-century poem (7) *canmil canmoles* 'a hundred thousand' praised God for Llywelyn ab Iorwerth's success in battle against Powys opponents. It has been pointed out that the line is capable of many interpretations, e.g. that 'God favoured a hundred thousand times this success'; see CBT VI, p. 315. Number (8), from a short eulogy for Llywelyn ap Gruffudd, states that in praising him the laud is in fact directed to God. Madog ap Gwallter in (9) has an interesting laud which opens with an adaptation of the *Gloria* or greater doxology, sung regularly at the beginning of all festal celebrations of the Mass. He quotes the phrase *pax in terra* 'peace on earth', adding to it *i'n terfynau* 'to our boundaries'. From the same poet comes example (10) which expresses *ffrwyth angau Dofydd, Duw a folych* 'as a result of the Lord's death, praise God'; in (11) God is praised as the *nefoedd lewych* 'light of heaven'.

---

[35] See G. Dumézil, *Servius et la fortune*, 82; also MWRL 27, 29 and *passim*.

[36] See Dom J. Froger, *Les Chants de la Messe aux viiie et ixe siècles* (Paris, 1950), 50, where, in speaking of the audience knowledge of the actual words of hymns and psalms, he asks *Dans quelle mesure comprenait-il? Quelles impressions faisaient sur lui tous ces textes latins qui, avec ou sans musique, frappaient son oreille durant deux ou trois heures?* Note also A.M. Allchin in Chapter 1 of *Praise Above All*, where he presents an insightful picture of 'the poetic act (as) ultimately a religious act, a sacred act'.

1. 24
Amendment of Life / Repentance

The examples which follow reveal the *Gogynfeirdd* in repentant and contrite mood and it is obvious that fear of hell and of punishment for
personal sin is very real for them as they turn to God pleading for
forgiveness. A re-reading of the prefatory note, on the 'Loving and
Merciful God', and the examples given in section 1. 14 *supra,* will show
clearly why the poets could approach God with assurance and confidence
that their prayer would be answered.[37] The fifteen citations have been
presented as: Confession of guilt, Recompense, Comments, Repentance
and Forgiveness.

Confession of guilt: In the six examples listed we find poets from
Meilyr Brydydd, often regarded as the first of the *Gogynfeirdd*, admitting
in (1) *digonais gerydd* 'I have done wrong', right through to where Llywelyn Fardd (II) in the thirteenth century (6) cries *dybwyf o'm camwedd* 'let
me come from my evil-doing', in confidence declaring *Duw a'm cymer*
'God will receive me'.

Recompense: The verb *diwyn* 'to pay back, to compensate' occurs in all
three citations. Gwalchmai (7) resolves 'to pay recompense' to God for
his sins and in (8) not only to God but also to St David. Finally, in (9)
Phylip Brydydd proclaims that *difwyn a gymer Duw fry* 'God will receive
recompense' on high.

Comments: Elidir Sais in (10) notes the wisdom of *cymhennu* 'to settle,
put in order', which is the verb he uses in this and the next example to
denote making 'his peace with God'.

Repentance: In (13) Einion ap Gwalchmai hopes that by *diofryd arfau*
'rejection of arms' and turning instead to *creiriau Duw* 'treasures of God'
he will earn his forgiveness. What exactly these 'treasures' are is difficult
to say, but it is clear that the poet means to do penance and amend his
life. We have evidence that the *Gogynfeirdd* fought side by side with their
patrons in battle. See CBT VI, p. 369, where it is shown, from near
contemporary evidence, that Dafydd Benfras probably died while fighting
alongside Llywelyn ap Gruffudd. See also ByT 33–4 for a discussion on
poets in battle in Ireland and elsewhere, but note that J. Carney in *Studies*
62, p. 235, argues that Irish poets did not fight in battles. Compare PWP
27–8. In (14) the poet Daniel ap Llosgwrn Mew resolves on making *diau*
gerennydd 'certain peace' with God. *Cerennydd,* meaning 'friendship' or

---

[37] See MWRL 36–7; in Bl BGCC 284–5 there is a poem of seven triplets entitled 'Sut i
ennill maddeuant' ('How to merit / win forgiveness'); note the advice given by *Yr Eryr*
'The Eagle' in *ib.* 297–312 (poem 30, stanza 24), p. 305.

'kinship', was a term to describe 'the state of legal peace between two parties when outstanding claims between them have been justified'. *Cerennydd* could also mean 'reconciliation', see GPC.

Forgiveness: One example.

1. 25
Ejaculatory Greetings

In this section short greetings are listed under three headings:

Henbych well, which has three examples probably dating from the early and late thirteenth century.

Gwae, three examples from the twelfth and the thirteenth centuries. An imprecatory note characterizes examples (4) and (5).

Och, all of these eight examples come from twelfth- and thirteenth-century elegies. Gwalchmai, in an exaggerated expression of grief (7), sighs to God with regret that Judgement Day had not forestalled the death of Madog ap Maredudd.

1. 26
Miscellaneous References to God

Twenty-six citations which do not fit into any of the earlier sections are now collected and classed under four headings—Religious and moral practice, Exhortation, Exemplars of Virtue and Moral Questions.

Religious and moral practice: Example (1) must be understood within the general context of Gwalchmai's '*Gorhoffedd*'. With (2) can be associated (5), both recommending the practice of almsgiving *er Duw* 'for God's sake'. In three of these citations we see the great commandment of *caru Duw* '[to] love God' extolled—Meilyr ap Gwalchmai in (6) and (7) and Gwynfardd Brycheiniog in (13). Belief in God and trust in Him figure in (8) and (9). In (12) Gwynfardd Brycheiniog notes that St David undertook *er Duw ddioddeifiaint* 'for God's sake [voluntary] suffering' while in (14) Cynddelw recommends *talu i Dduw Ei ddylyed* 'Paying back to God what is His due'; this latter value is also stressed by Cynddelw in (15). Phylip Brydydd (17) comments on the virtue of remembering God's goodness in a crisis and not *difreinaw dawn Duw* 'depreciate God's gift'.

Exhortation: Warning is given against *hydraeth brad* 'treachery in word' in (18), and in (19) Dafydd Benfras warns that *rhy fychan i Dduw a ddiwygir* 'too little satisfaction is made to God'. In (21) Bleddyn Fardd suggests that in grief the mourner should keep faith in God otherwise terror would prevail.

Exemplars of virtue: Cynddelw (22) recommends St Tysilio for his decision to remain celibate: *diofryd gwragedd* 'renouncing women'. In the elegy for Llywelyn ab Iorwerth, Dafydd Benfras (23) points out that in exchange for extensive success his patron had devoted to God *ei ddihewyd* 'his yearning', while in (24) an anonymous poet speaks of a person choosing *er Duw ddifröedd* 'exile for the sake of God'.

Moral questions: There are two challenging questions, one on the command to love God and the other on the question of belief in God, one from Dafydd Benfras and the second from Gruffudd ab yr Ynad Coch.

1. 27
References to the Word 'God'

Twenty-six references are given in this section with comments on particular points of interest.

Number (1) from Gwalchmai is an example of the erotic which comes from a *gorhoffedd*, a type of boastful composition peculiar to the *Gogynfeirdd* period.[38] Two references to Church feast days or liturgical practice occur in (3) and (8). Gwalchmai (3) refers to *cain fedydd fy Nuw* 'the excelling baptism of my God', and here again we see use of the word God when in fact Jesus is meant. *Ystwyll* 'Epiphany' celebrated on 6 January suggests it as being the day on which this baptism of Jesus took place.[39] In (8) *Dyrwest Duw* 'God's fasting' refers to Christ's fast for forty days in the wilderness (Mk 1) which is still commemorated in the observance of the season of Lent, the forty days of preparation for Easter.[40] Judgement Day is referred to in (7) and indirectly in (11). Example (14) mentions [*y*] *fagl aur ei phen* 'the gold-topped crozier' received by St David from the Patriarch of Jerusalem when the saint went there on pilgrimage. The significance of the crozier, a symbol of episcopal office, is that it claims that St David had been made bishop in Jerusalem by the Patriarch in accordance with the direction—*mihi in episcopatum benedicendo consecrabis*—of the angelic visitor who appeared to him on the night before the arrival of David and his companions. In (14) there is a

---

[38] See MWRL 55–6.

[39] See ODCC 465 and J. Fisher, 'The Welsh Calendar', THSC, 1894–5, for remarks on this feast celebrated on 6 January. See also E.G. Willis, *A History of Early Roman Liturgy* (London, 1994), where he maintains that in certain churches the account of the Lord's baptism was read from Jn 2:1–11 or Lk 3:21–2 on the feast of the Epiphany.

[40] See Mk 1:12–13; Mt 4:13–17; Lk 4:1–2.

description of divine intervention at the Senate of Llanddewibrefi. St David was unable to communicate with all present as the large crowd assembled. However, by miraculous intervention, a hillock rose up beneath his feet, according him a view and easy command of the situation.[41] The second part of that example refers to crossing the sea on a stone. Many saints are reputed to have had a similar miraculous voyage— St Declan to Ireland, St Finbarr to Wales—and here St David seems to have been transported in a similar manner. In (20) Llywarch ap Llywelyn makes a clear statement on the true nature of the Incarnation which shows God being born as a human person; compare (24), in which Madog ap Gwallter expresses a similar idea, and see also (26) where Bleddyn Fardd's reference to the death of *Un Mab Mair, mawr lias Duw nef* 'the only Son of Mary, great death of [the] God of heaven' is the only killing to which that of Llywelyn ap Gruffudd can be likened.

1. 28
Un Duw One God

That there is only one God is a basic doctrine of both Old Testament and New Testament revelation. See Dt 6:4 (Mk 12:29) *Audi Israel, Dominus Deus tuus, Deus unus est* 'Listen Israel: Yahweh our God, is the one Yahweh'. See also Is 43:10, 15. 'No good was formed before me, nor will be after me'.

There are only two examples of *Gogynfeirdd* references to *Un Duw*. Example (1) demonstrates the beliefs of the *Gogynfeirdd*; earlier in the same poem there is a reference to the 'three persons' and so we are on safe ground in accepting that the *Gogynfeirdd* believed in the unity of God and also in the threeness of persons. In fact we have here evidence of their belief in the Trinity, which will be treated in section 5 *infra*. Both references are cited in the Appendix.

1. 29
Deus Dëws God

Both the Latin and the Welsh forms occur and the Latin form may be due to the sense of the context, e.g., *diwallus Dëus*. Similarly, the *Dëws* form would meet metrical requirements, especially when combined with words like *crëws, mynnws, ystyriws*. From a glance through the references it is quite clear that the Latin form can occur at any time throughout the *Gogynfeirdd* period. In (2) Gwalchmai refers to God's accepting baptism

[41] See J.W. James, *op.cit.* for a mid-twelfth-century source for this and other incidents mentioned in the examples cited here; *baculus gloriosis coruscus miraculis* is how the crozier is described.

on the Epiphany. Note (3) includes a reference to the feeding of the five thousand with five loaves and two fish (Mt 14:15–21). Noteworthy, too, is the fact that four of the examples cited, (13), (14), (15) and (16), come from the poetry of Dafydd Benfras.

2. 1
Tad Father

It is as first person of the Blessed Trinity that we think here of God the Father. In both the Apostles' and the Nicene Creed we say *Credo in unum Deum Patrem omnipotentem,* 'I believe in God the Father Almighty'.

Although the examples in this section will not be classed and dealt with in subsections, some references are brought together for comment because of their similar themes or emphases. Gwalchmai in (1) and Meilyr ap Gwalchmai in (8) associate Mary with God the Father, she being called *Mam ei Thad* 'Mother of her Father'. In mentioning this relationship with the Godhead does the poet, perhaps, wish to give a glimpse of her role in the Redemption? Gwalchmai in Poem 3 (I 14) (37–47) *supra* provides a good example of the sophisticated literary device which plays with her threefold position as 'mother', 'daughter', and 'sister', and P. Ó'Dwyer, *op. cit.,* cites similar examples from Irish sources. There is a certain homogeneity within (2), (10) and (12), where God the Father is addressed as *fy Rhên* 'My King' (2), *Tad tëyrneiddiaf* 'most regal Father' (10), *tud Rwyf hollawl* 'supreme Lord of His kingdom' (12). *Tad ysbrydawl* 'spiritual Father' is the description in (4), (14), and (18); *dwywawl* describes Him in (13). He is the 'heavenly Father from on high' in (11) and (17). Example (5) stands on its own with its reference to *Crog ein Tad* 'Cross / crucifixion of our Father'. This seems rather strange since it was Christ, the second person of the Blessed Trinity, who suffered and died on the Cross. There are other examples from the Middle Ages of God the Father being cast in the redemptive role. Ó Carragáin cites: 'Almighty God stripped himself When he willed to mount the gallows', and in the Antiphonary of Bangor Christ is referred to as 'Almighty God'.[42] Example (3) also connects God the Father, *difai Dad* 'blameless Father', with the suffering of the Passion. In (22) and (24) we have definite trinitarian references. Furthermore, in (22) there is mention of *gwir gariad* 'faithful love' which may link with the prayer to the 'Father of love' in (15). Other examples show the Father as of 'complete faith' and in (9) He is *Tad teg hynafiaeth* 'the Father of fine longevity' which seems an amazing description of the eternal God.

---

[42] See Éamonn Ó Carragáin, 'The Ruthwell Crucifixion Poem in its Iconographic and Liturgical contexts', *Peritia*, 6–7 (1987–8), 52–3.

2. 2
Cywirdad True Father

2. 3
Mawrdad Great Father

3. 1
Mab Son

There are thirteen examples of *Mab* Son in the *Gogynfeirdd* poems. In (1), (3) and (6) the second and third persons of the Blessed Trinity are named together. In (2) we see play on the dual relationship of Mother and Son already noted in section 2. 1. The word *Pab,* which occurs in (4) and (12), is translated in GPC 2662 as 'pope, bishop, priest', but it can also be used figuratively as in (4), where the Son is described as *Pab pennaf* 'the highest Father-priest'. The *Oxford English Dictionary* supports this, giving the Greek form *pappas* as 'father'. The second example is interpreted as 'priest'. Example (10) makes a clear statement of the Son in His role as Redeemer. Perhaps we have a reference to the signs of the zodiac in (11), which may emphasize God's universal knowledge of all that is in the heavens and on the earth. *The New Shorter Oxford English Dictionary,* as noted previously, describes *zodiac* as 'a belt of the celestial sphere extending about 8 or 9 degrees on each side of the ecliptic, within which the apparent motions of the sun, moon, and principal planets take place, and which is usu[ually] divided into twelve signs'.

3. 2
Mab Duw Son of God

There are forty-one references to *Mab Duw* in this section; eight refer to some aspect of the earthly life of Our Lord; four to His despoiling of hell and two give evidence of *Gogynfeirdd* hope for God's intervention by miraculous healing. Some occur in prayers of petition and praise or as 'ejaculations' to Him. Besides there are some described as moral comments and finally unclassified references. All will appear under subheadings with comments as may seem necessary or appropriate.

Events in the life of our Lord: References are to events as they appear in the Gospel narratives. In (6) there is mention of *llên a llyfrau* 'literature and books' predicting the Incarnation of the Son of the Lord God. Perhaps this points to the scriptural prophecies of Isaiah and those of the lesser prophets. Example (7) comments on the Birth of the Son of God mentioning *Nos Nadolig* 'Christmas night' as 'a night unlike evil nights'; Lk 2:7 merely states: 'she gave birth to a son'. In (8) there is reference to *Dyw Sul ... y ganed Mab Duw* 'on Sunday ... was born the Son of God' and this accords with an ancient tradition. 'On Sunday He was born of the Virgin ...'.[43] The baptism of the Son of God, noted in (1) and (2), speaks of Him redeeming mankind; He purchased *mad gerennydd* 'a felicitous reconciliation'. Elidir Sais gives a specific reference to the Resurrection in (3). Note that the Gospel (Jn 20:1) detail: 'very early on the first day of the week' becomes *Duw Sul ... awr y cyfyd haul* 'On Sunday ... when the sun arises'. The Son's Ascension into heaven is recorded by Einion ap Gwalchmai in (4).

The Son of God, despoiler of hell: Elidir Sais in the early thirteenth century and Gruffudd ab yr Ynad Coch later in that century supply the three references to the descent into hell by the Son of God on *y dydd gorau* 'the best day' as spoken of in (11)/(12). In examples (9) and (10) the opening of the gates of heaven to mankind by the redeeming act of the Son of God is mentioned.

Judgement Day: There is one example in the work of Dafydd Benfras.

God the Son as healer: Prayers for the restoration of health are common and addressed both to God the Father and God the Son. The two examples listed come from Llywarch ap Llywelyn and show that the poet understood something of the healing power of the *Son of God*. In the second example there is a rather clear indication of the poet's self-interest in asking for the recovery of his patron; in his illness *ni lwydd beirdd* 'he does not benefit poets'.

Prayer to the Son of God: In this section there are eight examples of prayer to the Son of God. The reference to God (16) as an avenger of wrong-doing throws light on the poet's concept of Him; certainly He seems to be reduced to a very human dimension. Then, in a thirteenth-century reference (20), we see belief in the efficacy of prayer to the saints.

In praise of the Son of God: Two examples are cited (24) and (25), both of which come from the twelfth century.

Ejaculations: These supplicatory sighs to the only Son of God come from Hywel ab Owain Gwynedd's twelfth-century compositions—one from a *gorhoffedd* and the other in an amorous outpouring, when he is obviously suffering the pangs of unrequited love.

Son of God's power over life and death: Three examples attribute supreme power over life and death to the Son of God; already we have seen many references to this divine prerogative in 1. 11 *supra*. In the second of these references (29), the Son described as *Dewin holl wybod* 'Seer

---

[43] See M. Herbert and M. McNamara, *Irish Biblical Apocrypha* (Edinburgh, 1989), 53.

of all knowledge' has done wrong to the poet in taking away Llywelyn ab Iorwerth.

Moral comment: Some of these examples express the poet's resolution to 'mend his ways' in accordance with Christian principles. Perhaps Dafydd Benfras (36) had heard a Franciscan sermon on the theme of Mt 19:23–4: 'It is easier for a camel to pass through the eye of a needle than for a rich man to enter the kingdom of heaven'. In example (37) the same poet speaks of his intention to choose *Mab Duw dewisaid* 'the chosen Son of God'. Note the play on the word *dewis*.

Unclassified examples: Various facets of the redeeming act of the Son of God appear in these citations with (41) focusing on the importance of loving Him.

3. 3
Mab Mair Son of Mary

There are five references to Jesus as the Son of Mary, all from poems composed in the thirteenth century and perhaps indicating the increased awareness of Mary's role. Example (2) is part of an 8-line *incipit,* where Einion ap Gwgon prays for inspiration to compose a eulogy worthy of his patron, Llywelyn ab Iorwerth. In it the poet requests a word of help from 'the strong Son of Mary' so that he can test or savour the homily style of St Paul. Does this suggest that Paul's letters were known, to some degree at least, by the *Gogynfeirdd?* Mention of the *pum gair heb gêl* 'the five words not hidden' in (4) presents a difficulty. In line 119 of this un-edited poem the word *llaswyr* occurs, which may be a reference to the *Parvum Officium, Gwasanaeth Mair* 'Psalter of Mary', though the mention of 'five' makes this unlikely; or the word *llaswyr* 'Rosary', a devotion which concentrates on the Five Joyful, Five Sorrowful and Five Glorious Mysteries of our salvation, may be a possibility. Could this *pum gair* refer to Mary's five-word reply to Gabriel *Fiat mihi secundum verbum tuum* (Lk 1:38)?

3. 4
Mab Mam Son of a Mother

The second person of the Blessed Trinity is described in example (1) as Son of a Mother *Mair ddinam, mawr ddoeth* 'holy Mary, most wise' and in (2) He is *Mab Fam forwyn, grefydd addfwyn, aeddfed eirau* 'Son of a virgin mother, gentle [her] faith, mature [her] words'.

3. 5
Mapgwas Child / Boy

Two examples, both in thirteenth-century dedications to God.

3. 6
Mab Rhad Son of Grace

The very description, Son of Grace, suggests supernatural intervention as in His miraculous conception. In general it seems that the miracles of the Old Testament and the New Testament were of interest and importance to the *Gogynfeirdd.*

4. 1
Yr Ysbryd Glân The Holy Spirit

The words of the Apostles' Creed *Credo in Spiritu Sancto* 'I believe in the Holy Spirit', the third person of the Blessed Trinity, must have been well known to the *Gogynfeirdd* and therefore it seems strange to find so few references to the Holy Spirit in their poetry. Because of the lexical nature adopted throughout this work example (3) has been included, though *Ysbryd* here strictly refers to Jesus who was betrayed by Judas, on what became known as Spy Wednesday, and handed over to the Jews on Thursday night. See Lk 22:47 and Ac 1:17.

4. 2
Glân Ysbryd Holy Spirit

Actually there is no difference in meaning between *Glân Ysbryd* and *Ysbryd Glân*. Both refer to the third person of the Blessed Trinity and both are used according to the metrical requirements of *Gogynfeirdd* composition.

5. 1
Trindawd Trinity

In dealing with the *Gogynfeirdd*, references to the Father, the Son and the Holy Spirit have been considered before proceeding to examine the Trinity; in choosing to follow this order of presentation, K. Rahner's reasoning has been the guide.[44]

---

[44] See K. Rahner, *The Trinity* (2nd ed., Norwich, 1975), *passim*.

The subject of the Trinity seems to have been of special interest to Welsh poets and scholars in medieval times and there is evidence of this in MS Ff.4, at Corpus Christi College, Cambridge. The original manuscript contained the text of the Juvencus poem,[45] fourth-century Latin verses on Gospel themes, with Welsh glosses in the margins. In addition this manuscript contains the earliest example of verse in Old Welsh. There are in all twelve quatrains, nine of which appear on part of page 1 of this MS and the other 3 on f. 42.[46] The manuscript seems to belong to the ninth or tenth century.[47] Sir Ifor Williams has established that three of the *englynion* are secular and nine religious in character. The main theme of the nine is praise of the Trinity.[48]

In another manuscript in the same Cambridge Library, there is further significant evidence of Welsh interest in the Trinity in the medieval period. Here in MS 199 is a copy of a substantial part of the *De Trinitate* treatise compiled in the fifth century by Augustine, Bishop of Hippo. This copy of the treatise emanated from the scriptorium in the Llanbadarn Fawr monastery and can be dated to the end of the eleventh century. It is generally accepted that it was written between 1085 and 1091 by Ieuan son of Sulien. This Sulien, who was Bishop of St David's during two periods in the eleventh and early twelfth centuries, was head of a family famous for its learning and scholarship.[49]

The twenty-two references to the Trinity in this section are presented under six separate titles—Unity of the Trinity, Trinity and Mercy, Hell's suffering, Judgement, Inspiration by the Trinity and Unclassified examples.

Unity of the Trinity: Five examples—three from poets of the twelfth century and two from the later thirteenth century—speak of the 'unity of the Trinity'. Meilyr Brydydd, in the closing couplet of his elegy for Gruffudd ap Cynan (1) prays that his patron may be *yn undawd Drindawd* 'in the unity of the Trinity'. In (2) Gwalchmai attributes his understand-

---

[45] See I. Williams, B vi (1931–3), 101–10, 205–24—the first entitled 'Tri Englyn y Juvencus', and the second 'Naw Englyn y Juvencus'. See also T. Arwyn Watkins on the orthography of these verses in 'Englynion y Juvencus' in *Bardos: Penodau ar y Traddodiad Barddol a Cheltaidd cyflwynedig i J. E. Caerwyn Williams*, ed. R. Geraint Gruffydd (Cardiff, 1982), 29–43.

[46] See ODCC 916–17 on Juvencus, and M. Lapidge, 'Latin Learning in Dark Age Wales' in *Proceedings of the Seventh International Congress of Celtic Studies Oxford 1983*, eds. D.E. Evans, J.G. Griffith and E.M. Jope (Oxford, 1986), 97–101.

[47] H. Bradshaw, *Collected Papers* (Cambridge, 1889), 284; also W.M. Lindsay, *Early Welsh Script* (Oxford, 1912), 16.

[48] For a comprehensive study of these *englynion* 'triplets' see Bl BGCC 3–16, also J.C.T. Oates, 'Notes on the later History of the Oldest Manuscript of Welsh Poetry: The Cambridge Juvencus' in CMCS iii (1982), 81–7.

[49] See Lapidge, *art.cit.* 71.

ing to the Creator, the Son and the Spirit, the unity of the Trinity, 'of the same stock as I am'. Gruffudd ab yr Ynad Coch's prayer in (4) is for *nawdd undawd Trindawd* 'the protection of the unity of the Trinity' and in (5) speaks of the *Undawd orau* 'best unity'.

Trinity and Mercy: A petition for mercy from the Trinity appears in four examples. In a dedication to God Elidir Sais pleads with the Trinity for mercy (6). Cynddelw also prays on his own behalf in (7), and in (8), which is an 'Appeasement Poem', prays *er bodd y Drindawd* 'on account of the favour of the Trinity' that he may receive mercy *tros waredd tros wawd* 'because of [his] compassion and because of [his] praise', from his alienated patron. Bleddyn Fardd (9), in the closing lines of his eulogy for Rhys ap Maredudd ap Rhys, prays that this patron be rewarded *Yn rhan drugaredd, yn rhad y Drindawd* 'In the lot / shareland of mercy, in the grace of the Trinity'.

Inspiration by the Trinity: There are two references to poets requesting inspiration from the Trinity. Seisyll Bryffwrch (10), in a twelfth century elegy, prays to the God of the Trinity *bwyf priawd prifiaith* 'May I be the possessor of fine language'. In order to do justice to Llywelyn ap Gruffudd, his patron, Dafydd Benfras (11) relies on *nerth y Drindawd* 'the power of the Trinity'.

Judgement: In a couplet from his dedication to God, Gwalchmai (12) states that God will save him from the Judgement of the Trinity, the Three in One.

Hell's suffering: The one reference to the suffering of hell comes from Gruffudd ab yr Ynad Coch (13) and asserts that only the Trinity, with its unique unicity, can tell of the hardships of the multitude held there in captivity.

Unclassified References to the Trinity: There are nine unclassified references to the Trinity. The first (14) is from an elegy written by an early Gogynfardd and is a plea for mercy which the poet regards as a gift from the Trinity. Note the use of *Rex,* one of the rare Latin words found in Welsh Court poetry. Another (21) is taken from an elegy by Llywarch ap Llywelyn. The remaining 7 occur in dedications to God; Cynddelw (20) in his *Ode to God,* attributes the rescuing of the Three Youths, Sadrach, Mesach and Adednego, from the fiery furnace to the power of the Trinity. The account of this incident is recorded in the Book of Daniel 3:8-41; the Song of thanksgiving, which these three sang glorifying and blessing God, was included as a Canticle in the Divine Office. Noteworthy, too, is the final example (22) where Gruffudd ab yr Ynad Coch portrays Christ reproaching us as He recalls what He himself has undergone to save us and presents a challenge by asking what have we done. He further justifies His sufferings by saying that they were necessary so that souls could be freed from sin to meet the Trinity in purity. We find a similar plea in an Anglo-Norman poem *Vous ke me veez*, translated 'You see me dying on the cross / and for love of you suffering so terrible a death / ... make just this effort for love of me, / and for the rest of your days keep from sin.' Both the Welsh and the Anglo Saxon references probably derive from the *Improperia* 'Reproaches' sung at the Good Friday Service. These Reproaches have a very long tradition; the oldest version appears in the *Pontifical of Prudentius*, bishop of Troyes in the ninth century. J.W. Tyrer comments that this is most likely of Gallican or Spanish origin, being possibly suggested by the use of Mi 6:3, 4 'O my people, what have I done to thee, or wherein have I saddened thee? answer me. I brought you out of the land of Egypt', 'thou hast prepared a cross for thy Saviour'. The Reproaches in their complete form were in use in Benevento in the eleventh century, but may not have been adopted at Rome till three or four centuries later.[50]

5. 2
Trined Trinity

There are eight examples of the word *Trined* and this form rather than *Trindawd* for the Trinity may on occasions have been more suited to metrical requirements. In (6) Llywelyn Fardd (II) speaks of the *tri nifer* 'three hosts' coming before the Trinity and comments that *trydy* 'the third' is led by Lucifer.

6. 1
Christ

Although the *Gogynfeirdd* would have been familiar with the title Jesus Christ, no example of it was found. This may be due to difficulty in accommodating the two words in a *cynghanedd* line. In section 1. 19 *supra* examples of God as the Saviour of mankind have been considered but

---

[50] See J.W. Tyrer, *Historical Survey of Holy Week and its Services and Ceremonial* (Oxford, 1932), 131, also *The Anglo-Norman Lyric*, ed. D.L. Jeffrey and B.J. Levy (Toronto, 1990), 80–1. This poem was probably inspired by the *Improperia* which formed an integral part of the Good Friday Liturgy. These question and answer Reproaches 'have an air of great antiquity' and, *pace* J.W. Tyrer, are still sung or recited. The celebrant begins with the formula *Popule meus quid feci tibi aut quo contristavi te? responde mihi. Quid eduxi te de terrs Egypti parasti crucem Salvatori tuo?* 'O my people, what have I done to thee, or wherein have I saddened thee? answer me. Because I brought thee out of the land of Egypt' (Mi 6:3–4), 'thou hast prepared a cross for thy Saviour'. Part of the responses are in Greek, part in Latin: *Agios o Theos; Sanctus, Deus* 'O holy God'. *Agios ischyros; Sanctus fortis* 'O holy, strong One'.

usually that role is given to the incarnate second person of the Blessed Trinity, referred to as Christ or as Jesus. In this section only the *Gogynfeirdd* references to Christ are considered. The role of Jesus is examined in the next section.

First we must examine why there had to be a saviour. Scripture supplies the answers: from the fall of our first parents, Gn 3, Satan was lord of the world,[51] but Christ's death breaks this satanic dominance as expressed in Jn 3:5 ff. and especially in v. 14.[52]

Sixty references to Christ are presented with subsections in accordance with the different emphases.

Christ as Creator: The word *Creawdr* 'Creator' is found eight times combined with Christ. This suggests that the *Gogynfeirdd* were not strict in adhering to the traditional roles of the three persons of the Blessed Trinity—that of Creator to God the Father, Redeemer to God the Son and Sanctifier to God the Holy Spirit. This can perhaps be interpreted as poetic licence when the poets, tempted by metrical convenience (e.g. alliteration of the initial *Cr-* in *Crist* and *Creawdr*), chose to depart from the accepted trinitarian role designations. Similarly, the *-awdr* rhyme in *Creawdr, Amerhawdr,* and *Llywiawdr* in (6) and (7) obviously fits the *cynghanedd*.[53] The word Amerhawdr has been considered already in section 1. 10 *supra*.

In (1) mention of the tomb of Christ may be a reference to His actual physical burial. If it is to the Holy Sepulchre in Jerusalem, it may refer to its being lost to Christendom, when that city fell to Saladin in 1187 AD; see CBT I 16.24 and footnote, also Poem 30 *supra*. Cynddelw in (2) initially blames Christ for the loss of his patron and then in the same breath refers to Him as *Creawdr trugar* 'the merciful Creator'. In (8) the thirteenth-century poet refers to Christ and to those who betrayed Him into the hands of His enemies—a reminder of the Spy Wednesday tradition in the Holy Week calendar. But since Christ is also referred to as Creator, we have Christ in the double role of Creator and Redeemer.

Humanity of Christ: In his 'Ode to God', Gwalchmai in (9) speaks of the repentant sinner who wishes to do penance 'Where Christ walked on the fair face of the earth'. In (10) Meilyr ap Gwalchmai expresses his belief in *Crist, diathrist athro* 'Christ, joyful teacher', before commenting in the next line that the believer / prophet / poet who does not have this faith is not an able / efficient / competent / one. Llywarch ap Llywelyn

---

[51] See Gn 14:30, 16:11, 2 Co 4:4, Ep 2:2, 6:2, 1 Jn 5:19.

[52] See Mt 8:29 ff., Lk 8:31 ff., Col 1:12–13. St Paul in 1 Tm 2:4 summarizes all the prophesies and the message of Jesus by saying: 'God wills that all be saved'.

[53] *Cynghanedd* 'harmony' is a strict and systematic pattern of alliteration and internal rhyme observed in much Welsh poetry. See MWRL 11.

refers in (11) to *Crist yng ngnawd* 'Christ in the flesh' as our privileged 'Brother', suggesting a very natural dimension of his understanding of the human Christ and of his close relationship with Him. Finally, example (12) emphasizes Christ's humanity through His *dybu Grist ym mru* 'Christ came to the womb' for our sakes. This links very closely with **7. 1. 1** and **7. 1. 2** *infra* where Mary's part in the Incarnation is highlighted.

Christ as Saviour: While the idea of Christ as Saviour is implicit in examples given under other headings below, the two which follow seem to state explicitly the saving role of Christ,—the one by the use of the word *gwared* and the second by the sense of the line; both come from the late thirteenth century, (13) from an elegy for a secular patron and (14) from a religious poem.

Christ and the cross: Gwalchmai in (15) refers to Christ *o groes edwyn cethri* 'through a painful cross of nails' and Gruffudd ab yr Ynad Coch (24) mentions *dolur archollau* 'the agony of [His] wounds', but the other eleven examples do not dwell on particular physical details of the crucifixion. The expression *croes rinweddawl* 'gainful [His] cross' in (16) brings to mind the hymn *Crux Fidelis* sung during the Adoration of the Cross on Good Friday.[54] Does (17) refer to Christ's establishing an assembly of followers which was later to become known as the Church? In (18) 'the cross' occurs with differing emphasis. In the first line of the couplet the 'sign of the cross' may refer to the cross gesture which the priest makes as he pronounces the words of absolution in the Sacrament of Penance. In the second line Einion ap Gwalchmai desires to carry the Cross in reparation for His sins. This may refer to the cross worn as an identification sign by the Crusaders who were medieval European soldiers engaged in holy wars to recover the Holy Land from the Muslims,[55] or, perhaps, it could express his willingness to accept any suffering that may come to him. Compare (23) below where Gruffudd ab yr Ynad Coch refers to John, i.e. John the Baptist, as *ben diwydon* 'foremost [of the] faithful ones' whom Christ blessed with *croes arwyddon* 'signs of [the] cross'.

Example (19) refers to the unrepentant thief crucified along with Jesus: one of the criminals hanging there abused him. 'Are you not the Christ?' he said. 'Save yourself and us as well.'[56] Two important points are made in (20); firstly, the poet asks Peter for help 'because of his relationship with Christ'. Peter, despite his ambivalence—a trait which would have

---

[54] See *Missal* 465.

[55] On the subject of the Crusades, see a summary in J.C. Brauer, *The Westminster Dictionary of Church History* (Philadelphia, 1971), 249–51.

[56] See Lk 23:39: *Unus autem de his qui pendebant, latronibus, blasphemabat eum, dicens: Si tu es Christus, salvum fac temetipsum et nos.*

appealed to one aware of his own sinfulness—had been chosen as leader of the Apostles by Christ. Yet he had denied that he knew Him at the very time when Christ was undergoing the agonies of scourging and crowning with thorns. Despite this he was the first to reach the tomb on Easter Sunday and find it empty; some days later Peter was challenged by Jesus on his love for Him and, as a result of his threefold protest of love, was reinstated with Christ's words 'Feed my lambs' and finally the 'Feed my sheep' command entrusted him with the care of the future Church.[57] Secondly Llywarch ap Llywelyn remarks that Christ took the Cross 'with dignity', and Dafydd Benfras (21) points out that Christ 'took up the cross as His own', which underlines Christ's willingness to suffer in order to redeem mankind. Gruffudd ab yr Ynad Coch notes that it was *er creulonder* 'because of cruelty' that Christ was crucified (22); this probably refers to the hatred which some of the Scribes and Pharisees bore to Jesus.

In (24) there is one of the very few references by the *Gogynfeirdd* to the Mass. This occurs within a 12-line litanic sequence of *Gwae* 'alas'! ['woe to'] warnings and here it is: 'Alas for [the] one who does not attend the fine Masses of Christ', which is obviously a reference to the importance attached by Gruffudd ab yr Ynad Coch to attendance at Mass. It is difficult to ascertain how frequently people were expected to attend Mass. The same poet in (25) seems to refer to what has become known as 'The seven words on the cross'. The example comes from the late thirteenth century. In considering the use made of heptads by the Gogynfeirdd, and in particular Gruffudd ab yr Ynad Coch, C. McKenna suggests possible sources from which they could derive. She interprets this reference as 'the seven perfect holy verses ... that Christ spoke', which is substantially the same as the translation given above. From whatever source the poet had his information the origin of the seven words is the New Testament[58]—(a) 'Father, forgive them; for they know not what they do'; (b) 'Today thou shalt be with me in Paradise'; (c) Seeing his mother and the disciple he loved standing near her, Jesus said to his mother, 'Woman, this is your son'. Then to the disciple he said, 'This is your mother'; (d) 'My God, my God, why have you forsaken me?' (e) 'I thirst'; (f) 'Father into thy hands I commend my spirit'; (g) 'It is consummated'.

The final example (27) is from Bleddyn Fardd's elegy for the three sons of Gruffudd ap Llywelyn and in view of the national loss and human tragedy being commemorated we can readily empathize with his cry

[57] See Mt 16:13–20 for Peter's declaration of faith; Jn 18:15–18 for Peter's denial; 21:7–17 Peter's restoration as head of the Apostles. However, it needs to be borne in mind that in this poem of petition the poet appeals to others of the Apostles, Thomas, Philip, Andrew and Paul.
[58] Lk. 23:34, Lk.23:43, Jn 19:26 ff. Mt 27:46, Mk 15:34, Jn. 19:28, Jn 19:30, Lk. 23:46.

Rhydrist y'n gwnaet Crist, croes oleuni 'Too sad has Christ, the light of the cross, made us'.

Christ and hell: Example (28) refers to Christ, whose Cross had been foretold by the prophets, and who will protect the poet Meilyr Brydydd from the pain of hell. Meilyr expresses his trust in *Crist croesddarogan* 'Christ of the foretold cross'. The full translation of this deathbed poem is given in Poem 25 *supra*. Cynddelw in (29) resorts to numerical correspondence: 'The five wounds of Christ brought the five ages from captivity', in an oblique reference to Christ's harrowing of hell. On the Ages of the World, see CBT IV, p. 294, note 170, also MWRL 89–90 on the historic background to this usage in medieval poetry. In several of the *Gogynfeirdd* poems the Ages of the World are mentioned and, depending on the rhythmic or other requirements of the context, the reference may be to four, five or six ages. Bleddyn Fardd in the third example (30) also deals with the harrowing of hell: *Crist a ddoeth i'r byd rhag bod Addaf A'i bobl yn uffern, gethern gaethaf* 'Christ came to the world lest Adam and his posterity, a host most captive, should have to remain in hell'. It may be of interest to cite MWRL here: 'The heroic view of the Redemption so congenial to the Welsh panegyrist was well grounded in patristic theology, which interpreted Christ's death as a payment of ransom to the devil, who had acquired a right to the souls of all men through the sin of Adam and Eve'.[59]

Christ as judge: Example (31) refers to Christ's coming in triumph to the General Judgement at the end of time and in (32) a special feature of Christ's attitude is revealed when He speaks reproachfully to the soul being judged.[60]

Statement of belief in Christ: The paucity of actual statements of belief in Christ in no way reflects a general lack of belief in Him. Gwalchmai in (33) reflects a firmness of faith in Christ, unlike Llygad Gŵr (37), who seems to have lost faith because of suffering and 'oppression' caused by Christ's taking away his patron. The other two examples dwell on the dire consequences of rejecting Him. Gwalchmai (33) refers to Christ as *neuedd gannwyll* 'a candle in time of need' or 'beacon light'. This same metaphor occurs in CBT VI 31.17, where Dafydd Benfras describes Llywelyn ab Iorwerth in battle to him as *cannwyll marchogion* 'the candle or beacon light, of the cavalry'. See also *Caindel Connacht, caindel Alban, amrae fiadat* translated as 'Connacht's candle, Britain's candle, splendid ruler', in *Iona* by Clancy and Márkus, pp. 146–7.

---

[59] See Part II footnote 14 and, on the five wounds of Christ, see Part II footnotes 31 and 60.
[60] See footnote 50 *supra*.

Christ, the source of inspiration: There are three examples of Christ as 'the awakener of [poetic] art', permitting 'speech' and providing 'wise inspiration' from the four elements.

Miscellaneous references to Christ: Apart from the classified references there are others which do not fit into any of the categories set out above. In (41) Elidir Sais promises to sing to Christ 'according to [the] custom of the law'. What does this law mean? We recall the poet Gwilym Du of Arfon referring to Elidir as *Elydyr gwir gwarant iawn ganon* and D. Myrddin Lloyd suggesting that *iawn ganon* is 'the standard for poets'. Is Elidir here announcing that henceforth, disillusioned in his role as a secular poet, he will devote his *awen* 'poetic inspiration' to praise God according to the best standards?

Prayers to Christ: Apart from Owain Cyfeiliog's complaint to Christ on the death of Moriddig (50), all examples in this section are framed as petitions to Christ. Ten times He is appealed to as 'Christ the Lord': seven times as *Crist Celi,* (48), (49), (52), (53), (54), (56), (57); once as *Crist Culwydd* (51) while in (58) the petition for grace is to *Crist, fawr Arglwydd rhwydd,* 'Christ mighty generous Lord'. In (59), which is from the same poem by Bleddyn Fardd, the prayer is for the protection of 'Christ Son of the true God', and in (60) the request is to the 'fair Christ' who, in virtue of the 'harshest sufferings' which He has endured, is 'just, bountiful, of the strongest defence'. Meilyr Brydydd (46), pleading on behalf of Gruffudd ap Cynan, asks 'Christ of perfect nature' 'to be merciful'. In (49) Christ is referred to as King; J. Pelikan would explain this emphasis as emanating from events of the fourth century, when Constantine declared the Roman Empire Christian. For the next thousand years it was necessary to accept Christ as the eternal King if one wanted to be a temporal king.[61]

7. 1
Iesu Jesus

The name Jesus was announced by the angel to Mary at the Annunciation: 'You are to conceive a Son and you must name him JESUS'.[62]

In *Gogynfeirdd* poetry there is a paucity of references to Jesus, which may be due to the attitude of respect and reverence among these poets for such a sacred name.[63] The examples which follow convey a sense of

[61] See J. Pelikan, *Jesus through the Centuries*, p. 53.

[62] Lk 1:32 *et paries filium, et vocabis nomen eius JESUM.*

[63] See Irénée Hausherr, *The Names of Jesus*, which elaborates on the reserve and reverence in which it was held by the early Christians, 3–61, under the headings 'Plurality of names', 'Names of Jesus in the Gospels', 'The remainder of the New Testament', 'The

the esteem in which the *Gogynfeirdd* held the name Jesus and their veneration for the incarnate Son of God. His coming down from heaven, His passion and redemptive sufferings, His descent into hell, implied in His meeting the 'three hosts' held captive there, His second coming as judge of the living and the dead all appear by direct mention or by implication within the twenty-four citations. Spoken of as Son of Mary, the poets see Him as the One to whom sinners may turn in repentance and receive forgiveness. Some of these examples reveal the existence of a rather personal relationship between the poet and Jesus. Individual examples will be considered under separate headings.

Jesus as Creator: Only one example casts Jesus in the role of Creator though that word does not occur, nor is a dependence on rhyme or initial alliteration with the form *Iesu* present in the line.

Jesus and Mary: Two examples occur in this section, both of which show Jesus as Son of Mary, who is referred to as daughter of her King in (2).

Passion of Jesus: The five references to the Passion of Jesus cover the period from His betrayal on Wednesday and His arrest on Thursday night to His crucifixion on Friday. In (5) Einion ap Gwalchmai utters a cry of malediction against those who perpetrated the *perygl fradau* 'dangerous treacheries' leading to the flagellation of Jesus. Here we have a reference to His betrayal by Judas, who is named as such in example (6). A brief account of this incident is given in each of the four Gospels. Mt 26:14–16 states that the chief priests paid Judas 'thirty pieces of silver', i.e. thirty shekels, the price the Law (Ex 21:32) fixed for a slave's life. In the 'Book of the Resurrection of Christ' ANT 183, we read: 'Jesus rose from the dead, and Abbaton (Death) and Pestilence came back to Amente (underworld) to protect it, but they found it wholly desolate, only three souls were left in it (those of Herod, Cain, and Judas) ...'. In (4) Elidir Sais, deploring the fact that one like Jesus *Iesu managu mwynglyd* of 'gentle and consoling speech' could be so treated, says of the capture of Jesus on Thursday, *A Difiau y'n dyfu ledfryd* 'And Thursday there came discouragement to us'.

Harrowing of hell: This sole example has been classed as the 'harrowing of hell' by associated inference, for in fact it does not mention hell but speaks of 'the five ages in bondage' when Jesus left heaven to come down and redeem them. See *supra* on the 'five ages of the world' in 6. 1 **Christ and Hell** and also Part II, *supra* where there are further

---

Apostolic Fathers' (selecting a number of the Fathers, whom she regards as deserving special attention, e.g. St Irenaeus, Origen, St Basil, etc.).

references to the Ages of the World in general. From the same poem comes the only example of Jesus as Judge.[64]

Prayer to Jesus: Einion ap Gwalchmai (11) prays that he may be able to make adequate atonement to Jesus for his sins and in (12) the poet invokes Jesus directly and with similar intimacy Madog ap Gwallter prays in (13). It may be worth noting that Hausherr reminds us that we never read in the Gospels that anyone addresses the master by his proper name nor as 'Lord Jesus'. The vocative does occur in Mark and Luke, but only from the demons speaking through the lips of someone possessed, and then only with the addition of the native town, 'Jesus of Nazareth' (Mk 1:24; Lk 4:34). The Gerasene demoniac uses the title 'Jesus, son of God most high'.[65] Gruffudd ab yr Ynad Coch (14) prays for the protection of 'the loving Jesus' who is *coron tangnefedd* 'crown of peace'.

In praise of Jesus: Cynddelw alone comments on his praise of Jesus, motivated perhaps by self-interest. This hope of reward from Jesus is an instance of the *laudo ut des* referred to previously in the short introduction to *Response in Praise* 1. 23 *supra*. These lines follow the poet's recommending the importance of praising God and his disapproval of anyone failing to do so. See CBT IV 16.118–19.

Miscellaneous references to Jesus: It is unlikely that the Joseph whose 'discourse' is referred to in (16) is the spouse of Mary, since Scripture records no word of his. Traditionally Joseph of Arimathea was connected with Glastonbury, and he may therefore be a possibility. In connection with this suggestion, see 'The Narrative of the Assumption' attributed to him in ANT 216–18. However, there is grounds for believing that this is a reference to Joseph the son of Jacob, since he has often been represented as prefiguring Christ the Redeemer. When the starving people[66] of Egypt turned to Pharaoh asking for food, they were told: 'Go to Joseph, and do what he tells you'. These words bring to mind Jn 2:5 when Mary at the Wedding Feast at Cana tells the servants: 'Do whatever he [Jesus] tells you' (see Part II Poem 6). In (17) Llywelyn Fardd (I) states unequivocally the purpose of his composition which is to keep Jesus in mind as he proceeds with his song of praise for Cadfan. Hywel ab Owain Gwynedd (18) expresses great confidence that Jesus will not blame him for immoderation in his love follies. Dafydd Benfras, on the other hand, in (20) is prepared to lay the blame for the death of Llywelyn ab Iorwerth on the 'relentless' Jesus. It is as a *gwrawl ... pen* 'heroic chief' and *pen rhiau* 'supreme king' that Jesus is described in (21)

---

[64] See Part II footnote 18.
[65] See NOJ 5–6 and Mk 10:47; Lk 18:38.
[66] See *Ite ad Joseph, et quidquid ipse vobis dixerat, facite;* Gn 41:55.

and 22), while He is shown to be all-powerful in (23). Finally Gruffudd ab yr Ynad Coch (24) stresses the need for amendment of life—*Bod yn ddir talu ger bron yr Iesu* 'it is necessary to make retribution before Jesus' if one has sinned.

8. 1
Alternative names for God

Part III 1–7 considers the Godhead under strictly orthodox titles in theological terms. Section 8 is different, not in style or sentiment, but in its use of multiple designations for God. Many of these have biblical parallels as *Arglwydd* Lord, *Brenin, Rhi, Rex* King, *Iudex* Judge, while others cannot be traced to scriptural or liturgical sources. In using these the poets have drawn on their own native cultural heritage and we find in descriptions of God words that have legal and military connotations, e.g. *Priawd, Priodor, Perchen* Master, Rightful Owner, Owner, *Gŵr* Warrior, all of which are also applied to their secular patrons. There are other titles in the heroic vein which echo a long-standing Welsh poetic usage, e.g. *Gwrda* noble One, *Llywiawdr* Ruler, *Naf, Ner, Peryf* Lord. In all, there are examples of fifty-six alternate names for God gleaned from the seven volumes of *Cyfres Beirdd y Tywysogion*. A great number of these have been translated by the word Lord.

The references appear throughout the period of *Gogynfeirdd* composition. Instead of presenting these examples in separate sections they are merely named in alphabetical order and the number of occurrences of the title appended in brackets.

Many of these names seem to have been used to meet the rhyme patterns or metrical requirements of the line or couplet, e.g. *Amherawdr* occurs in combination with *Creawdr* in all four examples listed.

Appendix

True God: **1. 1. 1** Ef yn un Duw gwir, yn gywiraf *He [is] one true God, the most faithful One* (Meilyr ap Gwalchmai, 'Ode to God', I 32.15); **1. 1. 2** Duw dewrwir, pellir pwyllawr—o'n cynnen *God strong and true, comprehensively is our discord considered* (Cynddelw, 'Ode to God', IV 17.3); **1. 1. 3** I'r gwir Dduw ydd wyf yn erchi *To the true God I make petition* (Hywel Foel ap Griffri, 'Request for the liberation of Owain ap Gruffudd', VII 23.23).

Eternal God: **1. 2. 1** Tragywyddawl Dduw tra gynanwyf Traethawd ohonawd a handdenwyf *Eternal God, while I may speak I shall take pains to make a song about You* (Gwalchmai ap Meilyr, 'Ode to God', I 14.55–6); **1. 2. 2** Gorau un, gorau gerennydd—i ddyn Yr hon Dduw tragywydd A gorau ail gerennydd, **1. 2. 3** Wedi'r hon Dduw, 'r hon Ddafydd *The best of all, the best reconciliation for man Is that with the eternal God And the second best reconciliation, After that with God, is that with Dafydd* (Gwilym Rhyfel, 'Appeasement of Dafydd ap Owain', II 28.57–60); **1. 2. 4** Tranc ar Dduw, traethaf na ellir! *God's death, I declare, is impossible!* (Cynddelw, 'Poem to St Tysilio', III 3.93).

God the Creator: **God as creator of heaven**: **1. 3. 1** Gorugost wormes …, Gorfawr Dduw gorfod, o Iddewon Am fedd Crist: Creawdr nef, ys angen! *You have caused oppression…, Immense victorious God, because of [the] Jews About the tomb of Christ: Creator of heaven, inevitable it is!* (Elidir Sais, 'In Praise of God and Dafydd ab Owain', I 16.19–21); **1. 3. 2** Rhoddesid ein Duw yn ein dechrau Rhodd bêr paradwys (parha golau!) **1. 3. 3** Rhy-n-parasai Duw heb ddim eisau *At our beginning God gave to us The fine gift of paradise (light abides!). God had made us without any need* (Meilyr ap Gwalchmai, 'Ode to God', I 33.34–6).

God as creator of human beings: **1. 3. 4** Rhy-i-gorug Duw ddau henefydd—o'i phlaid *God has created two elders on its behalf* (Llywelyn Fardd (I), 'Song to Cadfan', II 1.61); **1. 3. 5** O nerth Duw y'i cread! *Through the power of God was he created!* (Llywarch ap Llywelyn, 'In Praise of Dafydd ab Owain Gwynedd', V 1.10); **1. 3. 6** Duw o nef rhy-th-swynas *It is God from heaven who has created you* (*Id.*, 'In Praise of Llywelyn ab Iorwerth', V 18.30).

God as creator of the unique individual: **1. 3. 7** Ac yn orau dyn Duw rhy'i creas *And the best of mortals whom God has created* (Gwalchmai ap Meilyr, 'Exaltation of Owain Gwynedd', I 8.81); **1. 3. 8** Neb ni orug Duw, … tëyrn fal ti. *God did not make, … [another] king like you* (Gwilym Rhyfel, 'Appeasement of Dafydd ab Owain', II 28.25–8); **1. 3. 9** Ni wnaeth Duw neb dyn dwywawl ffydd *God did not make any man [with] holy faith [like him]* (Daniel ap Llosgwrn Mew, 'Elegy for Owain Gwynedd', II 18.36); **1. 3. 10** Dafydd hael, ei hafal (nid ffug) Dyn nis gŵyr a Duw nis gorug *Generous Dafydd, his like ([this] is not false) No one knows of him and God did not make him* (Llywarch ap Llywelyn, 'In Praise of Dafydd ab Owain Gwynedd', V 1.131–2); **1. 3. 11** Y gwnaeth Duw deifniawg ar honnaid, Rhodri hael, a'i hafal ni wnaid *God made known the man of generous substance, Generous Rhodri and his like was not made* (*Id.*, 'In Praise of Rhodri ab Owain Gwynedd', V 6.49); **1. 3. 12** Ni orug Duw dy gystaddl *God has made none equal to you* (*Id.*, 'In Praise of Gruffudd ap Cynan of Gwynedd', V 10.48); **1. 3. 13** Wyt gorau un gwron o'r fas A wnaeth Duw y dydd y 'n creas *You are the one best warrior of the multitude Whom God made on the day He created us* (*Id.*, 'In Praise of Llywelyn ab Iorwerth', V 18.35–6); **1. 3. 14** Duw, mal ef, nef Nêr-Bennaeth, Dyn cynna, nis gwna, nis gwnaeth *God, Prince-Lord of heaven, [one] like him, [That is] as good a warrior, He does not make, nor has He made* (*Id.*, 'In Praise of Llywelyn ab Iorwerth', V 20.15–16); **1. 3. 15** Er pan orau Duw ddyn gysefin, Ni wnaeth ei gystal, traws arial trin *Ever since God first created man, [He] did not make his equal, mighty [in the] fury of battle* (Dafydd Benfras, 'To Llywelyn ab Iorwerth', VI 25.13–14); **1. 3. 16** Ni ryorug Duw ddyn fal tydy *God did not make a man like you* (*Id.*, 'In Praise of Llywelyn ab Iorwerth', VI 26.52).

God as creator of plants and animals: 1. 3. 17 Can digones Duw o'i ddefnyddiau **1. 3. 18** (Duw a ddigones) lles llyseuau *Since God made from His materials (God did it) the virtue of plants* (Meilyr ap Gwalchmai, 'Ode to God', I 33.29–30); **1. 3. 19** Duw a wna ddeubryd ffryd a ffrwythau. Diffrwythwyd daear drwy gareddau—dyn; Dinam bwyad, Duw a'i gorau *The God who makes the two forms of streams and fruits. Earth was made sterile through the transgressions of man; Without blemish it would have been [otherwise, it was] God who made it* (ib. 39–41); **1. 3. 20** Deuddegfed dydd, Duw ddigawn Anifeilaid môr mawrddawn *On the twelfth day, God makes Animals of the sea great its blessing* (Llywelyn Fardd (I), 'Signs before Judgement Day', II 5.17); **1. 3. 21** A ffrwythau a doniau, Duw ryddigawn *Both crops and gifts, God it is who created them* (Cynddelw, 'Deathbed Poem', IV 18. 6); **1. 3. 22** Duw a'n dyfu, dyn yn crëu creaduriau *God came to us, [a] man creating creatures* (Madog ap Gwallter, 'Ode to God', VII 32.7).

God the Creator until Judgement: 1. 3. 23 Duw Creawdr Llywiawdr a'm llywo—hyd Frawd *May God the Creator and Ruler guide me until Judgement Day* (Meilyr ap Gwalchmai, 'Ode to God', I 30.31).

God of heaven: **heaven on high or above: 1. 4. 1** Cyfarchaf, Dduw Naf, nefawl Dad—celi *I pray, O Lord God, heavenly Father on high* (Llywarch ap Llywelyn, 'In Praise of Dafydd ab Owain Gwynedd', V 1.1); **1. 4. 2** Boed yn nef a'th hendref a'th hafod,—tëyrn, Teÿrnas Duw uchod! *Let your winter and summer dwellings be in heaven, [O] chieftain, [In] the kingdom of God on high!* (*Id.*, 'In Praise of Rhys Gryg of Deheubarth', V 26.145–6); **1. 4. 3** Diwygaf, honnaf hynny, Difwyn a gymer Duw fry *I make recompense [for it], that I proclaim, Recompense God accepts on high* (Phylip Brydydd, 'Appeasement of Rhys Gryg', VI 12.43–4); **1. 4. 4** Duw fry am frenin Aberffraw *May God from on high be [as a fortress] around the king of Aberffraw* (Dafydd Benfras, 'In Praise of God and Llywelyn ab Iorwerth', VI 24.92).

Heaven as refuge: 1. 4. 5 Duw a'm gad cariad i mywn caerau—nef *God who will grant me love within the battlements of heaven* (Einion ap Gwalchmai, 'Ode to God', I 27.19); **1. 4. 6** Duw nefoedd, fy noddfa yn geugant *God of heaven, my refuge for sure* (Meilyr ap Gwalchmai, 'Ode to God', I 31.4); **1. 4. 7** Poed Ef, fy Nuw nef, fo fy ninas *Let Him, my God of heaven, be my defence* (*Id.*, 'Ode to God', I 33.103); **1. 4. 8** Can Dduw nef yn ei fawr noddfa *With the God of heaven in His great refuge* (Dafydd Benfras, 'Progress of Llywelyn ap Gruffudd', VI 35.91).

Abodes of heaven, including references to **Light** and **Throne: 1. 4. 9** Archaf arch i Dduw addodau—nef Na ddoto Pedr gloau I'm lluddias i'm haddas, i'r mau *I present a petition to God of the dwellings of heaven That Peter may not place obstacles To prevent me from my desert, from what is mine* (Einion ap Gwalchmai, 'Ode to God', I 27.87–9); **1. 4. 10** Ar Dduw addef nef fy llef llwyprawd *To the home of God in heaven will go my cry* (*Id.*, 'Ode to God', I 28.43); **1. 4. 11** Gan Dduw yn lleufer, llewychant,—llu bedydd *With God in light, they [will] shine, host of Christendom* (Meilyr ap Gwalchmai, 'Ode to God', I 31.9); **1. 4. 12** Yn lleithig Duw Gwledig y gwledychant *From the throne of the Lord God they shall rule* (*ib.* 31).

Banquet in heaven: 1. 4. 13 Diofelid Duw hwy ac eu tad Yn y wenwledd, fry yn y wenwlad *May God cause them and their father to be free from care In the blessed banquet, in the blessed land on high* (Dafydd Benfras, 'Elegy for Dafydd ap Llywelyn', VI 30.37–8).

General references to heaven: 1. 4. 14 Cedwid Duw o nef nerth Merfyniawn! *May the God of heaven protect [him who is] the support of the tribe of Merfyn!* (Cynddelw, 'Exaltation of Owain Gwynedd', IV 3.48); **1. 4. 15** Duw o'r nef a'i gwarawd *God of heaven delivered him* (*Id.*, 'Appeasement of the Lord Rhys', IV 9.38); **1. 4. 16** Tref ydd aeth Duw nef o'i dangnefedd *[The] village where the God of heaven went from His peace* (Anon., 'Lament of the Pilgrim', VI 36.8); **1. 4. 17** Duw o nef a fo nerth iddaw! *May the God of heaven be his strength!* (Llygad Gŵr, 'In Praise of Gruffudd ap Madog', VII 26.36).

God is Holy: **1. 5. 1** A Duw gwyn yn gwybod *And holy God knowing [of it]* (Cynddelw, 'A Quatrain to a Monk', IV 15.2); **1. 5. 2** Tra fai ddywawl Dduw yn ei ddwywdid Ar y llen falchwen ni fylchid—ei braint Ydd ysgarawdd henaint ac ieuenctid *While God was holy in His divinity On the fair and proud curtain the privilege of which was not broken Where old age departed from youth* (Phylip Brydydd, 'First Ode of Contention in the Presence of Rhys Ieuanc', VI 14.30–2).

God is all-knowing: **1. 6. 1** Duw a ŵyr eu manag *God knows their expression* (Elidir Sais, 'Elegy for Ednyfed Fychan and Tegwared ab Iarddur', I 18.22); **1. 6. 2** Hoed a'n cyferyw, cyfarwydd Yw Duw am ein diheurwydd *Worry has come to us, but proficient Is God with regard to [imparting] certainty to us* (Id., 'Elegy for Hywel ab Arthen', I 19.1–2); **1. 6. 3** Gwypid Duw, gwybod a ddarfu *God knows, knowing what happened* (Id., 'Ode to God', I 21.24); **1. 6. 4** Nis gŵyr namyn Duw ac a'i dywaid *Only God and those who express it know* (Owain Cyfeiliog, 'The Drinking-horn of Owain', II 14.134); **1. 6. 5** A Duw yn gwybod ei ddefodau *And God knew his customs* (Gwynfardd Brycheiniog, 'Song to St David', II 26.251); **1. 6. 6** Nis gŵyr namyn Duw a dewinion—byd A diwyd dderwyddon, O eurdorf eurdorchogion, Ein rhif yn Rhiweirth afon *No one knows but God and the diviners of the world And reliable wise men, Of a host of warriors wearing gold torques, Our number / strength in the River Rhiweirth* (Cynddelw, 'Elegy for Madog ap Maredudd, Llywelyn his son and the warband of Powys', III 8.21–4); **1. 6. 7** Cerddgar cyfarwar (cyfarwydd—yw Duw) *Joyful lover of poetry (fully learned is God)* (Id., 'Elegy for Owain Gwynedd', IV 4.47).

Almighty/Supreme God: **1. 7. 1** Boed ef y byddwyf gwedi beddrawd Cyd â'r un Duw mawr yn Ei undawd *Grant that, after my burial, I may be In the company of the One great God in His Unity* (Einion ap Gwalchmai, 'Ode to God', I. 28.47–8); **1. 7. 2** O gysgawd tafawd, da yr awr—y medrais Ymadrawdd o Dduw mawr *Through protection of my tongue, good was the time when I could Speak with [the help] of the august God* (Einion Wan, 'Appeasement of Dafydd ap Llywelyn', VI 6.29–30); **1. 7. 3** Nawdd Duw mawr, deg Wawr dewaint Gyd â nawdd naw mil o saint *Protection of the great God, fair Lord of midnight darkness Together with the protection of nine thousand of the saints* (Phylip Brydydd, 'Appeasement of Rhys Gryg', VI 12.31); **1 7. 4** Duw mawr, Amherawdr dyniaddon *Great God, Emperor of men* (Hywel Foel ap Griffri, 'Request for the liberation of Owain ap Gruffudd', VII 22.1).

God is Just in His Judging: **1. 8. 1** Duw a fynn dyfod i'w orsedd Hydr a llaw, nid lle i'w omedd *God insists upon the coming to His throne Of the strong and the weak, it is no place to refuse Him* (Gruffudd ap Gwrgenau, 'Elegy for Gruffydd ap Cynan', II 31.25–6); **1. 8. 2** Duw â'r nef ni'th wŷl hân, Â'i senedd lariedd lydan, Â'i saint gloyw ardduniaint glân *God will see that you will not be debarred from heaven, From His assembly of spacious hospitality, [Nor] from His saints of brilliant and holy adornments* (Llywarch ap Llywelyn, 'Elegy for Hywel ap Gruffudd of Merioneth', V 13.2–4); **1. 8. 3** Gwedi llarydad, Duw deg gyfreithiau *After a generous father, [Thee] God of just laws* (Dafydd Benfras, 'Elegy for Gruffydd ap Llywelyn', VI 29.64).

An Angry God: **1. 9. 1** Gwae a goddwy Duw dogn berthidau *Woe to the one who may anger God of the fullness of riches* (Meilyr ap Gwalchmai, 'Ode to God', I 33.38); **1. 9. 2** Iolaf-i Dduw i ddifwyn Ei fâr *I pray to God in order to placate His anger* (Cynddelw, 'Ode to God', IV 16.40); **1. 9. 3** Pan wnêl Duw dangos Ei faran, Dyddwyre, dyddaered arnan *When God may show forth His anger, It will erupt and come down upon our heads* (ib. 207–8); **1. 9. 4** A minnau, mynnaf gyweithas, Bodd Duw im, a dianc o'i gas *As for me I desire fellowship, God's good pleasure towards me, and fleeing His anger* (Llywarch ap Llywelyn, 'Ode to the Hot Iron', V 15.19–20); **1. 9. 5** Rhag dy fâr, câr cerdd lochi, Mal gwirion, gwared, Dduw, fi *From your anger, friend patronizing poetry, As an innocent one, deliver me, O God* (Phylip Brydydd, 'Appeasement of Rhys Gryg', VI 12.11–12).

God as King: **Brenin: 1. 10. 1** Duw Dewin, Breienin breinawl *God the Magician, privileged King* (Elidir Sais, 'Ode to God', I 22.3); **1. 10. 2** Can ein Duw fry freenhiniaeth! *Kingship on high with our God!* (Cynddelw, 'Ode to God', IV 17.118); **1. 10. 3** Wrth Dduw ydd iolaf hynny, Werthefin Freienin fry *To God I pray for that, The supreme King on high* (Llywarch ap Llywelyn, 'Welcoming Gruffudd ap Llywelyn', V 29.11–12); **1. 10. 4** Wrth Dduw fry, Freienin coeth … Llawer cerddawr, gwawr gwawdfaith, Ar fâr am dy farwoliaeth *Against God on high, illustrious King … Many a poet, lord extensive your renown, [Is] in rage because of your death* (Y Prydydd Bychan, 'Elegy for Rhys ap Llywelyn', VII 15.5–8); **1. 10. 5** Nid oes, Frenin, Dëws domin, dimyn eisau *There is not, O King, Lord God, [the] least trace of defect* (Gruffudd ab yr Ynad Coch, 'Ode to God', VII 41.10).

Rhi: 1. 10. 6 Cyfarchaf-i, Dduw, cyfarchwel iawn I foli fy Rhi rhwydd, rhadlawn *I beg you, O God, for a fitting conversion To praise my generous and blessed King* (Cynddelw, 'Deathbed Poem', IV 18.1–2).

Rhwyf: 1. 10. 7 Duw a'm rhodd Rhwyf fodd feddyliaid *God grant that I consider the will of the Prince* (Cynddelw, 'Ode to God', IV 16.147).

Dofydd: 1. 10. 8 Duw Dofydd, Duw parchrydd, parchraith *God the Ruler, God great his honour, fully lawful His honour* (Seisyll Bryffwrch, 'Elegy for Owain Gwynedd', II 22.2); **1. 10. 9** Penydwr pennaf ei grefydd A gredws Duw, Dëws Ddofydd *A penitent of greatest devotion Who believed in God, Lord King* (Cynddelw, 'Poem to St Tysilio', III 3.197–8).

Gwledig: 1. 10. 10 A'm rhoddwy Gwledig gwleidiaddon Drefred gwlad wared worchorddion *May the King of kings grant to me A dwelling-place in the land of the multitude of salvation* (Cynddelw, 'Poem to St Tysilio', III 3.241–2).

Naf: 1. 10. 11 Arddunedig Dduw, arddelw ohonawd A wnaf, Arglwydd Naf, nerth pob ciwdawd *O revered God, avow You I shall, Lord [and] Sovereign, strength of all peoples* (Einion ap Gwalchmai, 'Ode to God', I 28.37–8).

Meddu: 1. 10. 12 Duw a fedd o'i fuddugoliaeth *God governs by virtue of His victory* (Elidir Sais, 'Elegy for Rhodri ab Owain', I 15.30); **1. 10. 13** Moesen a'i dywawd, a Duw a'i medd *It is Moses who said that, and God will arrange it* (*Id.*, 'Ode to God', I 23.32); **1. 10. 14** Breuddwyd a'i dywaid, a Duw a'i medd *A vision proclaims it, and God makes it possible* (Hywel ab Owain Gwynedd, '*Gorhoffedd*', II 6.26); **1. 10. 15** Drwy eirioled Dewi, a Duw a fedd *Through the intercession of [Saint] David, and it is God who governs* (Gwynfardd Brycheiniog, 'Song to St David', II 26.291); **1. 10. 16** Nid meddwl meddu hefyd, Namyn o Dduw, ddim o'r byd *Nor thinking of gaining possession either, Except by God, of any part of the world* (Cynddelw, 'Elegy for Madog ap Maredudd, Llywelyn his son and the warband of Powys', III 8.71–2).

God of Life and Death: Gallael: 1. 11. 1 Can rygallas Duw draig Powys *Since God has snatched away the dragon of Powys* (Gwalchmai ap Meilyr, 'Elegy for Madog ap Maredudd', I 7.135); **1. 11. 2** Trist wyf: trais Duw rhy'i gallas *I am sad: God's violence has taken him away* (Bleddyn Fardd, 'Elegy for Dafydd Benfras', VII 44.15).

Dwyn: 1. 11. 3 A Duw a'i dug i arnaf *And God took him from me* (Cynddelw, 'Elegy for Rhirid Flaidd', III 25.3); **1. 11. 4** Trwm a barthed yd berthyn Y dug Duw dewis ar ddyn *This a sad locality to which [it] belongs That God took from it the choice of men* (*Id.*, 'Elegy for Ednyfed, Lord of Crogen', III 27.19–20); **1. 11. 5** Mawr Dduw! a ddycych beunoeth Mor wael na welir drannoeth *Great God! the one whom you may call away each night How wretched that he is not seen next day* (Gwernen ap Clydno, 'Quatrains', VI 21.3–4); **1. 11. 6** Golau y dug Duw ein diebryd—fry *Openly God took aloft that which was due to us* (Dafydd Benfras, 'Elegy for Llywelyn ab Iorwerth' VI 27.59); **1. 11. 7** Truan y gwnaeth Duw ddwyn cariad—Cymry *Sadly did God act in taking away the darling of Wales* (*Id.*, 'Elegy for Dafydd ap Llywelyn', VI 30.29); **1. 11. 8** Duw a'i dug rhagon, ddeon ddiwedd *God took him from us, downfall of nobles* (*ib.* 69); **1. 11. 9** Tri gŵr a ddug Duw o'r dyniaddon *Three warriors whom God took away from amongst men* (*Id.*, 'Elegy for Llywelyn ab Iorwerth, Gruffudd ap Llywelyn and Dafydd ap Llywelyn', VI 31.57); **1. 11. 10** Rhyddug Duw o'i gartref *God has taken him away from his home* (Bleddyn Fardd, 'Elegy for Owain Goch ap Gruffudd ap Llywelyn', VII 49.14); **1. 11. 11** Duw a ddug ataw (buddwaglaw byd) *God took [him] to Himself (empty reward [is the] world)* (*Id.*, 'Elegy for Dafydd ap Gruffudd ab Owain', VII 55.1).

Lladd: 1 11. 12 Lladdawdd Duw arnam am ddwyn lleurwydd—frwyd *God struck us in taking away from us the source of light* (Dafydd Benfras, 'Elegy for Llywelyn ab Iorwerth', VI 27.19); **1. 11. 13** Dwyn ein llyw, Duw ry-n-lladdawdd *Our leader has been taken away, God has stricken us* (Y Prydydd Bychan, 'Elegy for Cynan ap Hywel', VII 6.4).

Trais: 1. 11. 14 Trais Duw, dwyn hael o an byd, **1. 11. 15** Ac wedi trais Duw, tristyd *It was God's violence the taking one of noble stock from our world, And after the violence of God, sadness* (Einion Wan, 'Elegy for Llywelyn ab Iorwerth', VI 5.23–4); **1. 11. 16** Rhy-m-gorau angau angen orddwy—drais Am drawsfab Goronwy, Rhy-m-dirwaen Duw, rhy-m-dirwy *Death has caused me violence of oppression of loss For the strong son of Goronwy, God saddens me, He punishes me* (*Id.*, 'Elegy for Hywel ap Goronwy', VII 47.1–3).

Prayers: 1. 11. 17 Duw damnawdd eirioes einioes Einiawn *O God, protect the life of Einion [that is full] of faith* (Cynddelw, 'Elegy for Rhirid Flaidd and his brother Arthen', III 24.139); **1. 11. 18** Gwnaed Dduw ei ddiwedd-ef, ddi-fefl hebrwng, Yni fo ei orffen ar ffordd deilwng *Let God make his demise, perfect [funeral] cortege, So that his death may be in a worthy manner* (Einion ap Madog ap Rhahawd, 'In Praise of Gruffudd ap Llywelyn', VI 23.27–8).

Extreme grief: 1. 11. 19 Nid adawo Duw dyn yn fyw—bellach *May God not leave anyone alive further* (Cynddelw, 'Elegy for Madog ap Maredudd, Llywelyn his son and the warband of Powys', III 8.45); **1. 11. 20** Peris Duw eu dygngudd rhagon *God caused their lamentable concealment from us* (Dafydd Benfras, 'Elegy for Llywelyn ab Iorwerth, Gruffudd ap Llywelyn and Dafydd ap Llywelyn', VI 31.51).

General references: 1. 11. 21 I'm dyddwyn o'm Duw i'm dylyed O gadwent present près efrifed *To be borne by my God to my deserts From the tumult of this life with its very great oppression* (Gwalchmai ap Meilyr, 'Ode to God', I 14.89–90); **1. 11. 22** Pan fynno Duw dy ddifuriaw O ddyllest present a phreswyl fraw *When God may wish to uproot you From the order of the present world with its constant fear* (Meilyr ap Gwalchmai, 'Ode to God', I 33.46–7); **1. 11. 23** Na cherydd i Dduw ddwyn yr Eiddaw! *Do not re-*

proach God for taking away that which is His! (*ib.* 51); **1 11. 24** Hir ni
mynnwys Duw dyniawl einioes *God did not intend human life to be abiding*
(*ib.* 59); **1. 11. 25** Gobwylled fy Nuw-i fy nihenydd *May my God consider
my destiny* (Hywel ab Owain Gwynedd, 'Gorhoffedd', II 6.41); **1. 11. 26**
Can digones Duw ein diflan—ferroes *Since God has fashioned our transient
short life* (Cynddelw, 'Ode to God', IV 16.195); **1. 11. 27** Truan ydd
edfyn dyn pan dwyller, Tru, Dduw, ei ddifant pan ddifäer *Miserably does
man pine [away] when he is deceived, Sad, O God, is his destruction when he is
destroyed* (Llywelyn Fardd (II), 'Ode to God', VI 10.43–4); **1. 11. 28** Mal
y dug o'i deg enrhydedd Y dwg Duw bawb yn y diwedd *As he has taken
[him] from his fair dignity God finally will take everyone* (Anon., 'Lament of
the Pilgrim', VI 36.47–8); **1. 11. 29** Ni fedd namyn Duw ddigyfoethi—
dyn *Only God has the right to dispossess a person* (Hywel Foel ap Griffri,
'Request for the liberation of Owain ap Gruffudd', VII 23.35).

Wise God: 1. 12. 1 Ar gyfoeth Duw ddoeth Ei ddetholi *By God's authority, whose choosing is wise* (Einion ap Gwalchmai, 'Elegy for Nest
daughter of Hywel', I 26.51); **1. 12. 2** Mynnid ymeiriawl greddfawl
graddau Men yd wedd, Duw doeth, i'th gyfoethau *The intercession of the
steadfast achieves the hierarchies [of heaven] Where it befits Your powers, [O]
wise God* (*Id.*, 'Ode to God', I 27.103–4); **1. 12. 3** Cedwid Duw dewrddoeth gyfoeth Cadfan *May God, wise and courageous, protect the kingdom of
Cadfan* (Llywelyn Fardd (I), 'Song to Cadfan', II 1.178); **1. 12. 4** Duw
doeth i deithi teÿrnedd, Teÿrnas wenwas wirionedd *Wise God with [the]
attributes of kings, One who is [the] truth of the blessed dwelling of the kingdom
[of heaven]* (Cynddelw, 'Poem to St Tysilio', III 3.3–4).

Faithful, Strong, Supporting God: 1. 13. 1 Ac a'm bo, o'm budd ym-
weddwyd, Bod Duw i'm diau gadwyd *And [grant] me, deprived of my
profit, That God is certainly saving me* (Gwalchmai ap Meilyr, 'Gwalchmai's
Dream', I 12.29–30); **1. 13. 2** A'm Duw a'm diwyd arbed Erbyn brawd
Trindawd Trined *And God will faithfully rescue me Ready for the judgement of
the Trinity the Three in One* (*Id.*, 'Ode to God', I 14.109–10); **1. 13. 3**
Edifeiriawg da, Duw nwy gomedd *The good repentant one, God does not
refuse him* (Elidir Sais, 'Ode to God', I 23.14); **1. 13. 4** Canys gorau Duw
diwyd Gwared plant rhag pla a thristyd *For the faithful God caused The redemption of [His] children from plague and sadness* (*Id.*, 'Ode to God', I 24.3–
4); **1. 13. 5** Coelaf Dduw a'r saint a braint eu bro *I shall put my trust in
God and the saints and the privilege of their region* (Meilyr ap Gwalchmai,
'Ode to God', I 30.20); **1. 13. 6** Duw terwyn torfoedd gogoniant *Steadfast God of the hosts of glory* (*Id.*, 'Ode to God', I 31.3); **1. 13. 7** Cedwis
Duw urddas, yn ŵr ac yn was, I fab Eneas, eurwas fyged *God defended the
dignity, as man and youth, Of the son of Eneas, [one of the] honour [of] an excellent youth* (Llywelyn Fardd (I), 'Song to Cadfan', II 1.11–12); **1. 13. 8**

Dra safo Duw ganthaw *As long as God supports him* (Llywarch Llaety, 'In Praise of Llywelyn ap Madog', II 16.46): **1. 13. 9** Dothyw i Ddewi yn ddeheueg, Gan borth Duw, porth dyn yn ddiatreg *There came to [Saint] David skilfully, With the help of God, help of man immediately* (Gwynfardd Brycheiniog, 'Song to St David', II 26.150–1); **1. 13. 10** Ac onid trech celwydd no gwirionedd Neu ddarfod dawn Duw yn y diwedd, Ys mi a feflawr o'r gyngheusedd *And if lying be not stronger than truth Or that the grace of God finally comes to an end, I shall be disgraced as a result of the contention* (Phylip Brydydd, 'Second Ode of Contention in the presence of Rhys Ieuanc', VI 15.39–41); **1. 13. 11** Am drais Duw, nid oes gyhyd *As to the force of God, nothing is as great* (Dafydd Benfras, 'Elegy for Llywelyn ab Iorwerth', VI 27.81); **1. 13. 12** Pedwaredd ar ddeg, pan ddug achwaneg, Dwyn Cedewyng deg, Duw a'i nertha! *The fourteenth [expedition], when he extended his possession further Was the possessing of fair Cedewain, God will strengthen him!* (Id., 'Progress of Llywelyn ap Gruffudd', VI 35.63–4); **1. 13. 13** Duw, dy nawdd rhag tawdd tanllachar—uffern *[O] God, [give] your protection against the fiery molten state of hell* (Bleddyn Fardd, 'Elegy for Dafydd ap Gruffudd ap Llywelyn', VII 52.1).

***Loving and Merciful God*: God as loving friend: 1. 14. 1** Caru Duw, diwelling ymddired, Cyrchaf Câr cerennydd afneued *[In order] to love God, it is generous to believe [in Him], I turn to a Friend of the fulness of reconciliation* (Gwalchmai ap Meilyr, 'Elegy for Madog ap Maredudd', I 7.1–2); **1. 14. 2** Duw a brŷn yn brifgar *God redeems him as a best friend* (Cynddelw, 'Ode to God', IV 16.12); **1. 14. 3** Carws Duw dy fod, fydohen—Gymro *God loved your being, a Welshman seeking out all the world* (Llywarch ap Llywelyn, 'In Praise of Gruffudd ap Cynan of Gwynedd', V 10.81); **1. 14. 4** A'th garo, ddewr, Dduw dy Dad! *May God, your Father, love you, brave warrior!* (ib. 100).

God of mercy: 1. 14. 5 A'm bo i gan Dduw, a'm bo—trugaredd *May I receive from God, may I receive mercy* (Meilyr ap Gwalchmai, 'Ode to God', I 30.1); **1. 14. 6** Ac ef a'n gwrthfyn wrth nad ofnawg Ar drugaredd Duw, ar Drugarawg *And he will welcome us, since he is not afraid, To God's mercy, to the merciful One* (Gwynfardd Brycheiniog, 'Song to St David' II 26.39–40); **1. 14. 7** Caffael trugaredd trugarawg—Arglwydd, Trugar Dduw hywydd, rhwydd, rhinweddawg *[May you] have the mercy of the merciful Lord, The compassionate God, ready, generous, virtuous* (Llywarch ap Llywelyn, 'In Praise of Llywelyn ab Iorwerth', V 24.73–4); **1. 14. 8** A Duw, 'n ein diwedd-ni, gwaredd gwirion *And God, at our end, [You are] clemency for the innocent* (Anon., 'In Praise of Llywelyn ab Iorwerth', VI 19.33); **1. 14. 9** Ac yn y gorffen (gorffawg—anrhydedd) Trugaredd gan Dduw trugarawg! *And in the end (honour to one of great stature) Mercy from the merciful God!* (Llygad Gŵr, 'In Praise of Llywelyn ap Gruffudd ap

Madog', VII 28.27–8); **1. 14. 10** Gan Dduw ni cheffir dim cywira, Eithr gwirionedd a gwâr dangnefedd A gwir drugaredd, fal y gwedda *[That] on God's part there will be no arguing, Rather, truth and gentle peace And genuine mercy, as is fitting* (Gruffudd ab yr Ynad Coch, 'Ode to God', VII 42.10–12).

God as refuge: 1. 14. 11 Duw, dy nawdd, na'm cawdd i'm camwedd! *Lord, [extend] your protection, do not punish me in my sin!* (Cynddelw, 'Poem to St Tysilio', III 3.2).

Mercy implied: 1. 14. 12 Ystyriwn, cwynwn cedwyr arfoll—naf Ni ad Duw yng nghyfrgoll *Let us consider, let us mourn for a lord who was wont to receive warriors Whom God will not let suffer perdition* (Gruffudd ap Gwrgenau, 'Quatrains to his Friends', II 32.5–6); **1. 14. 13** Golwg Duw arnaw a ddodir, A fo gwan wrth wan, wrth iawnwir *God's [affectionate] gaze will be bestowed upon him, Who is meek towards the meek, towards the faithful and just* (Cynddelw, 'Poem to St Tysilio', III 3.104–5); **1. 14. 14** Gan faddau o Dduw ei ddodi—yng nghrogwedd *Since God has forgiven his being put upon the cross* (Hywel ap Griffri, 'Request for the liberation of Owain ap Gruffudd', VII 23.29).

***God the Giver*: Benevolence of God: 1. 15. 1** Ni'm hethremyg Duw â digfryd oseb *God will not belittle me with a gift of angry intent* (Gwalchmai ap Meilyr, 'Gwalchmai's Dream', I 12.11); **1. 15. 2** Duw Dofydd, Rheg-ofydd rheithlau *[O] Lord God, [the] Giver of enlightened law* (Einion ap Gwalchmai, 'Ode to God', I 27.8); **1. 15. 3** Duw gwerthfawr, Gwerth-efin gwyniaith *God of great benefit, [One who is] the height of marvel* (Seisyll Bryffwrch, 'Elegy for Owain Gwynedd', II 22.3); **1. 15. 4** Ni bo cyfyng Duw i'm cyfedd *Let God not be tight-fisted towards my companion* (Gruffudd ap Gwrgenau, 'Elegy for Gruffudd ap Cynan', II 31. 47); **1. 15. 5** Can Dduw Rhên, yn rhan westifiant Can ddiwedd pob buchedd, bych sant *Through the bestowal of the Lord God, in a region of joy At the end of every life, may you be a saint* (Llywarch ap Llywelyn, 'In Praise of Llywelyn ab Iorwerth', V 23.207–8).

Dawn: 1. 15. 6 Aswynaf nawdd Duw (diamau—dy ddawn) *I beg God's protection (unquestionable is your gift)* (Cynddelw, 'Appeasement of the Lord Rhys', IV 10.1); **1. 15. 7** Can rhydd Duw Ddofydd ddawn ehelaeth *Since the Lord God bestows bounty in abundance* (Id., 'Ode to God', IV 17.97); **1. 15. 8** Difreinaw dawn Duw, nid dyn a'i medd *Man cannot dishonour a gift of God* (Phylip Brydydd, 'Second Ode of Contention in the presence of Rhys Ieuanc', VI 15.16); **1. 15. 9** Cedawl Dduw, Ei ddawn a iolir *Generous God, His favour is requested* (Dafydd Benfras, 'Elegy for Gruffudd ab Ednyfed', VI 33.42).

Rhoddi: 1. 15. 10 Duw Rhoddiad a'm rhydd cyngweiniant *God-Gift-giver who gives me remorse of conscience* (Meilyr ap Gwalchmai, 'Ode to God' I 31.2); **1. 15. 11** Rhoddes Duw Dofydd, defnydd—o'i foli, Dewi ar Frefi, fryn llewenydd *The Lord God placed, [this is] cause for praising him, [Saint] David on Brefi, hill of happiness* (Gwynfardd Brycheiniog, 'Song to St David' II 26.108–9); **1. 15. 12** Dawn cyflawn cywlad ormes, Dafydd, Duw it a'i rhoddes. **1. 15. 13** Rhoddes Duw dri dawn i drinwychydd—naf *A complete gift [to be the] oppression of [your] enemy, Dafydd, God gave it to you. God gave three gifts to the lord brave in battle* (Gwilym Rhyfel, 'Appeasement of Dafydd ab Owain', II 28.7–9); **1. 15. 14** Ni wnaeth Duw fwlch ar falch naf ... **1. 15. 15** Yn rhodd Duw a'i ganiad *God did not put a defect on the splendid lord ... Through God's gift and consent* (Cynddelw, 'In Praise of Llewelyn ab Iorwerth', IV 13.4–6); **1. 15. 16** Duw Rheen dy-m-rhydd gymwynas *The Lord God will give me a gift* (Llywarch ap Llywelyn, 'In Praise of Llewelyn ab Iorwerth', V 18.1); **1. 15. 17** Dawn i'm rhwyf, Duw a'i rhoddes. **1. 15. 18** Rhoddes Duw i'm llyw llafn waedlif—ysgwr *God gave power to my chieftain. God gave to my ruler of the bloodstained spear* (Einion Wan, 'In Praise of Madog ap Gruffudd', VI 2.12–13); **1. 15. 19** Ni ddwg Duw y dawn a roddo! *God does not take back the gift He may give!* (Llygad Gŵr, 'Ode to Gruffudd ap Madog', VII 25.84).

Rhannu: 1. 15. 20 Fy Nuw, fy neirthiad, fad rad rannu *My God, my support, [One who] distributes a good gift* (Gwynfardd Brycheiniog, 'In Praise of the Lord Rhys', II 25.1); **1. 15. 21** Hanbych well, Ddafydd, ddawn gaffael—fal Turn Teÿrnged o'r Israel, O Dduw, ddeon archafael *Let there be prosperity for you, Dafydd, with the gift to receive like Turn Tribute like that of Israel, From God who exalts noblemen* (Gwilym Rhyfel, 'Quatrains to Dafydd ab Owain', II 27.1–3); **1. 15. 22** Rhannws Duw Ddews ddonion—anghymwys, Anghymes i'i feibion *The Lord shared various gifts, Innumerable to his sons* (Llywarch ap Llywelyn, 'In Praise of Rhodri ab Owain Gwynedd', V 4.15–16); **1. 15. 23** Neud Duw a'i rhannws yr hael reiniad *God gave the generous giver* (Dafydd Benfras, 'Elegy for Dafydd ap Llywelyn', VI 30.32).

***God of Joy*: 1. 16. 1** Dduw a Mair, a chwair in chwerthin (Chwerddyd bryd!) o bryder chwefrin? *O God and Mary, will laughter come to us (The mind rejoices!) from wild anxieties?* (Elidir Sais, 'Appeasement of Llywelyn ab Iorwerth', I 17.10–11); **1. 16. 2** Llawen Duw Ddofydd ddydd yd gaffad—Cadfan *Joyful was the Lord God on the day Cadfan was begotten* (Llywelyn Fardd (I), 'Song to Cadfan', II 1.107); **1. 16. 3** Bwyf gwas Duw, gwesti dialar *Let me be a servant of God, the blessed and joyful sustainer* (Cynddelw, 'Ode to God', IV 16.24).

God the Miracle-worker: 1. 17. 1 Trugaredd a'th fo o'th feinin—gaerwedd O garu Duw Ddewin! *May you have mercy in your stone fortress Through loving God [the] Miracle-worker!* (Elidir Sais, 'Appeasement of Llywelyn ab Iorwerth', I 17.30–1); **1. 17. 2** Duw, Dewin gwerthefin gwyrthau *[O] God, supreme Wonder-worker of miracles* (Einion ap Gwalchmai, 'Ode to God', I 27.1); **1. 17. 3** Gwerthefin Ddewin Dduw, i'm gwared *God most high, Miracle-worker, [is] my succour* (Llywelyn Fardd (I), 'Song to Cadfan', II 1.1); **1. 17. 4** Gwyrthau Duw a ddangosan *They will show the marvels of God* (*Id.*, 'Signs before Judgement Day', II 5.39); **1. 17. 5** Ponid gwan truan trymder—pechadur, … Na chred i Dduw, ddewin ffyddlonder *Is not the sinner's burden unfortunate and wretched, … That [he] believes not in God, prophet of faithfulness* (Gruffudd ab yr Ynad Coch, 'Ode to God', VII 38.1, 6).

The Rewarding God: 1. 18. 1 Cadwn fraint dewaint, can ys defawd; Duw Nêr ni gymer gam esgusawd *Let us uphold the midnight [service] prerogative, for it is the custom; The Lord God will not accept a false excuse* (Einion ap Gwalchmai, 'Ode to God', I 28.39–40); **1. 18. 2** Cymerawd ein Duw ein dihewyd Canys Ef a'n gorug ac a'n gweryd *God will accept our longing For it is He who made us and will save us* (Meilyr ap Gwalchmai, 'Ode to God', I 33.78–9); **1. 18. 3** Urddws Duw diwyrnawd Owain *God honoured steadfast Owain* (Cynddelw, 'Elegy for Owain Gwynedd', IV 4.95); **1. 18. 4** Duw a'm rhydd, o'm rheiddun ofan, Rhwydd obaith o waith y winllan *God will give me, because of my gift of craftsmanship, Great confidence from labour in the vineyard* (*Id.*, 'Ode to God', IV 16.221–2); **1. 18. 5** A minnau, magator o'm dlid Bodd i Dduw a bod yng ngleindid *And as for me, there is won on account of my endowment [as a poet] The benevolence of God and a dwelling in sanctity* (Llywarch ap Llywelyn, 'Threat to Gruffudd ap Cynan', V 8.43–4); **1. 18. 6** Caniad Duw, ys diau ei fod I'th gannerth cyn darmerth darfod *The consent of God, certainly it is A help to you before preparing yourself for death* (*Id.*, 'In Praise of Rhys Gryg of Deheubarth', V 26.139–40).

God the Saviour: 1. 19. 1 Duw a glyw fy llef i'm llugfrydiau. **1. 19. 2** Duw a'm gwnêl gochel ffrawdd oerfel ffrau Ffrwd uffern astrus, ffrawdd-us ffrydiau *God will hear my cry in my anxieties. May God ordain that I avoid the fierceness of the current's chill Of the flood of wicked hell, ferocious torrents* (Einion ap Gwalchmai, 'Ode to God', I 27.20–2); **1. 19. 3** Duw brein-iawg a brynwys Ei garant O'r poenau a'r pechawd a wnaethant *Privileged God who ransomed His friends From the pains and the sin they had committed* (Meilyr ap Gwalchmai, 'Ode to God', I 31.5–6); **1. 19. 4** Duw a'm dwg i'm dogn anrhydedd I'w wenwlad, i'w rad, i'w riedd *God will bring me to my share of honour To His blessed land, to His blessing, to His glory* (Cynddelw, 'Poem to St Tysilio', III 3.5–6); **1. 19. 5** Cyfoeth Duw a'n dug yng ngwynfyd *God's power brought us to happiness* (*ib.* 3.178); **1. 19. 6** Can gorau ein Duw ein datbrwy Trwy gethrau a chrau a chymwy *Since our God has purchased us With nails and blood and suffering* (*Id.*, 'Ode to God', IV 16.181–2); **1. 19. 7** Gogwn Dduw, pryffwn y proffwydi, Nad adwg o'i ddawn ei ddaioni *I know that God, chief of the prophets, Will not withdraw His goodness [to me] because of His grace* (Llywarch ap Llywelyn, 'Threat to Dafydd ab Owain', V 2.47–8); **1. 19. 8** Milfeirdd mawrfrydig, rhyddanfones—Duw Dyn ym myd a'n gwares *[You] a thousand excellent poets, God sent a Man to this world who redeemed us* (*Id.*, 'In Praise of Rhodri ab Owain Gwynedd', V 5.63–4); **1. 19. 9** Rhybo Duw rhebydd ddadwyrain *Let God be the restoration of the lord* (Llywelyn Fardd (II), 'To Owain ap Gruffudd ap Gwenwynwyn', VI 8.37); **1. 19. 10** Mal gwirion, gwared, Dduw, fi *As an innocent one, save me, O God* (Phylip Brydydd, 'Appeasement of Rhys Gryg', VI 12.12); **1. 19. 11** Nawdd y Grog ddeau, ddonion ddanfon, A gymeraist, Dduw, er Dy ddynion *[The] protection of the auspicious cross sending forth blessings Which You have undertaken [O] God, for the sake of Your people* (Gruffudd ab yr Ynad Coch, 'Ode to God', VII 39.5–6).

Will of God: **Mynnu** to will to wish: **1. 20. 1** Ar a fynnwy Duw, nid egrygi—iddaw Arfeiddaw treiddaw trag Eryri *The one whom God wishes, it is not vanity for him To venture to cross Snowdonia* (Llywelyn Fardd (I), 'Song to Cadfan', II 1.133–4); **1. 20. 2** A fyn Duw, dybydd byth wy foli *Whatever God ordains, will always come to praise Him* (Gwynfardd Brycheiniog, 'Song to St David', II 26.194); **1. 20. 3** A Duw a'i mynnwys, Mynyw i Ddewi *And God insisted that Menevia should be [Saint] David's* (*ib.* 242); **1. 20. 4** Wrth fy Nuw, na fyn fy niddawl *Towards my God, who does not wish to see me impoverished* (Llywarch ap Llywelyn, 'In Praise of Dafydd ab Owain Gwynedd', V 1.155); **1. 20. 5** Wrth a fynno Duw, dim ni ellir *Against what God wishes, nothing can be done* (Dafydd Benfras, 'Elegy for Gruffudd ab Ednyfed', VI 33.4).

Bodd Duw: 1. 20. 6 Can fodd Duw yd fu'n ei ddilen, Tud wledig, elwig elfydden *According to God's pleasure was he in his withdrawal, Ruler of a region [with its] rich land* (Cynddelw, 'Poem to St Tysilio', III 3.135); **1. 20. 7** Gŵr a wnaeth o'r dwfr y gwin, Gan fodd Duw, a diwedd gwirin *He who made the wine from the water, According to God's will, and a holy end* (Dafydd Benfras, 'To Llywelyn ab Iorwerth', VI 25.42–3); **1. 20. 8** Gan faddau o Dduw ei ddodi—yng nghrogwedd Gan fyned i'r bedd, bu bodd Celi *Since God forgave [the act of] putting Him upon the cross And going to the grave, it was the will of God* (Hywel Foel ap Griffri, 'Request for the liberation of Owain ap Gruffudd', VII 23.29–30).

Llunio to devise, plan, intend: **1. 20. 9** Fal wrth Dduw ei hun yd lunied *As though it had been fashioned according to [the plan of] God Himself* (Llywelyn Fardd (I), 'Song to Cadfan', II 1.36); **1. 20. 10** Duw ei hun yn ei luniaw *God himself planning it* (*Id.*, 'Signs before Judgement Day', II 5.30).

Miscellaneous examples of God's will: 1. 20. 11 Iawn i Dduw ddifanw eu rheuedd *Right it is for God to depreciate their wealth* (Cynddelw, 'Poem to St Tysilio', III 3.34); **1. 20. 12** Delw yd orau Duw ei ddewisaw, **1. 20. 13** Dewised ei Dduw ei ddwyn ataw *Just as God chose him, So let his God choose to take him to Himself* (*Id.*, 'Elegy for Rhirid Flaidd and his brother Arthen', III 24.89–90); **1. 20. 14** A bid Duw yn ganiad *And may God be [the One to grant] permission* (Llywarch ap Llywelyn, 'Elegy for Hywel ap Gruffudd of Merioneth', V 13.6); **1. 20. 15** Nid adwna Duw a wnêl *God will not undo that which He may ordain* (ib. 22); **1. 20. 16** Nog a adwys Duw, yn y dognir—ced Haelfab Ednyfed, neb ni edir *[No more] than what God permitted, where is distributed the gift Of the generous son of Ednyfed, no one will be allowed to remain* (Dafydd Benfras, 'Elegy for Gruffudd ab Ednyfed', VI 33.29–30).

God Source of Inspiration: Awen: 1. 21. 1 Dëws Reen, ry-m-aw-i awen (amen, ffiad) *Lord God, grant me inspiration (amen, so be it)* (Anon., 'In Praise of Cuhelyn Fardd', I 2.1); **1. 21. 2** Duw Ddofydd dy-m-rhydd rheiddun awen—bêr *The Lord God shall give to me a gift of sweet inspiration* (Llywarch ap Llywelyn, 'In Praise of Gruffudd ap Cynan of Gwynedd', V 10.1).

Dawn: 1. 21. 3 Ac i Dduw o'i ddawn ydd archaf arch iawn, Awdl ffrwythlawn ffrwyth gymwyn *I make fair petition to God in His grace [for] A powerful ode rich in its effect* (Gwalchmai ap Meilyr, 'Elegy for Madog ap Maredudd', I 7.31–2); **1. 21. 4** Traethaf ohonaw, honnaid farchawg, Tra ym donnwy Duw dawn ardderchawg *I shall sing about him, a famous knight, As long as God may endow me with an excellent gift* (*Id.*, 'In Praise of Rhodri ab Owain', I 11.46–7); **1. 21. 5** Cyfarchaf i Dduw cyfarch-ddawn—foliant I filoedd enwogawn *I beseech God for a eulogy with an intercessory talent On behalf of [the] splendid hosts* (Cynddelw, 'To the Retinues of Powys', III 10.21–2); **1. 21. 6** Cadair bair beryf, caniad Duw gennyf Cadr ddeisyf heb ddisudd Dawn cyflawn, digawn, digyfludd, Digardd gerdd i ged ddiorchudd *Lord who is chief of the assembly, let me have the permission of God [To present] a strong petition without constraint [For] a perfect gift, unstinted, [coming] without impediment, A faultless poem for [one] of known beneficence* (*Id.*, 'Song to Hywel ab Owain Gwynedd', IV 6.1–4); **1. 21. 7** O brydest, o ddyllest a ddulliaf, O ddawn Duw can doddyw ataf *In poetry, in the manner in which I shall organize it, Through the gift of God because of its coming to me* (ib. 286–7); **1. 21. 8** Cyfarchaf i Dduw, o'i ddawn—huanaidd *I pray to God in virtue of His* *brilliant power* (Llywarch ap Llywelyn, 'Ode to Llywelyn ab Iorwerth', V 17.1).

Rhoddi: 1. 21. 9 Duw ry-m-rhoddwy, rheiddun arlwy, erlid cyngor Rhodd fodd fedru, rhif brif brydu, brydest ragor *May God, gift-giver, grant that I follow advice To grasp the gift [which gives] satisfaction, [that is] composing an excellent poem with the utmost excellence* (Gwynfardd Brycheiniog, 'Song to the Lord Rhys', II 24.1–2).

Parablu 'to speak', **prifiaith** 'fine language', **ceinfolawd** 'excellent paean': **1. 21. 10** Ar Dduw fy enaid, cyfraid cyfrau, Eiriolwch, sefwch yn eich swyddau! *To [the] God of my soul, [in] need of speech, Make a request, do your share!* (Einion ap Gwalchmai, 'Ode to God', I 27.97–8); **1. 21. 11** Pâr im, Dduw, parablu ohonawd *Grant me, O God, to speak of You (Id., 'Ode to God', I 28.2); **1. 21. 12** Duw Drindawd, bwyf priawd prifiaith *God [who is] Trinity, may I be the possessor of fine language* (Seisyll Bryffwrch, 'Elegy for Owain Gwynedd', II 22.4); **1. 21. 13** Cyfarchaf-i, Dduw, cyfarchaf,—ceinfolawd Ar draethawd a draethaf *I beseech, O God, I beseech, an excellent paean I shall intone in verse* (Cynddelw, 'Deathbed Poem', IV 18.15–16); **1. 21. 14** Cyfarchaf i Dduw o ddechrau—moliant, Mal y gallwyf orau Clodfori ... *I shall first ask for praise to God, So that I may best Extol ...* (Llygad Gŵr, 'In Praise of Llywelyn ap Gruffudd', VII 24.121–3).

Response in prayer: **Poet prays on behalf of a living patron: 1. 22. 1** Duw yn gymorth, yn nerth, yn borth, yn ganhorthwy *Let God be a succour, a strength, a support, a help* (Anon., 'In Praise of Hywel ap Goronwy', I 1.1); **1. 22. 2** Duw ganddudd, eu budd parth ag atan! *God be with them, let their benefit be [directed] towards us!* (Llywelyn Fardd (I), 'Song to Cadfan', II 1.168); **1. 22. 3** Bodd Duw a gaffwy a goffaaf *I will commemorate whomsoever may receive God's favour* (Id., 'In Praise of Owain Gwynedd', II 2. 26; **1. 22. 4** As dewiso Duw y diweiriaf—o'r gwŷr *Let God choose the most faithful of men* (ib. 51); **1. 22. 5** Galwaf-i Dduw Arglwydd am arglais—Owain *I call upon God concerning the anger of Owain* (Id., 'Appeasement of Owain Fychan', II 3.21); **1. 22. 6** Nawdd Duw yn awch cylch, calchdöed—Owain *God's protection all around you, [men of] Owain clad in coloured armour* (ib. 53); **1. 22. 7** Dos, a Duw gennyd, yn hyfryd,—yn hawdd *Go, and God be with you pleasantly, with ease* (Llywarch Llaety, 'In Praise of Llywelyn ap Madog', II 16.57); **1. 22. 8** Arglwydd Dduw, heddiw boed hawddamor—llary *Lord God, today let the generous one have good fortune* (Cynddelw, 'Exaltation of Owain Gwynedd', IV 2.39); **1. 22. 9** Cedwid Duw, a'n cedwis heb wad, Cadr heddwch hyddyn am winllad *May God, who protected us without doubt, protect The fair peace of a person ready with a gift of wine* (Llywarch ap Llywelyn, 'In Praise of Dafydd ab Owain Gwynedd', V 1.33–4); **1. 22.**

10 Glyned Duw Trined i'm trugarddawn—fi O fawrnen Merfyniawn *Let the Triune God abide with my merciful gift-giver who will be Of the great lord of the stock of Merfyn* (*Id.*, 'In Praise of Gruffudd ap Cynan of Gwynedd', V 10.53–4; **1. 22. 11** Doeth ateb, Duw a'th atwy Tair oes byd hefyd yn hwy *[The one] of wise answer, may God permit you to remain For three ages of the world and also longer [than that]* (*Id.*, 'Ode to Llywelyn ab Iorwerth', V 22.35–6); **1. 22. 12** Can cymeri, Dduw, ddifwyn ynni—dyn, Cymer Lywelyn, lyw cadeithi *O God, since you accept man's unprofitable energy, Accept Llywelyn, the war leader* (*Id.*, 'Ode to Llywelyn ab Iorwerth', V 25.57–8); **1. 22. 13** Am unig treisig y trawsiolaf—Dduw A ddigawn iach o glaf *On behalf of a masterly hero I pray earnestly to God Who can make of a sick man a healthy one* (*Id.*, 'Request for the recovery of Madog ap Gruffudd Maelor', V 27.1–2); **1. 22. 14** Cadw, Dduw, Lywelyn lyw ongyr—aelaw, Ei alon niw hesgyr *O God, defend Llywelyn, ruler of frequent spear strikes, His enemies cannot rid themselves of him* (Einion Wan, 'Ode to Llywelyn ab Iorwerth', VI 1.5–6).

Blessings: 1. 22. 15 Ys bendico Duw ddwywawl weinydd *Let God bless the godly servant* (Llywelyn Fardd (I), 'Song to Cadfan', II 1.40); **1. 22. 16** Bendith Dduw gennwch, gynreinion! *May God's blessing be with you, princes!* (Cynddelw, 'To the Retinues of Powys', III 10.11).

Sefyll: 1. 22. 17 Wedi Cedifor cadfarchawg—a saif, Sefid Duw gan Fadawg *After Cedifor the warrior still stands, May God support Madog* (Llywelyn Fardd (I), 'Elegy for Cedifor ap Genillyn', II 4.25–6); **1 22. 18** Ysef a'u herly, arlwy garthan—ddyn, Dra safo Duw ganthaw *That man is an amazingly strong supporter, As long as God supports him* (Llywarch Llaety, 'In Praise of Llywelyn ap Madog', II 16.45–6).

Ejaculations: 1. 22. 19 Erglyw, O Dduw, fy ngweddi *Hear, O God, my prayer* (Gwalchmai ap Meilyr, 'In Praise of Dafydd ab Owain', I 10.4); **1. 22. 20** I Dduw uchaf erchi *To the most high God I make intercession* (*ib.* 37); **1. 22. 21** Duw a'm dwg yno, anaw dremyn *May God bring me there on a profitable journey* (*Id.*, 'Ode to God', I 14.71); **1. 22. 22** I gan Dduw gogoned! *From God [may you] have glory!* (Llygad Gŵr, 'Ode to Gruffudd ap Madog', VII 25.32).

Help of God's special friends: 1. 22. 23 Porthwyr Duw, poed wynt fy ngheraint! *Let God's assistants be friends to me!* (Cynddelw, 'Poem to St Tysilio', III 3.74); **1. 22. 24** Bernid Duw ein dwyn i wenblaid *May God decree that we be brought to the blessed host* (Cynddelw, 'Ode to God', IV 16.153).

Conversion: 1. 22. 25 Duw a'm gwnêl o'm gwaith golaith gwelïau *May God arrange that I because of my own effort avoid wounds* (Einion ap Gwalchmai, 'Ode to God', I 27.23); **1. 22. 26** Duw a'm gwnêl goglyd selwyd Suliau *May God see that I eschew the foul sin of [desecrating] Sundays* (*Id.*, 'Ode to God', I 27.24); **1. 22. 27** Duw a'm differo o'm daffarau *May God defend me from my intentions* (*Id.*, 'Ode to God', I 27.25); **1. 22. 28** Duw, dwg fi atad, y Mawrdad mau! *[O] God, bring me unto You, my Great Father!* (*Id.*, 'Ode to God', I 27.26); **1. 22. 29** Bodd Duw a haeddwyf, Rhwyf a'm rhifo *Let me please God, may the Lord deem me worthy* (Meilyr ap Gwalchmai, 'Ode to God', I 30.5); **1. 22. 30** Ni rygollwyf Dduw o ddewredd byd *Let me not lose [sight of] God because of the splendour of the world* (Cynddelw, 'Ode to God', IV 17.61); **1. 22. 31** Bwyf gwas Duw cyn gwesti daear *May I be a servant of God before [entering] a habitation in [the] earth* (Llywelyn Fardd (II), 'Ode to God', VI 9.16); **1. 22. 32** A! Duw a'm troswy o'm trasalwder—ataw *O may it be God who may turn me from my wickedness towards Him* (*Id.*, 'Ode to God', VI 10.1).

Special favours: 1. 22. 33 Boed canhorthwy Duw im ddyhudded—anian *Let God's assistance be to me fulfilment [to my] nature* (Llywelyn Fardd (I) 'Song to Cadfan', II 1.15); **1. 22. 34** Can Dduw ni bo cwyn ddielw Cuddfedd, ceinddiwedd Cynddelw *With God let it not be [an occasion of] unprofitable grief The secret grave, a happy end [for] Cynddelw* (Cynddelw, 'Elegy for Dygynnelw', III 30.11–12); **1. 22. 35** Archaf i Duw ddwy uned: Un ffydd â chrefydd, a chred *I ask God for two petitions: One faith with devotion, and belief* (Llywelyn Fardd (II), 'Ode to God', VI 10.95–6); **1. 22. 36** Rhag tri gelyn dyn, Duw, a'm noddych *From the three enemies of man, O God, defend me* (Madog ap Gwallter, 'Ode to God', VII 33.13).

Nawdd: 1. 22. 37 A'm dyfynno Duw i'm dyfynnu—nef Ar Ei nawdd a'i deulu *May God call me, to summon me to heaven Under His protection and that of His household* (Elidir Sais, 'Ode to God', I 21.41–2); **1. 22. 38** Yn olau ys bo fy anwylyd Ar nef, ar nawdd Duw a'i diffryd! *Light may my love be For heaven, for God's refuge and His protection!* (*Id.*, 'Ode to God', I 24.41–2); **1. 22. 39** Nawdd merthyri Duw, deon dragywydd *[The] protection of the martyrs of God, eternal [His] princes* (Gruffudd ab yr Ynad Coch, 'Ode to God', VII 39.27).

'God be with' prayers: 1. 22. 40 Duw gennyf, Duw, Peryf perffaith *Let God be with me, God, the perfect Lord* (Seisyll Bryffwrch, 'Elegy for Owain Gwynedd', II 22.1); **1. 22. 41** Eilyw a'm doddyw, Duw i'm gwared! *Grief has come to me, God deliver me!* (Cynddelw, 'Elegy for Cadwallon ap Madog ab Idnerth', III 21.146); **1. 22. 42** Ys bo Duw gydag ef! *Let God be with him!* (Einion Wan, 'Ode to Madog ap Gruffudd', VI 2.22); **1. 22. 43** Duw gennyf, gennyt-ti bwyf gydymddaith *May God be with me, may I be a companion to you* (Llywelyn Fardd (II), 'Ode to God', VI 10.59).

The poet prays for deceased patrons and others: 1. 22. 44 Go-gwypo ei Dduw o'i ddiweddawd *May God be mindful of his end* (Meilyr Brydydd, 'Elegy for Gruffudd ap Cynan', I 3.39); **1. 22. 45** Galwaf Dduw gan ddeifniawg adfar *I call upon God in sadness after [the death of] one qualified to rule* (Gwalchmai ap Meilyr, 'Elegy for Madog ap Maredudd', I 7.47); **1. 22. 46** Nis ddiddolwy Duw o'i deÿrnles *Let not God keep him from his kingly benefit* (Cynddelw, 'Elegy for Cadwallon ap Madog ab Idnerth', III 21.103); **1. 22. 47** Dëws dominws, Duw, boed gwirion! *Lord, God, O God, let him be without fault!* (ib. 209); **1. 22. 48** Dygen yw hebod bod byd, Dygynnelw, a Duw gennyd! *Painful it is that life goes on without you, Dygynnelw, and may God be with you!* (Id., 'Elegy for Dygyn-nelw', III 30.7–8); **1. 22. 49** As duch Duw yn ei dangnefedd *May God bring him to His peace* (Id., 'Elegy for Owain Gwynedd', IV 4.121); **1. 22. 50** A'th garo, ddewr, Dduw dy Dad! *O brave one, may God your Father love you!* (Llywarch ap Llywelyn, 'In Praise of Gruffudd ap Cynan of Gwynedd', V 10.100); **1. 22. 51** Boed i gyda'i Dduw fo ei ddiwedd *May his end be with his God* (Dafydd Benfras, 'Elegy for Dafydd ap Llywelyn', VI 30.92); **1. 22. 52** Llywiawdr braint y saint, synied wrthaw—Dduw *May God, guardian of the saints' privilege, take care of him* (Bleddyn Fardd, 'Elegy for Llewelyn ap Gruffudd', VII 51.33); **1. 22. 53** I Dduw ydd archaf, Naf, eu noddi *I ask God, [the] Lord, to protect them* (Id., 'Elegy for the three sons of Gruffudd ap Llywelyn', VII 54.37); **1. 22. 54** I Dduw ydd archaf (Naf ni'm ennyd) Llehäu Dafydd yn lle diwyd *I ask God (a Lord who will not refuse me) To place Dafydd in the dwelling of the faithful one* (Id., 'Elegy for Dafydd ap Gruffudd ab Owain', VII 55.25).

Response in Praise: **Prayers of praise: 1. 23. 1** Tra'm oedd o'm dawn Duw i'i gymwyll *While I might have God to praise with my talent* (Gwalchmai ap Meilyr, 'Ode to God', I 14.27); **1. 23. 2** Duw Arglwydd, erglyw Dy foliant *O Lord God, listen to Your praise* (Meilyr ap Gwalchmai, 'Ode to God', I 31.1); **1. 23. 3** Moladwy un Duw, un diffyniad—ysydd *Praiseworthy is the one God, the sole protector there is* (Llywelyn Fardd (I), 'Song to Cadfan', II 1.95); **1. 23. 4** Molaf Dduw uchaf, archaf weddi—iddaw *I praise God the most high, I present a petition to Him* (ib. 145); **1. 23. 5** Duw a folaf er eirioled—im *I shall praise God so that [He accepts] intercession on my behalf* (Gwynfardd Brycheiniog, 'Song to St David', II 26.196); **1. 23. 6** Molawd Duw, molaf a'i dywaid *Praise of God, I extol those who proclaim it* (Cynddelw, 'Ode to God', IV 16.118); **1. 23. 7** Canmil canmoles Duw hyn *A hundred thousand praised God for this* (Anon., 'In Praise of Llywelyn ab Iorwerth and his family', VI 20.76); **1. 23. 8** Neud i Dduw mal y dadferaf *It is [as] to God that I proclaim* (Dafydd Benfras, 'In Praise of Llewelyn ap Gruffudd', VI 34.18); **1. 23. 9** 'I Dduw *gloria, pax in terra* i'n terfynau, Heddwch i'r byd, iechyd i gyd gwedi angau' *'Glory to God, on earth peace to our boundaries. Peace to the* *world, complete salvation after death'* (Madog ap Gwallter, 'Ode to God', VII 32.27–8); **1. 23. 10** Ffrwyth angau Dofydd, Duw a folych *As a result of the Lord's death, praise God (Id.*, 'Ode to God', VII 33.44); **1. 23. 11** A'th folaf, Duw Naf, nefoedd lewych *I shall worship You, Lord God, light of heaven (ib.* 73).

Amendment of Life / Repentance: **Confession of guilt: 1. 24. 1** Digonais gerydd yng ngŵydd Duw Ddofydd *I have done wrong in the sight of the Lord God* (Meilyr Brydydd, 'Deathbed Poem', I 4.7); **1. 24. 2** Cyfarchaf i Dduw, ddwywawl weini, Cyfarchwel a ddêl i ddaeoni *I beseech God, [as] divine service, [For] conversion that will come to goodness* (Gwalchmai ap Meilyr, 'Ode to God', I 14.1–2); **1. 24. 3** A cymryd i gan Dduw ddiwynni *And obtaining from God the eradicating of lust (ib.* 11); **1. 24. 4** Cymryd oedd einym cymodlonedd—cwbl Cyn cablu o Dduw ar ein buchedd *Ours it was to accept complete reconciliation Before God found fault with our life* (Elidir Sais, 'Ode to God', I 23.27–8); **1. 24. 5** Duw a'm dwg o'm drwg i dramwy Ei dremyn, i dremid ofrwy *God will lead me from my evil ways to follow His way, to the beauty of [His] pathway* (Cynddelw, 'Ode to God', IV 16.163–4); **1. 24. 6** Dybwyf o'm camwedd, Duw a'm cymer *Let me come from my evil-doing, God will receive me* (Llywelyn Fardd (II), 'Ode to God', VI 10.54).

Recompense: 1. 24. 7 Ac ysim-i Dduw a ddiwycwyf—o'm drwg *And I have a God to whom I shall pay recompense for my evil* (Gwalchmai ap Meilyr, 'Ode to God', I 14.63); **1. 24. 8** I Dduw a Dewi y diwycwyf *Let me make amends to God and to [Saint] David* (Gwynfardd Brycheiniog, 'Song to St David', II 26.78); **1. 24. 9** Diwygaf, honnaf hynny, Difwyn a gymer Duw fry *I shall make atonement [for it], I proclaim that, God will receive recompense on high* (Phylip Brydydd, 'Appeasement of Rhys Gryg', VI 12.43–4).

Comments: 1. 24. 10 Cymhennaf yw in cymhennu—â Duw *Wisest it is for us to put things in order with God* (Elidir Sais, 'Ode to God', I 21.29); **1. 24. 11** Cymhennaf i ddyn cyn ei ddiwedd Cymodi â Duw cyn mud ym medd *It is wisest for man before his end To make peace with God before removing to a grave (Id.*, 'Ode to God', I 23.25–6).

Repentance: 1. 24. 12 Bwyf gwas Duw, cyn no'm gostegu *Let me be a servant of God, before being muted* (Elidir Sais, 'Ode to God', I 21.37); **1. 24. 13** Mynnid im gyreifiaint mwyniant creiriau—Duw / A diofryd arfau *Recourse to the treasures of God And the eschewing of arms will achieve my forgiveness* (Einion ap Gwalchmai, 'Ode to God', I 27.107–8); **1. 24. 14** Moch gwnelwyf, mal y gwna dedwydd, Mi â Duw diau gerennydd *Soon, as a blessed man does, may I make Certain peace between me and God* (Daniel ap Llosgwrn Mew, 'Elegy for Owain Gwynedd', II 18.28–9).

Forgiveness: 1. 24. 15 Archaf reg yn deg, a digerydd—wyf, I erchi i'm Rhwyf rhwydd gerennydd, I Dduw gysefin, ddewin Ddofydd *I ask rightly for a favour, and I am blameless, In interceding for ready forgiveness, To God first, foreseeing Lord* (Gwynfardd Brycheiniog, 'Song to St David', II 26.81–3).

Ejaculatory greetings: **Henbych well: 1. 25. 1** Hanbych well o Dduw ac o ddyn *May your state be better because of God and man* (Llywarch ap Llywelyn, 'Ode to Llywelyn ab Iorwerth', V 19.38); **1. 25. 2** Henbych well, O Dduw, od eddewy *Hail to Thee, O God, if you make a promise* (Dafydd Benfras, 'In Praise of Llywelyn ab Iorwerth', VI 26.1); **1. 25. 3** Hanbych well hyd bell, bwyll ardderchawg, O Dduw yn gyntaf naf niferawg *Hail to Thee for [a] long [time], one of excellent disposition, By God's will, the foremost lord with an army* (Llygad Gŵr, 'In Praise of Llywelyn ap Gruffudd ap Madog', VII 28.1–2).

Gwae: 1. 25. 4 Gwae a goddwy Duw dogn berthidau *Woe to the one who may anger God of the fullness of riches* (Meilyr ap Gwalchmai, 'Ode to God', I 33.38); **1. 25. 5** Gwae a goddwy Duw trwy syberwyd *Alas for those who may offend God through pride* (ib. 70); **1. 25. 6** Gwae fi, Arglwydd Dduw, am eurgledd—ddidaich! *Woe is me, Lord God, because of the warrior splendid his sword unyielding!* (Anon., 'Lament of the Pilgrim', VI 36.45).

Och: 1. 25. 7 Och, Dduw, na ddoddyw Dyddbrawd can deryw Derwyddon weinifiad *Alas, O God, that Judgement Day has not come since there has died The minister / provider of poets* (Gwalchmai ap Meilyr, 'Elegy for Madog ap Maredudd', I 7.81–2); **1. 25. 8** Och Dduw! na ddaw ef etwaeth *Alas, O God! that he will not come again* (Elidir Sais, 'Elegy for Rhodri ab Owain', I 15.26); **1. 25. 9** Ochaf-i, Dduw, o ddyfod ei laith *I sigh, O God, because of the coming of his death* (Daniel ap Llosgwrn Mew, 'Elegy for Owain Gwynedd', II 18.1); **1. 25. 10** Ochaf-i, Dduw, na ddaw ef eilwaith—ym myd *I sigh, O God, that he will not come to the world again* (ib. 3); **1. 25. 11** Och hyd atat-ti, Dduw, a ddodaf—yn dde O weled fy lle ar lledeithaf *O God I shall give a sigh earnestly unto you Seeing my place on the [exposed] outermost edge [of the battle array]* (Phylip Brydydd, 'Elegy for Rhys Ieuanc', VI 16.13); **1. 25. 12** Och, Dduw, o ddyfod ein harglwydd *Woe [to us, O] God for the taking away of our lord* (Dafydd Benfras, 'Elegy for Llywelyn ab Iorwerth', VI 27.34); **1. 25. 13** Och pa wneir? Och Feir! Och Fihangel! Och hyd atad, Duw, er dwyn Hywel! *Alas what will happen? Alas Mary! Alas Michael! Alas unto you, O God, for the snatching away of Hywel!* (Llygad Gŵr, 'Elegy for Hywel ap Madog', VII 27.47–8); **1. 25. 14** Och hyd atat Ti, Dduw, na ddaw—môr tros dir! *A sigh unto Thee, O God, that the sea does not cover the land!* (Gruffudd ab yr Ynad Coch, 'Elegy for Llywelyn ap Gruffudd', VII 36.71).

Miscellaneous References to God: **Religious and moral practice:**
1. 26. 1 Gwyn ei fyd paddiw, Duw, yd rangwy Rhieinged rhwych wyry
wared lywy *Blessed, O God, he to whom comes The girlish favour of the gift of
a maiden [whose] aid [is] lovely* (Gwalchmai ap Meilyr, '*Gorhoffedd*', I 9.31–
2); **1. 26. 2** A adwy Creawdr, mad y'i crewyd, I waddawl er Duw diawd
a bwyd *He was created blessedly whom the Creator allows To bestow food and
drink for God's sake* (*Id.*, 'Gwalchmai's Dream', I 12.23–4); **1. 26. 3**
Edifeiriawg da, Duw a'i ceinmyn *The good repentant man, God will honour
him* (*Id.*, 'Ode to God', I 14.79); **1. 26. 4** Edifeirawg da, Duw a'u
cymerawd *The good repentant ones, God will receive them* (Einion ap
Gwalchmai, 'Ode to God', I 28.11); **1. 26. 5** Rhoddwn fwyd er Duw, a
diawd—beri, Crist Eli Celi, can ufylltawd *Let us give food [as alms] and
provide drink for God's sake, Christ Lord and Master, with [submissive] humility*
(Einion ap Gwalchmai, 'Ode to God', I 28.23–4); **1. 26. 6** Caru Duw i
bawb oedd bybyriaf Mal câr y saint braint breinolaf *To love God would be
the finest thing for all As the saints most favoured in privilege love* (Meilyr ap
Gwalchmai, 'Ode to God', I 32.7–8); **1. 26. 7** Can ys caru Duw di-
adneiraf—gwaith, Eilwaith rhag cyfraith y'i cyfrifaf *For loving God is the
most perfect activity, Henceforth I shall consider it preferable to [the] law* (ib. 9–
10); **1. 26. 8** Creded bawb i Dduw, Ddewrnaf—gogoned *Let all believe in
God, strong Lord of glory* (ib. 25); **1. 26. 9** Credu i Dduw a'i ddawn, ys
cyfiawnaf *Trusting in God and His grace, it is most righteous* (ib. 34);
1. 26. 10 Ernywiant i ddyn ei ddigoni Ar Dduw yn gollwng gwall
fynechi *It is affliction for man that he has been created [As one] giving
inadequate service to God* (*Id.*, 'Ode to God', I 33.14–15); **1. 26. 11** Nis
ceryddo Duw nis ceryddaf *Whom God may not rebuke him I shall not rebuke*
(Llywelyn Fardd (I), 'Exaltation of Owain Gwynedd', II 2.18); **1. 26. 12**
Ef cymerth er Duw ddioddeifiaint—yn deg *He obediently accepted suffering
for God's sake* (Gwynfardd Brycheiniog, 'Song to St David', II 26.19); **1.
26. 13** A charu Duw yn drech na phenaethau *And loving God more than
chieftains* (ib. 265); **1. 26. 14** Can dalu i Dduw Ei ddylyed *Paying back to
God what is His due* (Cynddelw, 'Ode to God', IV 17.138); **1. 26. 15** A
roddo i Dduw ei ddegfed—o'i law *[And since I am one] who would give to
God a tithe [of wealth received] from His hand* (*Id.*, 'Deathbed Poem', IV
18.60); **1. 26. 16** Ni mad aned neb, ni mad aner, O edrych ar Dduw a
ddifarner *No one has been born fortunate, or will be born fortunate, Who is
deprived of the sight of God* (Llywelyn Fardd (II), 'Ode to God', VI 10.31–
2); **1. 26. 17** Gŵr oedd yn gallu ei ddifâedd (Ac eisoes, eisoes yn y
dygnedd Difreinaw dawn Duw, nid dyn a'i medd) *He was a man who
could have caused his destruction (And yet, even in the crisis Man cannot depreciate God's gift)* (Phylip Brydydd, 'Second Ode of Contention in the presence of Rhys Ieuanc', VI 15.14–16).

Exhortation: 1. 26. 18 I'r un Duw, un Dyn, na fid hydraeth—brad *To the one God, one Man, let treachery not be vocal* (Cynddelw, 'Ode to God', IV 17.107); **1. 26. 19** Rhy fychan i Dduw a ddiwygir *Too little satisfaction is made to God* (Dafydd Benfras, 'Elegy for Gruffudd ab Ednyfed', VI 33.6); **1. 26. 20–1** Ystyried, O Dduw, ddamwain dychryn—cun, Can nid byw Llywelyn, Athrist hiraeth gaeth golyn; Eithr o Dduw, aruthr i ddyn *Let [the miserable one], O God, consider the terrible misfortune of [the] leader Since Llywelyn does not live, Very sad is the inexorable stab of yearning, Except [that which comes] from God, terror [comes] to man* (Bleddyn Fardd, 'Elegy for Llywelyn ap Gruffudd', VII 51.25–8).

Exemplars of virtue: 1. 26. 22 Ac er Duw diofryd gwragedd *And for the sake of God renouncing women* (Cynddelw, 'Poem to St Tysilio', III 3.28); **1. 26. 23** Ef rhoddai i Dduw ei ddihewyd *He devoted his [whole] yearning to God* (Dafydd Benfras, 'Elegy for Llywelyn ab Iorwerth', VI 27.100); **1. 26. 24** Can mynnwys er Duw ddifröedd—arnaw *Since for the sake of God, he chose exile [for himself]* (Anon., 'Lament of the Pilgrim'. VI 36.33).

Moral questions: 1. 26. 25 Pam na châr mab dyn Dduw a'i geisiaw? *Why does the son of man not love God and seek Him?* (Dafydd Benfras, 'In Praise of God and Llywelyn ab Iorwerth', VI 24.49); **1. 26. 26** Pani credwch chwi i Dduw, ddyniaddon ynfyd? *Will you not believe in God, senseless men?* (Gruffudd ab yr Ynad Coch, 'Elegy for Llywelyn ap Gruffudd', VII 36.69).

References to the Word 'God': 1. 27. 1 Ac os Duw o nef neu ym cynnydd Ceinfod gan lywy imi, lawr, i'm hunydd! *And if the God from heaven gives me success [There will be] happiness with the fair maid for me, a champion, in my sleep!* (Gwalchmai ap Meilyr, 'Gorhoffedd', I 9.167–8); **1. 27. 2** Cennym can ein Duw, neud de, Cyfryw atreg cof atre *What we have from God is consuming, Of the same nature as grief is a living memory* (Id., 'Meditation on Life', I 13.5); **1. 27. 3** Cain fedydd fy Nuw yn niw Ystwyll *And the excelling baptism of my God on the Epiphany* (Id., 'Ode to God', I. 14.32); **1. 27. 4** Bardd fyddaf i Dduw hyd tra fwyf ddyn *I shall be a poet to God as long as I may live* (Elidir Sais, 'In Praise of God and Dafydd ab Owain', I 16.10); **1. 27. 5** (Llawer a wna Duw er dyniaddon) *(God accomplishes much on behalf of men)* (ib. 16); **1. 27. 6** A'u peirch Duw Dofydd uchben *God Lord above respects them* (Id., 'Elegy for Ednyfed Fychan and Tegwared ab Iarddur', I 18.32); **1. 27. 7** Teirffordd y deuant, etifedd,—ar Dduw Yn y dyfydd pawb i'r Frawd gyhedd *In three ways will they, the race, come to God When all shall come to the place of judgement* (Id., 'Ode to God', I 23.7–8); **1. 27. 8** Dyrwest Duw bu deugein pryd *[For] forty days was God's self-denial* (Id., 'Ode to God', I 24.8); **1. 27. 9** Ni bydd dda gan Dduw ei diddoli *God will not be pleased to deprive* *her* (Einion ap Gwalchmai, 'Elegy for Nest daughter of Hywel', I 26.57); **1. 27. 10** Duw gŵyl goludawg, golychwn Di *Rich and gracious God, we beseech You* (Meilyr ap Gwalchmai, 'Ode to God', I 33.6); **1. 27. 11** Morudd, meidrawl ei ddefawd O blegid Duw, a'i dywawd *Morudd, whose practice was powerful On God's behalf, it was [Morudd] who said it* (Llywelyn Fardd (I), 'Signs before Judgement Day', II 5.5–6); **1. 27. 12** Annerch, er Duw ac er dyn, I gan Lywarch, Lywelyn! *Greeting, for the sake of God and man, from Llywarch to Llywelyn!* (Llywarch Llaety, 'In Praise of Llywelyn ap Madog', II 16.63–4); **1. 27. 13** Annerch, er Duw ac er dyn, I gan Lywarch, Lywelyn! *Greeting, for the sake of God and man, from Llywarch to Llywelyn!* (Llywarch y Nam, 'To thank Llywelyn ap Madog for dogs', II 17.11); **1. 27. 14** A'r fagl aur ei phen, fföwch rhegddi Fal rhag tân, tost yd wân, tyst Duw iddi *And the gold-topped crozier, fly from it As before fire, painfully it pierces, God is witness to it* (Gwynfardd Brycheiniog, 'Song to St David', II 26.186–7); A'i fryn gwyn uchaf uchel beri, A llech deg dros waneg a thros weilgi **1. 27. 15** A'i dyddug, dybu Duw wrth ei throsi *And its highest blessed hill which he causes [to be] high / elevated, And a fine stone which over [the] wave and over [the] sea Brought him, God came to transfer it* (ib. 189–91); **1. 27. 16** Can ni allaf-i ddim heb Dduw Trined *Since I can do nothing without God of the Trinity* (ib. 197); **1. 27. 17** Duw dinag, dinas tangnefedd *Generous God, sanctuary of peace* (Cynddelw, 'Poem to St Tysilio', III 3.1); **1. 27. 18** Yn afrifaw Duw yn afrifed *To hold God in infinite contempt* (*Id.*, 'Ode to God', IV 17.134); **1. 27. 19** Hanbych well o Dduw, ddiechwraint—deÿrn, Teÿrnedd westifiaint *Greetings from God, king [Rhodri] without fault, [Provider of] hospitality for kings* (Llywarch ap Llywelyn, 'In Praise of Rhodri ab Owain Gwynedd', V 7.3–4); **1. 27. 20** Arglwydd Dduw, yn ddyn y'th enid *Lord God, you were born as a man* (*Id.*, 'Threat to Gruffudd ap Cynan', V 8.2); **1. 27. 21** Dygn ein symud, Duw, ein Tad—ysbrydol *God, our spiritual Father, harsh [is] our being moved* (Dafydd Benfras, 'Elegy for Dafydd ap Llywelyn', VI 30.1); **1. 27. 22** Duw a'm gwnaeth hiraeth hir ofalon Dyfod corff Gruffudd, mwynfudd maon *God caused me long afflictions of longing [Because] the corpse of Gruffudd, fine treasure of [his] people, has come* (*Id.*, 'Elegy for Llywelyn ab Iorwerth, Gruffudd ap Llywelyn and Dafydd ap Llywelyn', VI 31.28); **1. 27. 23** Dwyn gwawr trylwyn, trwy hiraeth, Duw fry, dewr Frenin, a'i gwnaeth *Taking the skilful lord, causing yearning, God on high, [the] valiant King, did it* (Y Prydydd Bychan, 'Elegy for Blegywryd', VII 20.15–16); **1. 27. 24** Dduw, yn ddyn, a'r Duw yn ddyn yn un ddoniau *As God, as man, and the God [a] man, of the same endowments* (Madog ap Gwallter, 'Ode to God', VII 32.8); **1. 27. 25** I Dduw'n gyntaf y cyfarchaf, bennaf biau Nef a daear, a gwyllt a gwâr, Gwawr ysbrydiau *I greet God first, the Most High One who owns Heaven and earth, and [animals] wild and tame, Lord of spirits* (Gruffudd ab yr Ynad

Coch, 'Ode to God', VII 41.1–2); **1. 27. 26** Eithr Un Mab Mair, mawr lias Duw nef, dyn mal ef ni las *Except the Only Son of Mary, great death Of [the] God of heaven, no one like him was killed* (Bleddyn Fardd, 'Elegy for Llywelyn ap Gruffudd', VII 51.3–4).

Un Duw One God: **1. 28. 1** Un Duw ŷnt wyntau a diau dri *They are One God and truly Three* (Gwalchmai ap Meilyr, 'Ode to God', I 14.24); **1. 28. 2** Un Duw mawr o'r llawr, llwrw fy nghofion, Lleha-Di fi, fy Rhi, rhwng engylion *The One great God of the world, according to my thoughts, Mayest Thou place me, my King, among [the] angels* (Anon., 'To Llywelyn ab Iorwerth', VI 19.1).

Deus Dëws God: **1. 29. 1** Dëws Reen, ry-m-aw-i awen (amen, ffiad) *Lord God, grant me inspiration (Amen, so be it)* (Anon., 'In Praise of Cuhelyn Fardd', I 2.1); **1. 29. 2** Ystwyll ystyriws Dëws ddefnydd (Dirnad digymrad) gymryd bedydd *On the Epiphany the one of true essence of God considered (Unfailing comprehension) accepting baptism* (Gwalchmai ap Meilyr, 'Ode to God', I 14.33–4); **1. 29. 3** Bendigws Dëws dialaeth … Y pum torth a'r pysg, pasgaduriaeth—gwŷr *Blessed God blessed … The five loaves and fish, sustenance of warriors* (Elidir Sais, 'Elegy for Rhodri ab Owain', I 15.7); **1. 29. 4** Diwallus Dëus ni'm difanwo, Didwyll ei bwyll, a'i cyrbwyllo! *Let not the unfailing God scorn me, Without deceit is his thought, he who praises Him!* (Meilyr ap Gwalchmai, 'Ode to God', I 30.27–8); **1. 29. 5** Lluniwys i Ddëws ddewis edrydd—iddaw Pan ddoeth o Lydaw ar lydw bedydd *The Godhead prepared a choice habitation on his behalf When he came from Brittany [as leader] of a faithful host* (Llywelyn Fardd (I), 'Song to Cadfan', II 1. 37–8); **1. 29. 6** A gredws Duw, Dëws Ddofydd *Who believed in God, Lord [and] King* (Cynddelw, 'Poem to St Tysilio', III 3.198); **1. 29. 7** Dëws dominws, Duw, boed gwirion! *Lord God, O God, may [he] be without fault!* (Id., 'Elegy for Cadwallon ap Madog ab Idnerth', III 21.209); **1. 29. 8** Can cyrchws Dëws diardwy (Cyrch clodfawr am ddyrawr ddirwy) *Since God fetched the defenceless ones (Praiseworthy encounter sequel to bitter punishment)* (Id., 'Ode to God', IV 16.167–8); **1. 29. 9** Nid ef ym crëws Dëws difflais Er gwneuthur amhwyll, na thwyll, na thrais *The immutable God did not create me To accomplish inanity, deceit or violence* (Id., 'Deathbed Poem', IV 18.70–1); **1. 29. 10** Rhannws Duw Ddews ddoniau—anghymwys, Anghymes i'i feibion *The Lord God bestowed various gifts, Innumerable on His sons* (Llywarch ap Llywelyn, 'In Praise of Rhodri ab Owain', V 4.15–6); **1. 29. 11** Dëws yr Israel, dewis gyfaith *God of Israel, chosen race* (Llywelyn Fardd (II), 'Ode to God', VI 10.58); **1. 29. 12** Pan fynnws Dëws ddewis ardaith—arnaw *When God willed a chosen punishment for him* (ib. 69); **1. 29. 13** Ystyriwys Dëws ddawn iddaw *God arranged a gift for him* (Dafydd Benfras, 'In Praise of God and Llywelyn ab Iorwerth', VI 24.89); **1. 29. 14** Ystyriws Dëws dawn ity—er gaint *God gave consideration to [the] blessing which I have sung for you* (*Id.*, 'In Praise of Llywelyn ab Iorwerth', VI 26.45); **1. 29. 15** Ebrwyddws Dëws dawn i'm plegyd,—gŵr Goreang ei wryd *God hastened to bestow a gift to me, [that is] a man of Exceedingly great valour* (*Id.*, 'Elegy for Llywelyn ab Iorwerth', VI 27.47–8); **1. 29. 16** Dechreuws Dëws, hyd na'm dyhudd—dim *God has initiated [this] so that nothing comforts me* (*Id.*, 'Elegy for Gruffydd ap Llywelyn', VI 29.70); **1. 29. 17** Rhwyddhäws Dëws diofn rhagddaw *God made easy [the way] before the fearless one* (Llygad Gŵr, 'In Praise of Gruffudd ap Madog', VII 26.22); **1. 29.18** Nid oes, Frenin, Dëws domin, dimyn eisau *There is not, O King, Lord God, [the] least trace of defect* (Gruffudd ab yr Ynad Coch, 'Ode to God', VII 41.10).

Tad Father: **2. 1. 1** Hi yn Fam wy Thad, hi yn wyry heb wad *She the mother to her Father, she an undeniable virgin* (Gwalchmai ap Meilyr, 'Ode to God', I 14.41); **2. 1. 2** I'r Tad cyfarchaf (rhwyddaf fy Rhên) *I petition the Father (most generous [is] my King)* (Elidir Sais, 'In Praise of God and Dafydd ab Owain', I 16.1); **2. 1. 3** Difai Dad, rhag brad breuawl—gymhlegyd *Blameless Father, against the treachery of the mortal community* (*Id.*, 'Ode to God', I 20.5); **2. 1. 4** Tud Ysbryd ein Tad ysbrydawl *[In the] land of the Spirit of our spiritual Father* (*Id.*, 'Ode to God', I 22.26); **2. 1. 5** Duw Gwener, bu crai, bu creulyd Crog ein Tad: ein trais i gyd *Friday, it was harsh, bloody was The cross / crucifixion of our Father: our total oppression* (*Id.*, 'Ode to God', I 24.13–14); **2. 1. 6** Nid perthyn it, Tad mad, fy maddau *It does not belong to You, blessed Father, to put me one side* (Einion ap Gwalchmai, 'Ode to God', I 27.44); **2. 1. 7** Ef yw'r Tad, Ef yw'r mad mwyaf *He is the Father, He is the greatest good* (Meilyr ap Gwalchmai, 'Ode to God', I 32.19); **2. 1. 8** A'm heiriolwy Saint Esechïas Ar Fair fam ei Thad, ei theg urddas *May St Ezechias pray for me To Mary mother of her Father, her fine honour* (*Id.*, 'Ode to God', I 33.96–7); **2. 1. 9** I'r Mab rhad, i'r Tad teg hynafiaeth *To the blessed Son, to the Father of fine longevity* (Cynddelw, 'Ode to God', IV 17.108); **2. 1. 10** O ganiad y Tad tëyrneiddiaf *Through the consent of the most regal Father* (*Id.*, 'Deathbed Poem', IV 18.35); **2. 1. 11** Cyfarchaf, Dduw Naf, nefawl Dad—celi *I pray, O Lord God, heavenly Father from on high* (Llywarch ap Llywelyn, 'In Praise of Dafydd ab Owain Gwynedd', V 1.1); **2. 1. 12** Mab ein Tad, ein tud Rwyf hollawl, **2. 1. 13** Ac ein Taid ac ein Tad dwywawl *[The] Son of our Father, and our supreme Lord of [His] kingdom, Both our Ancestor and divine Father* (ib. 141–2); **2. 1. 14** A gaiff tud ein Tad ysbrydawl *[Those] who enjoy the land of the spiritual Father* (ib. 176); **2. 1. 15** A'th garo, ddewr, Dduw dy Dad! *O brave one, may God your Father love you!* (Llywarch ap Llywelyn, 'In Praise of Gruffudd ap Cynan of Gwynedd', V 10.100); **2. 1. 16** Ystyried Tad llwyrgred rhag llaw *Let the Father of complete faith consider him henceforth* (Dafydd Benfras, 'In Praise of God and Llywelyn ab Iorwerth', VI 24.90); **2 1. 17** Mawr y'th orug Duw Dad, Arglwydd fry

God the Father, Lord on high, has made you great (*Id.*, 'In Praise of Llywelyn ab Iorwerth', VI 26.7); **2. 1. 18** Dygn ein symud, Duw, ein Tad— ysbrydol *Worrying is our [being] changed, [O] God, our spiritual Father* (*Id.*, 'Elegy for Dafydd ap Llywelyn', VI 30.1); **2. 1. 19** Cyn bai Mab i'n Tad, rhad rhwy danwedd *Though He was Son of our Father, [of] blessing exceedingly fervent of its kind* (Anon., 'Lament of the Pilgrim', VI 36.15); **2. 1. 20** Cyfoethawg tlawd, a'n Tad a'n Brawd, awdur brodiau *[A Son] rich [yet] poor, our Father and our Brother, author of judgements* (Madog ap Gwallter, 'Birth of Jesus', VII 32.10); **2. 1. 21** Nawdd y Tad a'r Mab Rhad rhof a'm galon *[The] protection of the Father and the Son of Grace between me and my enemies* (Gruffudd ab yr Ynad Coch, 'Ode to God', VII 39.1); **2. 1. 22** Ydd archaf i'm Tad, Ysbryd a Mab Rhad Ran o'i wir gariad, fal y'm gorau *I pray to my Father, the Spirit and the Son of Grace [For] a share of His faithful love, as He created me* (*Id.*, 'Ode to God', VII 40.64–5); **2. 1. 23** Hardd Owain firain, fâr luchiaw—yng nghad, Haelfab rhad, ei Dad a'i dug ataw *Splendid fair Owain, terror-striking in battle, Generous [and] liberal son, his Father took him to Himself* (Bleddyn Fardd, 'Elegy for Owain Goch ap Gruffudd ap Llywelyn', VII 48.35–6); **2. 1. 24** Llehäu Dafydd yn lle diwyd, Lle mae'r Un a'r Tri trwy anwyl-yd—mad, Lle mae'r Mab a'r Tad a'r Teg Ysbryd *To Establish Dafydd in a place belonging to a faithful one Where are the One and the Three through good kind(ness), Where are the Son and the Father and the Holy Spirit* (*Id.*, 'Elegy for Dafydd ap Gruffudd ab Owain', VII 55.25–8); **2. 1. 25** Arglwydd Dad, na'm gad gyllestrigawl dân *Lord Father, do not allow me [to] go to the fierce fire* (*Id.*, 'Deathbed Poem', VII 57.7).

Cywirdad True Father: **2. 2. 1** Cywirdad Fab Rhad, rhifed—Ei wyrthau *True Father of the Son of Grace, His miracles were greatly esteemed* (Dafydd Benfras, 'Elegy for Gruffudd ab Ednyfed', VI 33.47).

Mawrdad Great Father: **2. 3. 1** I'r Mab, i'r Mawrdad, roddiad Reen *To the Son, to the Great Father, Lord gift-giver* (Cynddelw, 'Elegy for Rhirid Flaidd and his brother Arthen', III 24.2).

Mab Son: **3. 1. 1** O'r Mab, o'r Ysbryd, o'r iawnfryd fri *From the Son, from the Spirit, from the power of fine intent* (Gwalchmai ap Meilyr, 'Ode to God', I 14.18); **3. 1. 2** Hi yn ferch wy Mab y modd ysydd, Hi yn chwaer i Dduw o ddwywawl ffydd *She a daughter to her Son, the way things are, She a sister to God of holy faith* (*Id.*, 43–4); **3. 1. 3** Ac i'r Mab a'r Ysbryd gloywfryd Glân *And the Son and the Holy Spirit of excellent purpose* (Elidir Sais, 'In Praise of God and Dafydd ab Owain', I 16.2); **3. 1. 4** Ef yw'r Mab, Ef yw'r Pab pennaf *He is the Son, He is the highest Father* (Meilyr ap Gwalchmai, 'Ode to God', I 32.20); **3. 1. 5** see **2. 3. 2** *supra*; **3. 1. 6** A'r Mab a'r Ysbryd, glendyd gloywaf *And the Son and the Spirit, of [the] most resplendent sanctity* (*Id.*, 'Deathbed Poem', IV 18.36); **3. 1. 7** see

2. 1. 12 *supra*; **3. 1. 8** see **2. 1. 19** *supra*; **3. 1. 9** Mab a'n rhodded, Mab mad aned dan ei freiniau, **3. 1. 10** Mab gogoned, Mab i'n gwared, y Mab gorau *A Son was given to us, a Son [who was] born favoured, having privileges, Son of glory, a Son to redeem us, the best Son* (Madog ap Gwallter, 'Birth of Jesus', VII 32. 1–2); **3. 1. 11** Y Mab ydoedd a anydoedd dan ei nodau *The Son it was that had been born under its signs* (*ib.* 43); **3. 1. 12** Pan aned Mab, Arglwydd pob pab, popeth biau *When [the] Son was born, Lord of all priests, who owns everything* (*ib.* 62); **3. 1. 13** see **2. 1. 24** *supra*.

Mab Duw Son of God: **Events in the life of our Lord: 3. 2. 1** Deliesid Ieuan ieuang dedwydd Diau Fab Duw nef yn nwfr echwydd *The young and blessed John held The true Son of the God of heaven in running water* (Gwalchmai ap Meilyr, 'Ode to God', I 14.35–6); **3. 2. 2** Prynesid Mab Duw mad gerennydd *The Son of God purchased a happy reconciliation* (*ib.* 47); **3. 2. 3** Gwir Fab Duw, dangos Ei fywyd. Duw Sul (dwysaf cof) awr y cyfyd—haul, Cyfodes o'i weryd *[He], true Son of God, showing that He was alive. On Sunday (most profound memory) when the sun arises, He rose up from His grave* (Elidir Sais, 'Ode to God', I 24.20–2); **3. 2. 4** Goresgynnws Mab Duw, Difiau,—nef uchod *On Thursday the Son of God ascended to heaven above* (Einion ap Gwalchmai, 'Ode to God', I 27.63); **3. 2. 5** Nid gwallawg fradawg fradwriaeth—Mab Duw *Faulty and treacherous plotting was no part of the Son of God* (Cynddelw, 'Ode to God', IV 16.51); **3. 2. 6** Eisoes mai Ef, dangos o nef a wnaeth gwyrthau, Oedd Fab Duw Rhên, o'r hwn y cên llên a llyfrau *Yet heaven, that performed miracles, revealed that He Was Son of the Lord God, He of whom literature and books declare* (Madog ap Gwallter, 'Birth of Jesus', VII 32.17–18); **3. 2. 7** Hynny a wnaeth ganedigaeth deg wyn-eithau Un Mab Duw gwir, od edrychir ar y dechrau; Nos Nadolig: nos annhebyg i ddrygnosau, Nos lewenydd i lu bedydd: byddwn ninnau! *Those things brought about the birth of fine miracles Of the only Son of the true God, if the beginnings be looked at; Christmas night: a night unlike evil nights, A night of joy for the host of Christendom: let us also be [joyful]!* (*ib.* 57–60); **3. 2. 8** Dyw Sul, un hydr gun y ganed—Mab Duw *On Sunday, a certain great lord was born the Son of God* (Gruffudd ab yr Ynad Coch, 'Ode to God', VII 40 app. 1).

The Son of God, despoiler of hell: 3. 2. 9 Dug Mab Duw o dân ac ergryd, O oerwern uffern, wern weglyd *The Son of God led [souls] out from fire and terror, From the cold marsh of hell, redemption from its morass* (Elidir Sais, 'Ode to God', I 24.29–30); **3. 2. 10** I garu Mab Duw diamau, I gymryd penyd rhag poenau—uffern *To love the true Son of God, To do penance against [the] sufferings of hell* (Gruffudd ab yr Ynad Coch, 'Ode to God', VII 40.6–7); **3. 2. 11** Pan aeth un Mab Duw, y dydd gorau, I ddrws porth uffern gethern gaethau I wân heb annog, â'i grog a'i grau Y sarff aflawen yn ei enau *When the only Son of God went on the best day, To* *[the] entrance door of [the] hell [of the] evil and captive host To strike without persuasion, with His cross and His blood, The savage serpent in His mouth* (*ib.* 32–5); **3. 2. 12** Pan ddoeth Mab Duw ar ôl dioddau I ddrws porth uffern … *When the Son of God came after suffering To [the] entrance door of [the] hell* … (*Id.*, 'Ode to God', VII 40 app. 73).

Judgement Day: 3. 2. 13 A Mab Duw Ddyddbrawd a ddaw—i'w brofi *And the Son of God on the Day of Judgement will come to test him* (Dafydd Benfras, 'In Praise of God and Llywelyn ab Iorwerth', VI 24.15).

God the Son as healer: 3. 2. 14 Mab Duw nef, nodda fy udd *Son of the God of heaven, protect my lord* (Llywarch ap Llywelyn, 'Request for the recovery of Madog ap Gruffudd Maelor', V 27.7); **3. 2. 15** Un Mab Duw Ei Hun, o'i henaint—na ludd Gŵr ni lwydd beirdd o'i haint *The Only Son of God Himself, do not deprive of his old age A man whose illness does not benefit poets* (*ib.* 13–14).

Prayer to the Son of God: 3. 2. 16 Dielid Mab Duw ddygn alaeth—Hywel, *May the Son of God avenge the terrible sorrow of Hywel* (Peryf ap Cedifor, 'Elegy for Hywel ab Owain Gwynedd', II 21.9); **3. 2. 17** Archaf i Fab Duw, can ys digawn *I ask the Son of God, since it is [He] who will achieve it* (Cynddelw, 'Deathbed Poem', IV 18.11); **3. 2. 18** Mab Duw nef boed nerth wy rydid *Let the Son of heaven be a help to his freedom* (Llywarch ap Llywelyn, 'Threat to Gruffudd ap Cynan', V 8.40); **3. 2. 19** A'm rhoddwy Fab Duw dawn arwaneg *May the Son of God bestow an additional blessing upon me* (Dafydd Benfras, 'In Praise of Dafydd ap Llywelyn', VI 28.9); **3. 2. 20** Mab Duw o nef, drwy nerth saint, Boed gwâr wrth flaengar Fleddyn! *May the Son of God from heaven, through [the] power of saints, Be kind to Bleddyn who loved to be in the van [of the battle]!* (Y Prydydd Bychan, 'Elegy for Bleddyn ap Dwywg', VII 17.15–16); **3. 2. 21** Nis plyco Mab Duw yn dragywydd! *Let the Son of God not cast him down forever!* (Llygad Gŵr, 'In Praise of Llywelyn ap Gruffudd', VII 24.104); **3. 2. 22** Ar ddehau Mab Duw bo ei dynged … ef Drwy gaffael porth nef yn agored *May his destiny be at the right hand of the Son of God Finding the gate of heaven open* (*Id.*, 'Elegy for Hywel ap Madog', VII 27.3–4); **3. 2. 23** Crist Fab Duw diwyll, hanbwyll honaf! *Christ Son of the true God, think of me!* (Bleddyn Fardd, 'Elegy for Llywelyn ap Gruffudd ap Llywelyn', VII 50.2).

In Praise of the Son of God: 3. 2. 24 Ni thäwn, pei byddwn celfydd, O foli Mab Duw diwenydd *Were I skilful, I would not cease from praising the blessed Son of God* (Daniel ap Llosgwrn Mew, 'Elegy for Owain Gwynedd', II 18. 24–5); **3. 2. 25** I foli Mab Duw dibechawd *To praise the sinless Son of God* (Cynddelw, 'Appeasement of the Lord Rhys', IV 9.3).

Ejaculations: 3. 2. 26 Wi a un Mab Duw! mawr a rhyfedd, Mor yw eilon mygr, maint y rheufedd! *O only Son of God! a great wonder, How excellent are the steeds, so great the wealth!* (Hywel ab Owain Gwynedd, '*Gorhoffedd*', II 6.19–20); **3. 2. 27** Oi a un Mab Duw o deÿrnas—nef, Cyn addef goddef, gwae fi na'm llas! *O only Son of God from the kingdom of heaven, Before acknowledging [i.e. experiencing] suffering, woe is me that I have not been killed!* (*Id.*, 'Ode to a Maiden', II 11.15–16).

Son of God's power over life and death: 3. 2. 28 Mab Duw a'i dug i'w gyfoeth *The Son of God took him to His Kingdom* (Einion Wan, 'Elegy for Llywelyn ab Iorwerth', VI 5.19); **3. 2. 29** Anrheithwys Mab Duw, Dewin—holl wybod *The Son of God took [him], Seer of all knowledge* (*ib.* 49); **3. 2. 30** Drwg, Fab Duw, y daethost ataf *Damagingly, O Son of God, you came to me.* (Dafydd Benfras, 'Elegy for Gruffydd ap Llywelyn', VI 29.114).

Moral comment: 3. 2. 31 Ny bydd dadwoddau dedwyddyd—mab dyn Gan Fab Duw o'i wynfyd *There will be no undoing of human happiness With the Son of God in His blessedness* (Elidir Sais, 'Ode to God', I 24.39–40); **3. 2. 32** Un Mab Duw ddiffwys Ei ddaffar *Only Son of God, immense His plan* (Cynddelw, 'Ode to God', IV 16.3); **3. 2. 33** Mab Duw byw, fy llyw a'm lleha O'm lle drwg, a'm dyddwg i'm da *Son of the living God, my Ruler who will settle me From my wretched place, and who will bring me to my well-being* (*ib.* 81–2); **3. 2. 34** Ni chasa Mab Duw dedwydd *The Son of God does not hate [the] fortunate one* (Einion Wan, 'Appeasement of Dafydd ap Llywelyn', VI 6. 20); **3. 2. 35** Mab Duw, dylyaf dy bwyllaw *Son of God, I am bound to consider You* (Dafydd Benfras, 'In Praise of God and Llywelyn ab Iorwerth', VI 24.1); **3. 2. 36** Ni bydd â Mab Duw diymadaw A fo mynws byd yn ei bydiaw *He will not be united with the Son of God Whom the wealth of the world endangers* (Dafydd Benfras, 'In Praise of God and Llywelyn ab Iorwerth', VI 24.17); **3. 2. 37** Mab Duw dewisaid dewisaw—a wnaf *The chosen Son of God, Him will I choose* (*ib.* 19); **3. 2. 38** Can gaffael yn dda dra heb drengi Gan fab Duw didwyll gymodi *By getting as a blessing a thing that does not fade From the Son of God of sincere covenanting* (Llygad Gŵr, 'In Praise of Llywelyn ap Gruffudd', VII 24.65–6).

Unclassified examples: 3. 2. 39 O ddawn mawr Mab Duw dylyaf—arddelw *In virtue of the great gift of the Son of God I am entitled to protection* (Cynddelw, 'Privileges of the Powys Warriors', III 11.5); **3. 2. 40** Ni wrthyd Mab Duw dadolwch! *The Son of God does not refuse appeasement!* (*ib.* 162); **3. 2. 41** I garu Mab Duw yn ei wiw gaerau *To love the Son of God in His fine fortresses* (Gruffudd ab yr Ynad Coch, 'Ode to God', VII 40 app. 1).

Mab Mair Son of Mary: **3. 3. 1** Gwae ddiwarth, ddiwyl, ddiolaith—am ei air, Ni lawer lefair o Fab Mair maith *Alas for the one without shame, impudent, headless concerning his word, Who does not speak at length of the great Son of Mary* (Llywelyn Fardd (II), 'Ode to God', VI 10.65–6); **3. 3. 2** A gair anghyfair Mab Mair meidrawl I brofi pob peth o bregeth Bawl *And the word of succour of the strong Son of Mary To test every part of [St] Paul's sermon* (Einion ap Gwgon, 'In Praise of Llywelyn ab Iorwerth', VI 18.5–6); **3. 3. 3** Cedwid un Mab Mair cenau cyniwair *May the only Son of Mary keep the swiftly attacking young warrior* (Dafydd Benfras, 'Progress of Llywelyn ap Gruffudd', VI 35.33); **3. 3. 4** Mab Mair o'r pum gair heb gêl *The Son of Mary of the five words not hidden* (Gruffudd ab yr Ynad Coch, 'Ode to God', VII 40 app. 123); **3. 3. 5** Eithr Un Mab Mair, mawr lias Duw nef, dyn mal ef ni las *Except the Only Son of Mary, great death Of [the] God of heaven, no man like him has been killed* (Bleddyn Fardd, 'Elegy for Llywelyn ap Gruffudd', VII 51.3–4).

Mab Mam Son of a Mother: **3. 4. 1** Mab Mam, Mair ddinam, mawr ddoeth *Son of a Mother, holy Mary, most wise* (Einion Wan, 'Elegy for Llywelyn ab Iorwerth', VI 5.20); **3. 4. 2** Mab Fam forwyn, grefydd addfwyn, aeddfed eirau *Son of a virgin mother, gentle [her] faith, mature [her] words* (Madog ap Gwallter, 'Birth of Jesus', VII 32.3).

Mapgwas Child/Boy: **3. 5. 1** Mapgwas Mair o Iesu *Jesus, child of Mary* (Elidir Sais, 'Ode to God', I 21.2); **3. 5. 2** A'm heirolwy Mair ar ei Mapgwas *May Mary pray for me to her Boy* (Meilyr ap Gwalchmai, 'Ode to God', I 33.98).

Mab Rhad Son of Grace: **3. 6. 1** = **2. 1. 9** *supra* (IV 17.108); Iolaf-i ... **3. 6. 2** Bwyf gwastad gan Fab Rhad rheithgar, *I ask ... That I may always be with the just Son of Grace* (Llywelyn Fardd (II), 'Ode to God', VI 9.13–15); **3. 6. 3** Ni ddoto fy Rhên, Fab Rhad,—ei bechawd yn erbyn fy mrawd, ddefawd ddifrad *Let not my Lord, Son of Grace, hold his sin Against my brother, of loyal practice* (Dafydd Benfras, 'Elegy for Dafydd ap Llyw-elyn', VI 30.17–18); **3. 6. 4** = **2. 2. 1** *supra* (VI 33.47); **3. 6. 5** Heb gnawdawl dad, hwn yw'r Mab rhad, rhoddiad rhadau *Without a father of flesh, He is the grace-filled Son, giver of blessings* (Madog ap Gwallter, 'Birth of Jesus', VII 32.4); **3. 6. 6** see **2. 1. 21** *supra;* **3. 6. 7** see **2. 1. 22** *supra.*

Yr Ysbryd Glân The Holy Spirit: **4. 1. 1** see **3. 1. 1** *supra;* **4. 1. 2** see **2. 1. 4** *supra;* **4. 1. 3** Am dduw Merchyr Brad dybu bryd—Iddas Bred-ychu ein Hysbryd *On Spy Wednesday came Judas's purpose, To betray our Spirit* (Elidir Sais, 'Ode to God', I 24.9–10); **4. 1. 4** I'r Ysbryd uchel o'r un echen, *To the most exalted Spirit of the same origin* (Cynddelw, 'Elegy for Rhirid Flaidd and his brother Arthen', III 24.3); **4. 1. 5** see **3. 1. 6** *supra;* **4. 1. 6** I Rên a'r Ysbryd gydamgeledd *To [the] Lord and the Spirit a mu-*

tual concern (Anon., 'Lament of the Pilgrim', VI 36.16); **4. 1. 7** see **2. 1. 22** *supra;* **4. 1. 8** Archwn i'r Ysbryd, Celi, o'th blegyd *We ask the Spirit, Lord, on Your account* (Gruffudd ab yr Ynad Coch, 'Ode to God', VII 43.43); **4. 1. 9** see **2. 1. 24** *supra.*

Glân Ysbryd Holy Spirit: **4. 2. 1** Ac i'r Mab a'r Ysbryd gloywfryd Glân *And the Son and the Holy Spirit of excellent purpose* (Elidir Sais, 'In Praise of God and Dafydd ab Owain', I 16.2); **4. 2. 2** Ef yn Ysbryd Glân gloyw-af—Ei ddefnydd *He [is] the Holy Spirit most brilliant His nature* (Meilyr ap Gwalchmai, 'Ode to God', I 32.21); **4. 2. 3** Nawdd y Glân Ysbryd cywyd cofion *[The] protection of the Holy Spirit [is the] objective [of my] thoughts* (Gruffudd ab yr Ynad Coch, 'Ode to God', VII 39.2).

Trindawd Trinity: **Unity of the Trinity**: **5. 1. 1** Yn undawd Drin-dawd, drwy rybuched *In the unity of the Trinity, through desire,* (Meilyr Brydydd, 'Elegy for Gruffudd ap Cynan' I 3.171); **5. 1. 2** O Drindawd undawd undras â mi *From the unity of the Trinity, of the same stock as I am*: (Gwalchmai ap Meilyr, 'Ode to God', I 14.19); **5. 1. 3** Yn undawd Drindawd yn dragywydd *In the unity of the Trinity eternally.* (*ib.* 54); **5. 1. 4** Nawdd Undawd Trindawd y Tri Pherson *[The] protection of the Unity of the Trinity of the Three Persons* (Gruffudd ab yr Ynad Coch, 'Ode to God', VII 39.21); **5. 1. 5** Onid y Drindawd, Undawd orau *Except for the Trinity, the best Unity* (*id.*, 'Ode to God', VII 40.53).

Trinity and Mercy: **5. 1. 6** Amgyrwyf, Drindawd, Dy drugaredd! *I desire your mercy, O Trinity!* (Elidir Sais, 'Ode to God', I 23.30); **5. 1. 7** As rhoddwy Trindawd trugaredd! *May the Trinity grant unto Him mercy!* (Cynddelw, 'Elegy for Owain Gwynedd', IV 4.138); **5. 1. 8** Delw y'm bo, er bodd y Drindawd, Trugaredd tros waredd tros wawd *So that I may have, with the favour of the Trinity, Mercy because of [my] compassion and because of [my] praise* (*id.*, 'Appeasement of the Lord Rhys', IV 9.9–10); **5. 1. 9** Yn rhan drugaredd, yn rhad—y Drindawd, Yn rhydd o'th bechawd ddefawd ddifrad! *In mercy's lot, in the grace of the Trinity, Free from your sin according to trustworthy custom!* (Bleddyn Fardd, 'Praise of Maredudd ap Rhys', VII 46.29–30).

Inspiration by the Trinity: **5. 1. 10** Duw Drindawd, bwyf priawd prifiaith I edmyg dinag, dinas mawrfaith—clod *God [who is] Trinity, may I be the possessor of fine language On behalf of one generous and honourable, great and extensive protector of a famous one* (Seisyll Bryffwrch, 'Elegy for Owain Gwynedd', II 22.4–5); **5. 1. 11** Traethwys fy nhafawd trwy nerth y Drindawd *My tongue proclaimed through the power of the Trinity* (Dafydd Benfras, 'Progress of Llywelyn ap Gruffudd', VI 35.1).

Judgement: **5. 1. 12** A'm Duw a'm diwyd achub Erbyn brawd Trin-dawd Trined. *And God will faithfully rescue me Ready for the judgement of the*

Trinity the Three in One (Gwalchmai ap Meilyr, 'Ode to God', I 14.109–
10).

Hell's Suffering: **5. 1. 13** Nis adrawdd tafawd, nis traetha ceudawd,
Onid y Drindawd, Undawd orau, Poenedig gethern pobl mywn myg-
wern, Poenofiaint uffern gethern gaethau. *Tongue cannot describe, mind
cannot tell, Except for the Trinity, the best Unity, The grieving crowd of people
in a smoking marsh, The torment of [the] captive and evil host of hell* (Gruffudd
ab yr Ynad Coch, 'Ode to God', VII 40.52-5).

Unclassified Examples: **5. 1. 14** Rex rhadau wrno, rhy-n-bo-ni
gardawd, Rheg rhy-d-eirifam yn rhan Drindawd. *King most exalted His
blessings, may we have mercy, A gift which we extol by the power of the Trinity*
(Meilyr Brydydd, 'Elegy for Gruffudd ap Cynan', I 3.3-4); **5. 1. 15**
Prydestawd o'r Drindawd draethu, *Proclaiming a song about the Trinity*
(Elidir Sais, 'Ode to God', I 21.27); **5. 1. 16** Trindawd a'm dyco
diguedd *Let the Trinity take me from my sadness* (id., 'Ode to God', I 23.5);
5. 1. 17 Molawd i'r Drindawd mal gweddïau *Praise the Trinity in the form
of prayers* (Einion ap Gwalchmai, 'Ode to God', I 27.106); **5. 1. 18** Yn
edrinaw fry rhag y Drindawd *Echoing on high before the Trinity* (id., 'Ode
to God', I 28.44); **5. 1. 19** Yng ngheinffawd y Drindawd y trigiant *In the
fair blessedness of the Trinity they will abide* (Meilyr ap Gwalchmai, 'Ode to
God', I 31.17); **5. 1. 20** Can diffyrth Trindawd tri macwy—o dân *Since
the Trinity rescued the three youths from the fire* (Cynddelw, 'Ode to God',
IV 16.185); **5. 1. 21** Drwy ganiad y Drindawd *By permission of the Trinity*
(Llywarch ap Llywelyn, 'Elegy for Iorwerth ap Rhotbert of Arwystli',
V 28.30); **5. 1. 22** Medd Crist Celi Ri: rhaid oedd yna Bod gleindid
parawd yn erbyn Trindawd Rhag trallawd pechawd ddeddfawd ddifa
*Says Christ the Lord and King: it was necessary there That there be ready purity
to meet the Trinity Against the calamity of sin of destructive nature* (Gruffudd ab
yr Ynad Coch, 'Ode to God', VII 42.50–2).

Trined: **5. 2. 1** Cerennydd ysydd herwydd Trined, I Gristiawn ys iawn ei
gyrhaedded *There is reconciliation because of the Trinity, For a Christian right it is
to attain it* (Meilyr Brydydd, 'Elegy for Gruffudd ap Cynan', I 3.157); **5. 2.
2** A chynnif oedd well no gwall rëi, Rhybuched Trined, tra ni belli *And toil
which would be better than evil riches, The will of the Trinity, a force that would not
fail* (Gwalchmai ap Meilyr, 'Ode to God', I 14.15–16); **5. 2.3** see **5. 1. 5**
supra; **5. 2. 4** see **1. 27. 11** *supra*; **5. 2. 5** see **1. 22. 38** *supra*; **5. 2. 6** Rhag
deulin Trined tri nifer—a ddaw A'r trydy i law y Lusiffer A'r ddau ar ddeau
yng ngoleuder, Yng ngolau drefad a fad foler *Into the presence of the Trinity
will come the three hosts And one of the three led by Lucifer And the [other] two on
the right hand in light, In the dwelling of light which will be blessedly praised*
(Llywelyn Fardd (II), 'Ode to God', VI 10.25–8); **5. 2. 7** Gwae ni gred
Trined cyn rhyred rhaith *Alas for him who does not believe in the Trinity before*

the onrush of judgement (*ib.* 67); **5. 2. 8** I'm dyddwyn i'r porth parth â Thrined *To bring me to the entrance leading to the Trinity* (*ib.* 90).

Christ: **Christ as Creator: 6. 1. 1** Am fedd Crist: Creawdr nef, ys angen! *About the tomb of Christ: Creator of heaven, inevitable it is!* (Elidir Sais, 'Ode to God and Dafydd ab Owain', I 16.21); **6. 1. 2** Neu ry-m-coddes Crist, Creawdr trugar *Christ, the merciful Creator, caused pain to me* (Cynddelw, 'Elegy for Rhirid Flaidd and his brother Arthen', III 24.32); **6. 1. 3** Gwrthyf ni bo trist Crist Creadur! *May Christ the Creator be not sorrowful in my regard!* (*Id.*, 'Ode to God', IV 17.90); **6. 1. 4** Crist Creawdr, Llywiawdr llu daear—a nef, A'm noddwy rhag afar *May Christ the Creator, Ruler of the host of earth and heaven, Protect me against sadness* (Llywarch ap Llywelyn, 'To Llywelyn ab Iorwerth', V 23.1–2); **6. 1. 5** Crist Creawdr, Ymherawdr a'n medd *Christ the Creator who rules us* (*Id.*, 'In Praise of Rhys Gryg of Deheubarth', V 26.1); **6. 1. 6** Crist Creawdr, Llywiawdr, llwrw saint *Christ the Creator, Ruler, [and] way [forward] of [the] saints* (Anon., 'In Praise of Llywelyn ab Iorwerth and his family', VI 20.3); **6. 1. 7** Rhydrist y'n gwnaeth Crist creaduriau *Too sad has Christ made us, [Lord] of created things* (Dafydd Benfras, 'Elegy for Gruffydd ap Llywelyn', VI 29.55); **6. 1. 8** A fradychwys Crist, Creawdr buchedd *[Those] who betrayed Christ, Creator of life* (Anon., 'Lament of the Pilgrim', VI 36.24).

Humanity of Christ: 6. 1. 9 Myn ydd ymddaeth Crist ar gain dyd-wed—daear *Where Christ walked on the fair face of the earth* (Gwalchmai ap Meilyr, 'Ode to God', I 14.85); **6. 1. 10** Coelaf i Grist, diathrist athro *I believe in Christ, joyful teacher* (Meilyr ap Gwalchmai, 'Ode to God', I 30.17); **6. 1. 11** Crist yng nghnawd, ein Brawd bu breiniawl *Christ in the flesh, our Brother was exalted [lit. privileged]* (Llywarch ap Llywelyn, 'In Praise of Dafydd ab Owain Gwynedd', V 1.140); **6. 1. 12** Dybu Grist ym mru, ym mhrudd-der,—eron *Christ came to the womb in wisdom for our sakes* (Llywelyn Fardd (II), 'Ode to God', VI 10.49).

Christ as Saviour: 6. 1. 13 Arglwydd Grist, mor wyf drist drostaw (Arglwydd gwir gwared i ganthaw) *Christ the Lord, how sad I am because of him ([The] Lord from whom true deliverance [comes] / lit. The Lord true is the deliverance [that comes]) from Him* (Gruffudd ab yr Ynad Coch, 'Elegy for Llywelyn ap Gruffudd', VII 36.37–8); **6. 1. 14** A Christ o'r diwedd i'n dwyn ataw *And Christ at the last to lead us to Him* (*Id.*, 'Ode to God', VII 43.48).

Christ and the cross: 6. 1. 15 Tir rygymyrth Crist o groes edwyn—cethri *The land which Christ has taken through the painful cross of nails* (Gwalchmai ap Meilyr, 'Ode to God', I 14.69); **6. 1. 16** Doniawg ddi-drist Grist groes rinweddawl *Generous and blessed Christ, gainful [His] cross* (Elidir Sais, 'Ode to God', I 20.7); **6. 1. 17** Cynnadl a wna Crist wedi crocwedd *Christ will make an assembly after the cross* (*Id.*, 'Ode to God', I

23.23); **6. 1. 18** Ar au pechodau puchswn arwydd—crog, Ymddwyn croes er Crist ar fy ysgwydd *Upon the deceit of sins I would have desired [to put] the sign of the cross, [And] to carry the cross for Christ's sake on my shoulder* (Einion ap Gwalchmai, 'Ode to God', I 29.5–6); **6. 1. 19** Lleidr na eill edrych Crist yn ei grocwedd *A robber who cannot look upon Christ in His crucified state* (Gruffudd ap Gwrgenau, 'Elegy for Gruffudd ap Cynan', II 31.20); **6. 1. 20** Archaf arch o Bedr o berthynas—Crist A ddug Grog yn urddas *I beseech Peter because of his relationship with Christ Who took the cross with dignity* (Llywarch ap Llywelyn, 'Ode to the Hot Iron', V 15.9–10); **6. 1. 21** Dydd y cymerth Crist crog yn eiddaw *The day Christ took up [the] cross as His own* (Dafydd Benfras, 'In Praise of God and Llywelyn ab Iorwerth', VI 24.22); **6. 1. 22** A Christ ym mhren crog er creulonder *And Christ on the wood of the cross because of cruelty* (Gruffudd ab yr Ynad Coch, 'Ode to God', VII 38.13); **6. 1. 23** Nawdd Ieuan liw ban, ben diwydon, A fendigawdd Crist croes arwyddon! *[The] protection of John [of] fine complexion, foremost [of the] faithful ones, Whom Christ blessed [with] signs of [the] cross!* (Id., 'Ode to God', VII 39.17–18); **6. 1. 24** Gwae ni chyrcho ffair offerennau—Crist Croes dolur archollau *Alas for [the] one who does not attend the fine Masses of Christ [On the] cross [of] agony of [His] wounds* (Id., 'Ode to God', VII 40.17); **6. 1. 25** Saith wers cyman glân cyn gloes angau—crog A gant Crist â'i enau *[The] seven perfect [and] holy words before the pain of death [on the] cross Which Christ uttered with His lips* (Ib. 29–30); **6. 1. 26** Na myned o Grist i'r grog erddaw *Nor in Christ's going to the cross on his behalf* (Id., 'Ode to God', VII 43.6); **6. 1. 27** Rhydrist y'n gwnaet Crist, croes oleuni *Too sad has Christ, the light of the cross, made us* (Bleddyn Fardd, 'Elegy for the three sons of Gruffudd ap Llywelyn', VII 54.10).

Christ and hell: 6. 1. 28 Crist croesddarogan a'm gŵyr, a'm gwarchan Rhag uffern affan, wahan westi *Christ of the foretold cross who knows me, [He] will direct me Past the pain of hell, the lodging set apart* (Meilyr Brydydd, 'Deathbed Poem', I 4.35–6); **6. 1. 29** Can dug pymwan Crist pymoes o gaeth *Since the five wounds of Christ brought the five ages from captivity* (Cynddelw, 'Ode to God', IV 17.109); **6. 1. 30** Crist a ddoeth i'r byd rhag bod Addaf A'i bobl yn uffern, gethern gaethaf *Christ came to the world lest Adam And his posterity, a host most captive, should have to remain in hell* (Bleddyn Fardd, 'Elegy for Llywelyn ap Gruffudd ap Llywelyn', VII 50. 9–10).

Christ as judge: 6. 1. 31 Crist a ddaw yn wâr, yn wrawl,—Dyddbrawd *Christ will come gently, doughtily on the Day of Judgement* (Elidir Sais, 'Ode to God', I 22.9); **6. 1. 32** Pobloedd trist, Crist a'u cennyw *Christ will see them, the sad multitudes* (Llywelyn Fardd (I), 'Signs before Judgement Day', II 5.58).

Statements of belief in Christ: 6. 1. 33 Credaf Grist nefoedd (neuedd gannwyll) *I believe in Christ [from] heaven (a candle in time of need)* (Gwalchmai ap Meilyr, 'Ode to God', I 14.31); Credadun yw Ef, credaf—i'w drawsglwydd, **6. 1. 34** Crist Arglwydd Culwydd, ac nis celaf *He is credible, I believe in His intention, Christ Lord and Master, and I shall not hide it* (Meilyr ap Gwalchmai, 'Ode to God', I 32.29–30); **6. 1. 35** Cyngeuddon a ddaw o ddiofryd—Crist *A curse comes [to us] from denying Christ* (Cynddelw, 'Ode to God', IV 17.35); **6. 1. 36** Crist, Celi, Culwydd, cŵl Ei ddiddawl *Christ, Lord, Chief, it is a sin to reject Him* (Einion ap Gwgon, 'In Praise of Llywelyn ab Iorwerth', VI 18.2); **6. 1. 37** Trist y'n gorug Crist (cred nid ymchwel) Trais dirgwyn ac nid trais dirgel *Sadly did Christ bring about for us (faith does not return) Oppression [bringing] terrible grief and not a secret oppression* (Llygad Gŵr, 'Elegy for Hywel ap Madog', VII 27.29–30).

Christ the source of inspiration: 6. 1. 38 Deffro Crist Celi ein celfyddyd *[The event] of Christ the Lord's awakening of our [poetic?] art* (Elidir Sais, 'Ode to God', I 24.24); **6. 1. 39** Crist fab Mair a'm pair o'm pedwar—defnydd Dofn awen ddiarchar *Christ Son of Mary will provide for me from the four elements of my being Profound, wise inspiration* (Llywarch ap Llywelyn, 'To Llywelyn ab Iorwerth', V 23.5–6). **6. 1. 40** Crist fab Duw dy-m-rhydd arllafar *Christ Son of God will permit me [to have] speech (ib. 7).*

Miscellaneous references to Christ: 6. 1. 41 I Grist y canaf, ar fraint canon, Ceinwawd o'm tafawd ar draethwawd drŵn *To Christ I sing, according to [the] custom of the law, An excellent eulogy with my tongue in fine song* (Elidir Sais, 'In Praise of God and Dafydd ab Owain', I 16.5–6); **6. 1. 42** Mynesynt fradwyr fredychu—Crist *Traitors had insisted on betraying Christ* (Id., 'Ode to God', I 21.15); **6. 1. 43** Mau foli Crist celi, Culwydd *My praising is for Christ from heaven, the Lord* (Dafydd Benfras, 'Elegy for Llywelyn ab Iorwerth', VI 27.1); **6. 1. 44** Crist a ŵyr, yn llwrw a ganaf *Christ knows, because of what I sing* (Id., 'Elegy for Gruffydd ap Llywelyn', VI 29.115); **6. 1. 45** Da y dewisaist-ti hwnnw I'th fyddin, Grist, Frenin fry *Well hast thou chosen that [man] For your army, [O] Christ, King on high* (Y Prydydd Bychan, 'Elegy for Rhys ap Llywelyn', VII 15.3–4).

Prayers to Christ: 6. 1. 46 Crist cyflawn annwyd, boed trugarawg *Christ of perfect nature, let him be merciful* (Meilyr Brydydd, 'Elegy for Gruffudd ap Cynan', I 3.89); **6. 1. 47** A dyfo mab Cynan (mawr amgyffred) Can Grist geinforawd gwlad ogoned *And may the son of Cynan come (a fine arrival [it will be]) With Christ [on] the pleasant journey of the land of glory (ib. 167–8);* **6. 1. 48** Archaf arch i Grist Celi *I ask Christ the Lord [the fulfilment of] a wish* (Gwalchmai ap Meilyr, 'In Praise of Dafydd ab Owain', I 10.37); **6. 1. 49** Crist Celi, fy Rhi, a'm rhyddhao *May Christ the Lord, my King, free me (Id., 'Ode to God', I 30.24);* **6. 1. 50** Ochan

Grist, mor wyf drist o'r anaelau! O goll Moriddig mawr ei eisiau *Alas O Christ, so sad am I because of the grief! Because of the death of Moriddig great is his loss* (Owain Cyfeiliog, 'The Drinking-horn of Owain', II 14.95–6); **6. 1. 51** Crist Culwydd, poed rhwydd y'm rhangwy *May Christ the Lord easily reach me* (Cynddelw, 'Ode to God', IV 16.161); **6. 1. 52** Caffwyf o ioli Crist Celi, ced *Let me receive a boon through worshipping Christ the Lord* (Cynddelw, 'Ode to God', IV 17.141); **6. 1. 53** Perchen fo Gruffudd, parch westi,—ar nef, Ar neill-law Grist Celi *May Gruffudd, an abode of honour, be a proprietor in heaven, At one side of Christ the Lord* (Llywarch ap Llywelyn, 'Elegy for Gruffudd ap Hywel', V 16.9–10); **6. 1. 54** Crist Celi, bwyf celfydd a gwâr Cyn diwedd gyfyngwedd gyfar *Christ the Lord, may I be able and obedient Before [coming to] the last restricted earth-dwelling* (*Id.*, 'To Llywelyn ab Iorwerth', V 23.3–4); **6. 1. 55** Cadr Grist, rhag cadwen Angau, Cadw Fadawg fynawg yn fau! *Fair Christ, against the on-slaught of death, Keep illustrious Madog as my own!* (*Id.*, 'Request for the recovery of Madog ap Gruffudd Maelor', V 27.27–8); **6. 1. 56** Crist Celi, poed mi, o'm meithfaint—synnwyr, A'i syniwy cyn henaint *Christ, Lord, let me, because of my extensive wisdom, [Be the one] who meditates upon Him before old age* (Anon., 'In Praise of Llywelyn ab Iorwerth and his family', VI 20.1–2); **6. 1. 57** Ys bo ei ddiwedd, ddawn berchi,—ar nef Ar neillaw Crist Celi *May his end, [he who] respects grace, be in heaven Beside Christ the Lord* (Llygad Gŵr, 'In Praise of Llywelyn ap Gruffudd', VII 24.67–8); **6. 1. 58** Crist, fawr Arglwydd rhwydd, rhad a archaf, **6. 1. 59** Crist Fab Duw didwyll, hanbwyll honaf! **6. 1. 60** Crist ddeddfawl gedawl, gadarnaf—arddelw, A borthes ei ddelw ddolur dycnaf *[O] Christ, mighty generous Lord, I seek a blessing, Christ Son of the true God, think of me! Christ just [and] bountiful, strongest defence, Whose body endured [the] harshest suffering* (Bleddyn Fardd, 'Elegy for Llywelyn ap Gruffudd ap Llywelyn', VII 50.1–4).

Jesus: Jesus as Creator: 7. 1. 1 Cymhennaf pennaeth yr wnaeth Iesu *The most powerful leader whom Jesus had made* (Gwynfardd Brycheiniog, 'In Praise of the Lord Rhys', II 25.10).

Jesus and Mary: 7. 1. 2 Bod Iesu ym mru Mair (merch ei Rhi!), Mair, mad ymborthes ei beichogi! *Of Jesus being in the womb of Mary (daughter of her King!) Mary, propitiously she bore her pregnancy!* (Meilyr Brydydd, 'Deathbed Poem', I 4.13–14); **7. 1. 3** Mawr a Ŵr, Ei ddawn a ddyfu—ym mhryd Mapgwas Mair o Iesu *Mighty warrior, His gift came in the form of Jesus, child of Mary* (Elidir Sais, 'Ode to God', I 21.1–2).

Passion of Jesus: 7. 1. 4 A Difiau y'n dyfu ledfryd, Daly Iesu managu mwynglyd *And Thursday there came discouragement to us, The taking of Jesus of gentle and consoling speech* (Elidir Sais, 'Ode to God', I 24.11–12); **7. 1. 5** Gwae ef a'u peris, perygl fradau, Pan wanpwyd Iesu yn Ei asau

Alas for him who caused [them], dangerous treacheries, When Jesus was pierced in His ribs (Einion ap Gwalchmai, 'Ode to God', I 27.55–6); **7. 1. 6** Gwerthu Iesu (ysy rhyfedd) A orug Iddas o ddigasedd *Judas (it is a thing to marvel at) Sold Jesus because of hatred* (Anon., 'Lament of the Pilgrim', VI 36.19–20); **7. 1. 7** Gwaed Iesu a fu, gwaed cu cwynych *The blood of Jesus it was flowed, precious blood which you should lament* (Madog ap Gwallter, 'Ode to God', VII 33. 57); **7. 1. 8** Iesu, Iesu, a fydd, a fu, trwy fudd gethrau *Jesus, Jesus, who shall be, who was, by virtue of the nails of blessing* (Gruffudd ab yr Ynad Coch, 'Ode to God', VII 41.7).

Harrowing of hell: 7. 1. 9 Pan ddoeth Iesu fry o'i frenhindawd Ydd oedd pym oes byd yn gyd gaethnawd, Yng ngafael … *When Jesus came from His kingdom on high The five ages of the world were in common bondage In distraint …* (Einion ap Gwalchmai, 'Ode to God', I 28.33–5).

Jesus as Judge: 7. 1. 10 Pan ddêl rhag Iesu trillu trallawd *When the three hosts of tribulation come before Jesus (ib. 7).*

Prayer to Jesus: 7. 1. 11 Rhydalwyf iawn yn rhadlawn rwydd Can edifarwch cyfrwydd—i'm Iesu *Let me atone graciously [and] extensively With ready repentance to my Jesus* (Einion ap Gwalchmai, 'Ode to God', I 29.18–19); **7. 1. 12** Carannawg Iesu, câr ymwedd *Dear Jesus, a friend standing with me* (Llywarch ap Llywelyn, 'In Praise of Rhys Gryg of Deheubarth', V 26.5); **7. 1. 13** Iesu, deg Iesu, im dangosych Dy wyneb, ni heb a ohebych *Jesus, fair Jesus, show me Your face, he whom you reject will not speak [praise]* (Madog ap Gwallter, 'Ode to God', VII 33.61–2); **7. 1. 14** Nawdd y Iesu caru, coron—tangnefedd *[The] protection of the loving Jesus, crown of peace* (Gruffudd ab yr Ynad Coch, 'Ode to God', VII 39.3).

In praise of Jesus: Am obrwy, am obrid fy rhaid, **7. 1. 15** Am Iesu caru cyrbwyllaid *For a reward, in order to deserve that which I must have, [I] delight in praising Jesus* (Cynddelw, 'Ode to God', IV 16.120–21).

Miscellaneous references to Jesus: 7. 1. 16 O Ddofydd y traeth trwy gyhydedd, O Iesu y traethwys Iosedd *Concerning the Lord is the discourse in poetry, Concerning Jesus did Joseph declaim* (Elidir Sais, 'Ode to God', I 23.17–18); **7. 1. 17** Coffáu Iesu ysy bwyllad—i'm ban A moli Cadfan gan ei ganiad *The purpose of my song is to bring Jesus to mind And with His permission to praise Cadfan* (Llywelyn Fardd (I), 'Song to Cadfan', II 1.91–2); **7. 1. 18** Ni'm cerydd Iesu, y Cyfarwydd *Jesus, the Guide, will not blame me* (Hywel ab Owain Gwynedd, 'Ode to a Maiden', II 7.20); **7. 1. 19** Na'th adws Iesu eisiwed *That Jesus did not permit you to [be in] need* (Llywarch ap Llywelyn, 'In Praise of Rhys Gryg of Deheubarth', V 26.112); **7. 1. 20** Mor draws fu Iesu am aesdrygwydd *How relentless was Jesus regarding the dire fall of [our] shield* (Dafydd Benfras, 'Elegy for Llywelyn ab Iorwerth', VI 27.5); **7. 1. 21** Gwrawl Iesu, Pen llu llarïedd *Heroic Jesus, Chief of a bounteous host* (Anon.,

'Lament of the Pilgrim', VI 36.54); **7. 1. 22** Iesu yw hwn a erbyniwn yn ben rhiau *Jesus is He whom we receive as supreme king* (Madog ap Gwallter, 'Ode to God', VII 32.11); **7. 1. 23** Nid oes allu 'n erbyn Iesu, na syn droau *There is no power [that will prevail] against Jesus, nor stupefied wrigglings* (Gruffudd ab yr Ynad Coch, 'Ode to God', VII 41.31); **7. 1. 24** O gwnaethost gamwedd, na ryfedda Bod yn ddir talu ger bron yr Iesu *If you have sinned, be not amazed That it is necessary to make retribution before Jesus [for that]* (*Id.*, 'Ode to God', VII 42.14–15).

Alternative Names for God: Section 8. *Amherawdr* Emperor (3); *Argledyr* Support (1); *Argledrydd* Defender (1); *Argleidriad* Supporter (1); *Arglwydd* Lord (43); *Brenin* King (18); *Cadair* Throne (1); *Câr* Friend (2); *Celi* Lord (13); *Creawdr* Creator (27); *Culwydd* Lord (10); *Cyfarwydd* Guide (1); *Cymroddedri* Prince of peace (1); *Cynghorwr* Counsellor (1); *Dewin* Miracle Worker, Prophet, Seer (7); *Dewrnaf* Strong Lord (1) *Dofydd* Lord, God (37); *Eli* Lord (1); *Emmanuël* Emmanuel (1); *Erchwyn* Supporter (1); *Gwawr* Lord, Master; *Gwledig* Lord, Ruler, Prince (11); *Gŵr* Warrior, God, Lord (28); *Gwrda* Noble One; *Hael* Generous One (2); *Hydrner* Strong One (1); *Llary* Generous One (1); *Llyw* Ruler (1); *Llywiawdr* Ruler (4); *Mechdeyrn* Lord, King (2); *Meidradur* Ruler (3); *Modur* Lord (2); *Mur* Support (2); *Naf* Lord (13); *Nêr* Lord (4); *Oen* Lamb (1); *Pab* Father (1); *Pair* Lord (2); *Pen* Head (1); *Perchen* Owner (1); *Peryf* Lord (3); *Priawd* Master (1); *Priodor* Rightful Owner (1); *Prynawdr* Redeemer (1); *Rhebydd* Leader (1); *Rheg, Rhegofydd* Benefactor (1); *Rhên* Lord (23); *Rex* King (5); *Rhi* King (17); *Rhiau* King, Head, Lord (8); *Rhoddiad* Gift-giver (4); *Rhwyf* Ruler, Prince, Chief (27); *Sywedydd* Master (1); *Tri* Three (Trinity) (6); *Trugar, Trugarawg* Merciful One (4).

Epilogue

We have considered the historic milieu of the court poets, their orientations as official members of the patron's household, and their involvement with, and concern for, the Church and matters both religious and secular. How do we sum up their position and performance? It cannot be disputed that, as recognized professionals, they were a body of artists confident in their creative ability. As members of the Church, they emerge equally confident, not hesitating to let their religious stance be seen clearly in and through their frequent laudatory and supplicatory addresses to God and the Trinity, to Mary, the saints and all the hosts of heaven. In their compositions we gain glimpses, or rather hints *sotto voce,* of contemporary theological trends and developments, and throughout their poems there is revealed a pervasive God-consciousness, which seems to have penetrated every department of their lives and careers both private and professional. In this they emerge as being securely within the main attitudinal ethos of their period. Certainly there are other nuances. The wider aspects of court poet humanity, expressed in ambition, self-interested competition and jealousies, as well as a possible ruthlessness of combative engagementism are not the concern of the present volume.

Throughout this study attention has been drawn to the liturgy as a source of inspiration for the poetry of the *Gogynfeirdd.* The fact that all liturgies were celebrated in Latin would not have prevented poets, even without any knowledge of the language, from appreciating the significance of ceremonial rituals. It was an essential duty of the officiating clergy to keep their congregations in touch with the meaning and import of Psalms, Canticles, hymns, and readings which occurred in the Mass and other liturgical rites. On countless occasions, as these warrior-poets call upon angels and archangels to see them safely into paradise, we hear haunting echoes of the antiphon *In paradisum deducant te Angeli* … which was chanted at every burial service when the coffin was brought in procession to its resting place.

Other sources of influence may be revealed by archaeological and epigraphic research. Already fragmentary remains from some sites suggest the possibility of instructional crosses of the type which are still above ground in other parts of Britain and Ireland. Pilgrims and crusaders brought back to Wales descriptions of Church architecture and ornamentation which they had seen on mainland Europe or the Middle East. This may well have fired native Welsh artists to build, decorate and ornament for themselves.

Miniatures of scriptural scenes in illuminated Missals or Service manuscripts, which were seen by the poets themselves or described to them,
could also account for certain references and graphic descriptions which
they have passed on to posterity. But perhaps the most significant source of
inspiration came from panegyrics delivered at funerals and commemorative
services for the dead, and from devotional homilies preached at Masses of
seasonal importance, or on festal and celebratory occasions.

It is not easy to establish where these poems were proclaimed. In general
reciters were specially trained to perform this privileged task. Elegies may
have been spoken in cemeteries, either at the actual internment or at the
Mass on the 'Month's Mind'. The intimacy of address to the deceased in
some of these suggests that the recital took place at or near the place of
burial or even within the Church itself. There is no evidence of such a
practice in medieval countries at this period, as far as we have been able to
ascertain.

Curtius remarks, 'If I were to sum up in two words what I believe is the
essential message of medieval thought, I would say: It is the spirit in which
it restated tradition, and this spirit is Faith and Joy'. Reflection on this
'message' could perhaps be useful in summarizing what the study of the
Welsh court poets and God has revealed. It is legitimate to conclude that
the poets accepted without question the Christian tradition and stated or
restated their understanding of it with unwavering faith. Their hardships, or
those of their patrons and country, did not divert them from the central
focus of this faith. Invariably they turned to God in every eventuality—at
times praying for deliverance, on occasions upbraiding Him for natural or
human disaster, or again praising His benevolence for gifts received.
Furthermore they lived in the certain conviction that the *fidei traditio*, with
its gift and promise of happiness in the life to come, would provide the
necessary support at the moment of greatest need.

Less obvious is their spirit of joy, though it reveals itself from time to
time. On the other hand *timor Dei* is all-pervasive, often finding expression
in horrific descriptions of infernal torments which await those whose
names do not appear in the Book of Life. From these *angst*-ridden
imaginings we may be tempted to see the poets as being in a 'slough of
despond'. If such was their position and attitude, no one could blame
them, in view of the ever-present threat, or maybe reality, of plague,
famine and war in the Wales of their day.

Valedictory lines of some *Gogynfeirdd* poems echo the lesser doxology
(Glory be to the Father …); following this example, let us end with its actual
words, so often heard at Masses and as the conclusion of intercessory prayers:

> *Gloria Patri et Filio et Spiritui Sancto, sicut erat in principio*
> *et nunc et semper in saecula saeculorum.*
> AMEN

Bibliography

Books

Anciaux, P., *La théologie du sacrament de pénitence au XIIe siècle* (Louvain, 1949).

Armstrong, R.J. and Brady, I.C., *Francis and Clare, the complete works* (New York, 1982).

Aulén, G., *Christus Victor* (New York, 1969).

Baldwin, J.D., *The Scholastic culture of the Middle Ages 1000–1300* (Heath Lexington, 1971).

Baring-Gould, S. and Fisher, J., *The Lives of the British Saints* (London, 1907–13).

Bartrum, P.C., *Early Welsh Genealogical Tracts* (Cardiff, 1966).

Bertoni, Giuilio, ed., *La Chanson de Roland* (Firenze, 1936).

Bloomfield, M.W., *The Seven Deadly Sins: An Introduction to the History of a Religious Concept, with Special Reference to Medieval English Literature* (Michigan, 1952).

Bowen, E.G., *Settlements of the Celtic Saints in Wales* (Cardiff, 1954).

Bowra, C.M., *Heroic Poetry* (London, 1964).

Brandon, S.G.F., *The Judgement of the Dead* (London, 1967).

Brauer, C., ed., *The Westminster Dictionary of Church History* (Philadelphia, 1971).

Brault, G.J., ed. and trans., *La Chanson de Roland* (Pennsylvania, 1978).

Brittain, F., ed., *Penguin Book of Latin Verse* (London, 1962).

Bromwich, R. ed., *Trioedd Ynys Prydein* (Cardiff, 1961).

Brown, R., *Little Flowers of St Francis* (New York, 1958) [trans. of an anonymous work called *Fioretti* from the Latin *Actus* of Uglino].

Browne, R. et alii, *The Jerome Biblical Commentary* (London, 1969).

Burrow, J.A., *Medieval Writers and their Work, Medieval English Literature and its Backgrouond 1100–1500* (Oxford, 1982).

J. Carney, *Early Irish Lyrics* (Dublin, 1967).

Charlesworth, R.H., *Pseudepigrapha*, Vol. 11 (Oxford, 1913).

Clancy, T. and Márkus, G., *Iona, The Earliest Poetry of a Celtic Monastery* (Edinburgh, 1995).

Colunga, A. and Turrado, L., *Biblia Sacra iuxta Vulgatam Clementinam* (6th ed., Madrid, 1982).

Conway Davies, J., ed., *Episcopal Acts and cognate Documents relating to Welsh Dioceses 1066–1272,* Vol. 1 (No. 1, Historical Society of the Church in Wales, 1946).

Curtius, E.R., *European Literature and the Latin Middle Ages,* trans. by
    W.R. Trask (London, 1953).
Davies, O and Bowie, F., *Celtic Christian Spirituality* (London, 1995).
Davies, R.R., *Conquest, Coexistence and Change: Wales 1063–1415* (Ox-
    ford, 1987).
Davies, R.T., *Medieval English Lyrics* (3rd ed., London, 1971).
Davies, W., *Wales in the Early Middle Ages* (Leicester, 1982).
    Patterns of Power in Early Wales (Oxford, 1990).
de Verteuil, M., *Your Word is a light for my Steps: Lectio Divina* (Dublin,
    1996).
De Vries, J., *Heroic Song and Heroic Legend* (London, 1973).
Deansley, M., *Sidelights on the Anglo-Saxon Church* (London, 1962).
Diehl, P.S., *The Medieval European Religious Lyric: an ars Poetica* (Berkeley,
    1985).
Dimock, J. F., *Giraldi Cambrensis Opera.* Vol VI *Itinerarium Kambriae et
    Descriptio Kambriae.*
Dronke, P., *The Medieval Lyric* (London, 1968).
Dumézil, G., *Servius et la fortune: Essai sur la fonction sociale de louange et de
    blâme et sur les éléments indoeuropéens de cens romains* (Paris, 1943).
Edwards, N. and Lane, A., *The Early Church in Wales and the West* (Ox-
    ford, 1992).
Edwards, O.T., *Matins, Lauds and Vespers for St David's Day* (Cambridge,
    1990).
Evans, D.S., *Medieval Welsh Religious Literature* (Cardiff, 1986).
Fox, Cyril, *Offa's Dyke: a field survey of the western frontier works of Mercia in
    the seventh and eighth centuries A.D.* (Cardiff, 1953).
Gibbs, M. and Lang, J., *Bishops and Reform, 1215–1272: with special refer-
    ence to the Lateran Council of 1215* (London, 1934).
Gruffydd, R.G. general ed., Cyfres Beirdd y Tywysogion
    I   *Meilyr Brydydd a'i Ddisgynyddion* (1994).
    II   *Llywelyn Fardd (I) ac Eraill* (1994).
    III   *Cynddelw Brydydd Mawr I* (1991).
    IV   *Cynddelw Brydydd Mawr II* (1995).
    V   *Llywarch ap Llywelyn* (1991).
    VI   *Dafydd Benfras ac Eraill* (1995).
    VII   *Bleddyn Fardd ac Eraill* (1996).
Haycock, M., *Blodeugerdd Barddas o Ganu Crefyddol Cynnar* (Llandybïe,
    1994).
Hausherr, I., *The Name of Jesus* (1891), trans. C. Cummings OCSO (2nd
    ed., New Riegel, Ohio, 1983).
Hughes, P., *The Church in Crisis* (London, 1961).
Hutton, E., *The Franciscans in England* (London, 1926).
Huws, Daniel, *Medieval Welsh Manuscripts* (Cardiff, 2000).

Jackson, K.H., *The Gododdin: the Earliest Scottish Poem* (Edinburgh, 1969).

James, J.W., *Rhigyfarch's Life of St David* (Cardiff, 1967).

James, M.R., *The Apocryphal New Testament* (16th ed., Oxford, 1986).

Jeffrey, D.L., *The Early Christian Lyric and Franciscan Spirituality* (Nebraska, 1975).

Jeffrey, D.L., *A Dictionary of Biblical Tradition in English Literature* (Grand Rapids, Michigan, 1992)

———— and Levy, B.J., *The Anglo-Norman Lyric* (Toronto, 1990).

Jenkins, D. and M.E. Owen, *The Welsh Law of Women* (Cardiff, 1980).

Jeremias, J., *The Prayers of Jesus* (Norwich, 1977).

Jones, A. et alii, *The Jerusalem Bible* (London, 1996).

Journet, C., *The Dark Knowledge of God,* trans. J.F. Anderson (London, 1948).

Jurgens, and Knowles, W.A., *The Faith of the Early Fathers,* Vol. 3 (Collegeville, 1979).

Kennedy, C.W., *Early English Christian Poetry,* trans. (New York, 1963).

Ker, W.P., *Medieval English Literature* (Oxford, 1969).

Knott, E., *Irish Classical Poetry* (Dublin, 1957).

Knowles, D. and Hadock, R.M., *Medieval Religious Houses: England and Wales* (London, 1971).

Lane, D.A., *The Reality of Jesus: An Essay in Christology* (Dublin, 1975).

Latourette, K.S., *A History of the Expansion of Christianity,* Vol. II, *The Thousand Years of Christianity A.D. 500–1500* (London, 1938).

Lefevre, G., OSB, *St Andrew's Daily Missal* (Brughes, 1962).

Le Goff, J., *The Birth of Purgatory* (Chicago, 1984).

Leon-Dafour, X, *Dictionary of Biblical Theology* (2nd ed., London, 1978).

Lewis, S., *Braslun o Hanes Llenyddiaeth Gymraeg I* (Cardiff, 1932).

Loomis, R.S., *Arthurian Literature in the Middle Ages* (Oxford, 1959).

MacNamara, M., *The Apocrypha in the Irish Church* (Dublin, 1975).

Macy, G., *The Theologies of the Eucharist in the Early Scholastic Period* (Oxford, 1984).

Maertens, T., *Bible Themes* (Brughes, 1964).

Migne, J.P., *Patrologiae cursus completus: Series latina* (Paris, 1844–5).

McKenna, C.A., *The Medieval Welsh Religious Lyric* (Belmont, 1991).

McKenna, L. ed., *Dánta do chum Aonghus Fionn Ó Dálaigh* (Dublin, 1919).

Philip Bocht O Huiginn (Dublin, 1931).

Aithdioghluim Dána, i, ii ITS (Dublin, 1939–40).

Dán Dé (Dublin, s.d.).

Minihane, J., *The Christian Druids* (Dublin, 1993).

Morris, C., *The Papal Monarchy. The Western Church 1050–1250* (Oxford, 1989).

Morris, J. ed. / trans., *Nennius, British History and the Welsh Annals* (Oxford, 1980).

Nash-Williams, V.E., *The Early Christian Monuments of Wales* (Cardiff, 1950).

Ó Cróinín, D., *The Irish Sex Aetates Mundi* (Dublin, 1983).

Ó Dwyer, P., O. Carm, *Céli Dé: Spirituality of the Reform Movement in Ireland 750–900* (Dublin, 1977).

Mary: a History of Devotion in Ireland (Dublin, 1988).

Okasha, E., *Hand-list of Anglo-Saxon non-runic inscriptions* (Cambridge, 1971).

Ó Muirgheasa, É., *Dánta Diadha Uladh* (Dublin, 1936).

Owen, M.E. and Roberts, B.F., ed., *Beirdd a Thywysogion* (Cardiff and Aberystwyth, 1996).

Owst, G.R., *Preaching in Medieval England* (Cambridge, 1926).

Pennar, M., *Taliesin Poems* (Lampeter, 1988).

Phillimore, E., *Annales Cambriae,* Cy. ix.

Poschmann, B., *Penance and the Anointing of the Sick* (Freiburg, 1964).

Pryce, H., *Native Law and Church in Medieval Wales* (Oxford, 1993).

Raby, F.J.E., *History of Christian-Latin Poetry* (Oxford, 1953).

Rahner, K., *Theological Investigations* I (London, 1960).

The Trinity (2nd ed., London, 1975).

Richter, M., *The Formation of the Medieval West* (Dublin, 1994).

Rivière, J., *Le dogme de la rédemption au début du Moyen Age* (Paris, 1934).

Silverstein, T., *Visio Sancti Pauli* (London, 1953).

Southern, R.W., *Medieval Humanism and other studies* (Oxford, 1970).

Stacey, R.C., *The Road to Judgment; from custom to court in Medieval Ireland* (Pennsylvania, 1994).

Stephenson, D., *The Governance of Gwynedd* (Cardiff, 1984).

Stock, B., *The Implications of Literacy* (Princeton, 1983).

Tristram, H., *Sex Aetates Mundi* (Heidelberg, 1985).

Tyrer, J.W., *Historical Survey of Holy Week,* Alcuin Club Collection No. xxix (Oxford, 1932).

Ullman, W., *A Short History of the Papacy in the Middle Ages* (London, 1972).

Vendryes, J., *La Poésie Galloise de XIIᵉ et XIIIᵉ Siècles dans ses Rapports avec la Langue* (Oxford, 1930).

Victory, S., *The Celtic Church in Wales* (London, 1977).

Wade-Evans, A.W., *Nennius's 'History of the Britons'*, trans. of *Historia Brittonum* (1938).

Warren, F.E., *Liturgy and Ritual of the Celtic Church* (2nd ed., Woodbridge, 1987).

Wilkinson, J., *Egeria's Travels* (London, 1971).

Williams ab Ithel, J., *Annales Cambriae* (London, 1860).

Williams, Glanmor, *The Welsh Church from Conquest to Reformation* (Cardiff, 1968).
> *The Welsh and their Religion* (Cardiff, 1991).

G.J. Williams and E.J. Jones, *Gramadegau'r Penceirddiaid* (Cardiff, 1933).

Williams, H., *Gildae De Excidio Britanniae* (London, 1901).

Williams, Ifor, *Canu Llywarch Hen* (Cardiff, 1935).
> *Canu Aneirin* (Cardiff, 1938).
> *Canu Taliesin* (Cardiff, 1960).

Williams, J.E.C., *The Poems of Taliesin* (Dublin, 1968).
> *Beirdd y Tywysogion: Arolwg* (Cardiff, 1970).
> *Canu Crefyddol y Gogynfeirdd* (Llandysul, 1977).
> *The Poets of the Welsh Princes* (Writers of Wales) (Cardiff, 1978, 2nd ed., 1994).

———— et alii, *Llywelyn y Beirdd* (Caernarfon, 1984).

Williams, S.J. and Powell, E., *Cyfreithiau Hywel Dda yn ôl Llyfr Blegywryd* (Cardiff, 1961).

Willis, E.G., *A History of Early Roman Liturgy* (London, 1994).

Woolf, R., *The English Religious Lyric in the Middle Ages* (Oxford, 1968).

———— and O'Donoghue, H., ed., *Art and Doctrine: Essays on Medieval Literature* (London, 1986).

Wrenn, C.L., *Beowulf*, fully revised by W.F. Bolton (London, 1973).

Theses

Davies, R.T., 'A Study of the Themes and Usages of Medieval Welsh Religious Poetry, 1100–1450' (B.Litt. Oxford, 1958).

Morgan, Ll., 'Y Saith Pechod Marwol yng nghanu Beirdd yr Uchelwyr' (Ph.D. Cymru [Aberystwyth], 1989).

Articles

Breeze, A., 'Madog ap Gwallter', YB xiii (1985).

Carney, J., 'Society and the bardic poet', *Studies,* 62 (1973).

Charles-Edwards. T., 'The Date of the Four Branches of the Mabinogi', THSC, 1970.

Davies, W., 'The Myth of the Celtic Church' in *The early Church in Wales and the West* (Oxford, 1992).

Diehl, P.S., 'Genres, Forms and Structures' in the *Medieval European Religious Lyric: an ars Poetica* (Berkeley, 1985).

Fitzgerald, J., 'Aquinas on the good', *Downside Review,* cv, 358 (1987).

Ford, P.K., 'Welsh *Asswynaw* and Celtic Legal Idiom', B xxvi (1974–6).

Hamp, E.P., 'Nodiadau Amrywiol—Miscellaneous Notes', B xxix (1980–81).

Hughes, K., 'The Celtic Church: is this a Valid Concept?' CMCS i (1981).

Jarman, A.O.H., 'The Welsh Myrddin Poems' in *Arthurian Literature in the Middle Ages*, ed. R.S. Loomis (Oxford, 1959).
    'The Heroic Ideal in Early Welsh Poetry' in W. Meid 9th ed. *Beiträge zur Indogermanistik und Keltogie* (Innsbruck, 1967).

John, C.N., 'The Celtic Monasteries in North Wales', TCHSG xxi (1960).

Jones, J.W., 'Observations on the Origin of the Division of Man's Life into Stages', *Archaeologia,* xxxv (1983).

Jones, T., 'Pre-Reformation Welsh Versions of the Scriptures', NLWJ iv (1946).

Lane, B.G., 'The Beaune Last Judgement and the Mass of the Dead', *Simiolus*, xix (1989).

Lewis, C., 'The Court Poets: Their Function, Status and Craft' in *A Guide to Welsh Literature* i, ed. A.O.H Jarman and G. Hughes.

Loth, J., 'Notes étymologiques et lexicographiques', RC xlii (1925).

Lloyd, D.M., 'The Poets of the Princes' in *A Guide to Welsh Literature* i (*vide* Jarman).

Lloyd-Jones, J., 'The Court Poets of the Welsh Princes', PBA xxxiv (1948).

McKenna, C.A., 'Welsh Versions of the Fifteen Signs before Doomsday Reconstructed' in *Celtic Folklore and Christianity: Studies in memory of William W. Heist*, ed. P.K. Ford (Santa Barbara, 1983).

Ó Carragáin, É., 'The Ruthwell Crucifixion Poem in its Iconographic and Liturgical contexts', *Peritia,* 6–7 (1987–8).

O'Reilly, J., 'Early Medieval Text and Image: The wounded and exalted Christ', *Peritia* 6–7 (1987–8).

Walker, D., 'Church in Wales' in *Medieval Wales* (Cambridge, 1990).

Watkins, T. Arwyn, 'Englynion y Juvencus' in *Bardos: Penodau ar y Traddodiad Barddol a Cheltaidd cyflwynedig i J. E. Caerwyn Williams*, ed. R. Geraint Gruffydd (Caerdydd, 1982), 29–43.

Williams, I., 'Mynydd Mynnau', B xvii (1956–8).

Williams, J.E.C., 'Purdan Padrig', NLWJ iii (1943–4).

Index

O

Ó Fearghal Óg, 139
och, 146, 184
Offa's Dyke, 5
Ordinary of the Mass, 13
Original Sin, 119
Owain ap Gruffudd ap Gwenwynwyn, 136
Owain ap Madog, 12
Owain Cyfeiliog, 21, 161
Owain Fychan, 141
Owain Gwynedd, 11, 21, 31, 118, 132, 136, 140, 141

P

Pab, 150
parablu, 140, 179
Paradise, 83, 94, 97, 118
paschal candle, 14
Paschal Time, 103
Passion, 105, 139, 149
    plays, 92
    poems, 17
Pater Noster, 125, 140
Patriarch of Jerusalem, 147
patronage, 1, 3, 5–8, 102
Paul, 90, 95, 100
Penance, sacrament of, 15, 103, 106, 120, 158
    poems, 16
pencerdd, 9, 31, 73, 109, 111
Penrhaith, 108
performance of poems, 9
Peter, 90, 94, 100, 107, 121, 158
Pharaoh, 163
Phylip Brydydd, 125, 130, 133, 137, 145, 146
Poets of the Princes. *See Gogynfeirdd*
Powys, 117
praise
    response to God, 143–44, 182
prayer, 140
    on behalf of a living patron, 140, 179
    response to God, 140–43, 179–82
prayers, 128, 142, 151, 171

'God be with', 143, 181
    for conversion, 142, 180
    for deceased patrons, 143, 182
    for help, 142, 180
    for special favours, 142, 181
    of praise, 144, 182
    to Christ, 161, 199
    to Jesus, 163, 201
    to the Son of God, 151, 192
Preface, 84
Priawd, 108
pride, 89, 92, 100
prifiaith, 140, 179
Prydydd Bychan, 126
Prydydd y Moch. *See* Llywarch ap Llywelyn
Psalms, 13, 14
Purdan Padrig, 103

R

Raphael, 97
reciter, 9
recompense, 145, 183
Red Book of Hergest. *See Llyfr Coch Hergest*
Redemption, 14, 92, 108, 111, 149, 160
refugium, 102
religious and moral practice, 146, 185
repentance, 84, 145, 144–46, 183–84
    poems, 17, 106
Resurrection, 13, 92, 107, 108, 151
rhannu, 133, 175
Rhi, 108, 126, 169
Rhirid Flaidd, 21, 138
rhoddi, 133, 140, 175, 179
Rhodri ab Owain Gwynedd, 11, 31, 139
rhwyf, 126, 169
Rhys ap Gruffudd, 21
Rhys ap Llywelyn, 128
Rhys ap Maredudd ap Rhys, 155
Rhys Gryg, 120
Rich Young Man, The, 93
Rimini, Council of, 2
Rogation Days, 103
Roman empire, 123
Roman Empire, 2, 161

WITHDRAWN
UNIVERSITY OF GLASGOW LIBRARY